6/05

D1489958

# Favorite
# Demonstrations

*for College Science*

# Favorite
# Demonstrations
## *for College Science*

*Brian R. Shmaefsky, Editor*

*An NSTA Press Journals Collection*

NATIONAL SCIENCE TEACHERS ASSOCIATION

Arlington, Virginia

NATIONAL SCIENCE TEACHERS ASSOCIATION

Claire Reinburg, Director
Andrew Cocke, Associate Editor
Judy Cusick, Associate Editor
Betty Smith, Associate Editor

JOURNAL OF COLLEGE SCIENCE TEACHING Lauren Beben, Managing Editor

ART AND DESIGN Linda Olliver, Director
PRINTING AND PRODUCTION Catherine Lorrain-Hale, Director
    Nguyet Tran, Assistant Production Manager
    Jack Parker, Desktop Publishing Specialist
SciLINKS Tyson Brown, Manager
    David Anderson, Web and Development Coordinator

NATIONAL SCIENCE TEACHERS ASSOCIATION
Gerald F. Wheeler, Executive Director
David Beacom, Publisher

LIBRARY OF CONGRESS CATALOGING-IN-PUBLICATION DATA

Favorite demonstrations for college science : an NSTA Press journals collection / Brian R. Shmaefsky, editor.
    p. cm.
  Includes index.
  ISBN 0-87355-242-3
  1. Science—Study and teaching (Higher) 2. Communication in science. I. Shmaefsky, Brian
  Q181.F28 2004
  507'.1'1—dc22

                    2003027269

*Featuring SciLinks®—a way to connect text and the Internet. Up-to-the-minute online content, classroom ideas, and other materials are just a click away. Go to page xvi to learn more about this educational resource.*

**About the Cover**—Safety Issues: The cover illustrates a classical Van de Graaff generator demonstration used to excite physics students for many years. Today, this demonstration should only be conducted under the supervision of a competent operator of the generator. High voltage passes through the body during contact. That is what caused the funky hairdo in the student who volunteered to have his body loaded with electrons. A demonstration such as this one can still be done. However, strict precautions must be exercised. It should only be done on healthy volunteers who do not have any prosthesis that can be affected by the electrical current (e.g., a pacemaker or other implanted device). Plus, it is best to do any Van de Graaff generator demonstration away from computers and instruments sensitive to electrical discharge.

# Contents

ix | Introduction

xi | About the Editor

xii | Discipline Cross-Reference Guide

xv | Safety Guidelines for Conducting Demonstrations

xvi | SciLinks

## Safety

3 | The Rules of Research: Keeping Your Favorite Demonstrations Safe
*Brian R. Shmaefsky* (December 2002/January 2003)

## General Science Principles

9 | A Bright Idea: Reinforcing Logico-Deductive Reasoning
*Jan Benjamin and Brian R. Shmaefsky* (September/October 2003)

13 | Using Fluorescent Dyes to Demonstrate Solution-Mixing Techniques:
How to Bring Sample-Preparation Skills up to Speed
*Brian R. Shmaefsky and Mary Jo Smith* (December 1993/January 1994)

## Natural Sciences

17 | Seasonal Size Variations of Martian Polar Caps: An Interdisciplinary
Approach to Planetary Studies
*D. Blane Baker, Robert Sproles, and Glenn Good* (October 2000)

23 | The Brine Shrimp as a Model Organism for Biology: Anthropods Useful in
Demonstrating Properties of Organisms
*Kimberly Boman and Brian R. Shmaefsky* (March/April 1997)

27 | Demonstrating an Interactive Genetic Drift Exercise: Examining the Processes of
Random Mating and Selection
*Ashley J. R. Carter* (March/April 2002)

31 | Microbe Wars: A Demonstration of Microbial Antagonism—A Vivid Example of
Microorganism Interaction
*Marty Fox* (September/October 1997)

**35** | **Floating Spinach Disks: An Uplifting Demonstration of Photosynthesis**
*Marty Fox, John J. Gaynor, and Judith Shillcock* (December 1998/January 1999)

**41** | **Differential Weathering: A Delicious Demonstration**
*Mark Francek* (October 2002)

**43** | **An Interactive, Fiery Model of Genetic Complementation: Shedding Light on a Conceptually Difficult Biological Topic**
*Kathryn Hajek Zuehlke* (September/October 1999)

**47** | **Chemical Evolution as a Body-Language Demonstration: A Geological Timescale Using Real People**
*Douglas Hayward* (March/April 1993)

**51** | **Electrophoresis for under Five Dollars: How to Do It, Cheap and Easy**
*Vincent J. Lumetta and Mitchel J. Doktycz* (March/April 1994)

**57** | **Demonstrating the "Greenhouse Effect": Illustrating Variations on an Atmospheric Phenomenon**
*David P. Martin* (December 1995/January 1996)

**63** | **Illustrating Heterochrony and Heterotopy: Two Developmental Patterns in the Evolution of Organismal Form**
*Terry O'Brien* (October 2001)

**69** | **A Vivid Demonstration of Fall Leaf Color Changes: Assessing the Environmental Factors That Affect Plant Metabolism**
*Brian R. Shmaefsky, Timothy D. Shmaefsky, and Kathleen M. Shmaefsky* (September/October 1998)

**73** | **An Interactive Classroom Method to Demonstrate DNA Structure: Teaching Polymerization by Real-Life Participation**
*Sharon L. Weldon and Marjorie A. Jones* (September/October 1994)

# Physical Sciences

**79** | **Chemistry at Work: Generating Electricity Using Single Displacement Reactions**
*Barbara A. Burke* (December 1996/January 1997)

**83** | **Simple "Jack-in-the-Box" Demonstrations for Physical Sciences Courses: Five Easy Demos**
*Theodor C. H. Cole* (November 1993)

87 | **An Eye-Opening Demonstration—The Catalytic Decomposition of Hydrogen Peroxide: Enhancing a Chemistry Lecture with a Common Eye-Care Product**
*Brendan R. Flynn* (December 1994/January 1995)

91 | **The Ammonia Lava Lamp: A Colorful Demonstration of Diffusion**
*Marty Fox, John J. Gaynor, and Judith Shillcock* (February 1996)

95 | **Stopping a Siphon Action by Reduction of Atmospheric Pressure: Demonstrating Physics with a Simply Constructed Apparatus**
*Robert M. Graham* (September/October 1995)

99 | **The Remsen Demonstration: "Nitric Acid Acts upon Copper"— A Colorful Slice of Chemistry's History**
*Myra Hauben and Geoff Rayner-Canham* (March/April 1996)

105 | **The Johnson DC Electric Motor Recipe: A New Twist to the Mystery of the Electric Motor**
*Douglas C. Johnson* (May 1997)

109 | **Sulfuric Acid: King of Chemicals—History, Chemistry, and Some Demonstrations of $H_2SO_4$**
*George B. Kauffman and Scott D. Pennington* (May 1993)

115 | **A Colorful Demonstration of Le Châtelier's Principle: Observing the Effect of Stress on a Solution Containing Iron(III) and Thiocyanate Ions**
*Arthur M. Last and Peter W. Slade* (November 1997)

121 | **From Lodestone to Neodymium: Demonstrating Lenz's Law— An Innovative Approach to Teaching Magnetic Properties**
*James H. Larson* (November 1994)

125 | **Visualizing Chemical Reactions with the Pop-It Bead Model: Modeling the Dynamic Nature of Chemical Equilibrium (Part One of Two Parts)**
*John Luoma and Susan Yochum* (March/April 1995)

131 | **Demonstrating Chemical Processes with the Transfer-Tube Model: Modeling the Dynamic Nature of Chemical Equilibrium (Part Two of Two Parts)**
*John Luoma and Susan Yochum* (May 1995)

137 | **Does Black Paint Radiate Heat Better Than White Paint? Demonstrating Differences in Emission of Infrared Radiation**
*David P. Martin and Randy D. Russell* (February 1995)

143 | **Demonstrating Allotropic Modifications of Sulfur: Re-creating Io's Volcanic Surface**
*Jillian L. McCarty and Veljko Dragojlovic* (December 2001/January 2002)

147 | **Demonstrating a Thermodynamics Fountain: Heating Up the Classroom with an Energy Transfer Exercise**
*Miodrag Micic and Roger M. LeBlanc* (May 2002)

151 | **The Conductivity of Solutions: Laying the Foundation of Modern Chemical Thought**
*Geoff Rayner-Canham* (September/October 1993)

155 | **La Fiesta Radioactiva: Distinguishing Alpha, Beta, and Gamma Emissions from Orange-Glazed Dinnerware**
*Ruth N. Russo* (March/April 1999)

161 | **Demonstrating the Principles of Column Chromatography: An Easy Introduction to a Useful Analytic Technique**
*Brian R. Shmaefsky, David Barnes, and Chris Martin* (November 1995)

165 | **The Roles of Different Mobile Phases in Liquid Chromatography: A Moving Demonstration of Chemical Interactions**
*Brian R. Shmaefsky, Timothy D. Shmaefsky, and Kathleen M. Shmaefsky* (February 2001)

169 | **A Limiting Reactant Demonstration: Making a Stoichiometric Concept Visible for Beginning Students**
*Janet Z. Tarino* (September/October 1996)

171 | **List of Contributors**

173 | **Index**

# Introduction

*"To be fruitful in invention, it is indispensable to have a habit of observation and reflection."*

—Abraham Lincoln
February 11, 1859

Lincoln's comment truly reflects the nature of successful college science teaching. Teaching higher-order-thinking skills in science is best achieved by having students examine and reflect about the scientific principles behind their observations. This can be achieved in many ways through a combination of classroom instruction and laboratory experiences. Classroom demonstrations are a popular way of stimulating students to carefully witness and process scientific principles.

A multitude of educational research studies published over the past 30 years supports the use of demonstrations in teaching. Demonstrations reinforce learning by allowing students to visualize abstract scientific concepts as concrete expressions. They particularly help students who rely on visual learning cues to better understand the concept. Demonstrations are also entertaining and foster learning by linking two or more senses with positive emotional imagery. In other words, students keep facts and concepts in their minds longer when the information presented to them is enlivening and easy to recall. Students are more likely to remember complex topics such as thermodynamics when they see a demonstration that accurately portrays the principles.

This book is a compilation of peer-reviewed classroom demonstrations tailored to upper-level high school and college science teaching. All of them were published between 1993 and 2003 in the "Favorite Demonstration" column of the *Journal of College Science Teaching*.

These demonstrations were selected for this compilation because they accurately convey scientific principles in a manner that kindles student inquiry. Many of them are useful as "attention grabbers" for science talks to young children and the public. However, these demonstrations alone do not instill science learning. They are part of an overall instructional strategy that convinces students to seek a complete understanding of scientific doctrine.

The first two sections of this book are applicable to all science disciplines. They present demonstrations that illustrate laboratory safety and general scientific principles. After all, each science discipline shares the common threads of scientific method and experimental techniques. The latter two sections, Natural Sciences and Physical Sciences, were difficult to assemble. Many of the demonstrations exhibited principles that spanned the artificial delineations between the sciences. So, they were placed into categories based on where the concepts are commonly taught in introductory college science classes. Teachers can browse through both sections for demonstrations that touch on topics taught in any science discipline.

Each demonstration uses equipment and materials that are currently available from scientific supply companies or local stores. However, the costs of the items may have changed since the original publication date. Overall, most of the demonstrations are inexpensive and simple to carry out. They also require a minimum of precious classroom time. Some of the demonstrations can be modified into student inquiry activities or laboratory sessions. How the demonstrations are used is up to the instructor, who can adapt or modify the demonstrations to particular instructional needs.

Dr. Brian R. Shmaefsky
Column Editor, "Favorite Demonstration"
*Journal of College Science Teaching*
Kingwood College, Kingwood, Texas

# About the Editor

Brian Shmaefsky is a professor of biology and the service learning coordinator at Kingwood College in Kingwood, Texas. He went from co-editor to editor of the "Favorite Demonstration" column in the *Journal of College Science Teaching* and has served the column for 10 years. Dr. Shmaefsky regularly teaches with demonstrations he adapted from his experiences as a biochemist for Sigma Chemical Company and from 20 years of college teaching. He has published dozens of papers and presented almost an equal number of presentations on science education and training. Dr. Shmaefsky has also authored books and trade journal articles about biotechnology, human disease, and technology transfer. He has two children, 12-year-old Kathleen and 15-year-old Timothy, who assisted in several science teaching articles, including two that appear in this book. Dr. Shmaefsky lives in north suburban Houston with his dog, Dusty.

# Discipline Cross-Reference Guide

**M**any topics covered in different science classes overlap. For example, general biology classes are replete with chemistry lectures needed to understand cell function. Biology, chemistry, and physics all share coverage of thermodynamics.

The cross-reference guide that follows shows the potential interdisciplinary use of many of the demonstrations in this book.

The following symbols are used to identify the disciplines suitable for each demonstration:

**B** = Biology
**C** = Chemistry
**Es** = Earth Sciences
**Gs** = General Science (applies to all sciences)
**P** = Physics

Demonstrations are in alphabetical order by the first author's last name. Note the discipline identity symbol at the end of each citation.

Baker, D. Blane, Robert Sproles, and Glenn Good. "Seasonal Size Variations of Martian Polar Caps: An Interdisciplinary Approach to Planetary Studies" (page 17). **Es**

Benjamin, Jan, and Brian R. Shmaefsky. "A Bright Idea: Reinforcing Logico-Deductive Reasoning" (page 9). **Gs**

Boman, Kimberly, and Brian R. Shmaefsky. "The Brine Shrimp as a Model Organism for Biology: Anthropods Useful in Demonstrating Properties of Organisms" (page 23). **B**

Burke, Barbara A. "Chemistry at Work: Generating Electricity Using Single Displacement Reactions" (page 79). **C**

Carter, Ashley J. R. "Demonstrating an Interactive Genetic Drift Exercise: Examining the Processes of Random Mating and Selection" (page 27). **B**

Cole, Theodor C. H. "Simple 'Jack-in-the-Box' Demonstrations for Physical Sciences Courses: Five Easy Demos" (page 83). **C, Gs, P**

Flynn, Brendan. "An Eye-Opening Demonstration—The Catalytic Decomposition of Hydrogen Peroxide: Enhancing a Chemistry Lecture with a Common Eye-Care Product" (page 87). **C**

Fox, Marty. "Microbe Wars: A Demonstration of Microbial Antagonism—A Vivid Example of Microorganism Interaction" (page 31). **B**

Fox, Marty, John J. Gaynor, and Judith Shillcock. "The Ammonia Lava Lamp: A Colorful Demonstration of Diffusion" (page 91). **C, P**

Fox, Marty, John J. Gaynor, and Judith Shillcock. "Floating Spinach Disks: An Uplifting Demonstration of Photosynthesis" (page 35). **B**

Francek, Mark. "Differential Weathering: A Delicious Demonstration" (page 41). **B, Es, P**

Graham, Robert M. "Stopping a Siphon Action by Reduction of Atmospheric Pressure: Demonstrating Physics with a Simply Constructed Apparatus" (page 95). **C, P**

Hauben, Myra, and Geoff Rayner-Canham. "The Remsen Demonstration: 'Nitric Acid Acts upon Copper'—A Colorful Slice of Chemistry's History" (page 99). **C**

Hayward, Douglas. "Chemical Evolution as a Body-Language Demonstration: A Geological Timescale Using Real People" (page 47). **B, C**

Johnson, Douglas C. "The Johnson DC Electric Motor Recipe: A New Twist to the Mystery of the Electric Motor" (page 105). **C, P**

Kauffman, George B., and Scott D. Pennington. "Sulfuric Acid: King of Chemicals—History, Chemistry, and Some Demonstrations of $H_2SO_4$" (page 109). **C**

Larson, James H. "From Lodestone to Neodymium: Demonstrating Lenz's Law—An Innovative Approach to Teaching Magnetic Properties" (page 121). **C, Es, P**

Last, Arthur M., and Peter W. Slade. "A Colorful Demonstration of Le Châtelier's Principle: Observing the Effect of Stress on a Solution Containing Iron(III) and Thiocyanate Ions" (page 115). **C, P**

Lumetta, Vincent J., and Mitchel J. Doktycz. "Electrophoresis for under Five Dollars: How to Do It, Cheap and Easy" (page 51). **B, C**

Luoma, John, and Susan Yochum. "Visualizing Chemical Reactions with the Pop-It Bead Model: Modeling the Dynamic Nature of Chemical Equilibrium (Part One of Two Parts)" (page 125). **B, C**

Luoma, John, and Susan Yochum. "Demonstrating Chemical Processes with the Transfer-Tube Model: Modeling the Dynamic Nature of Chemical Equilibrium (Part Two of Two Parts)" (page 131). **B, C**

Martin, David P. "Demonstrating the 'Greenhouse Effect': Illustrating Variations on an Atmospheric Phenomenon" (page 57). **B, Es, P**

Martin, David P., and Randy D. Russell. "Does Black Paint Radiate Heat Better Than White Paint? Demonstrating Differences in Emission of Infrared Radiation" (page 137). **Es, P**

McCarty, Jillian L., and Veljko Dragojlovic. "Demonstrating Allotropic Modifications of Sulfur: Re-creating Io's Volcanic Surface" (page 143). **C**

Micic, Miodrag, and Roger M. LeBlanc. "Demonstrating a Thermodynamics Fountain: Heating Up the Classroom with an Energy Transfer Exercise" (page 147). **B, C, Es, P**

O'Brien, Terry. "Illustrating Heterochrony and Heterotopy: Two Developmental Patterns in the Evolution of Organismal Form" (page 63). **B**

Rayner-Canham, Geoff. "The Conductivity of Solutions: Laying the Foundation of Modern Chemical Thought" (page 151). **C, P**

Russo, Ruth N. "La Fiesta Radioactiva: Distinguishing Alpha, Beta, and Gamma Emissions from Orange-Glazed Dinnerware" (page 155). **C, P**

Shmaefsky, Brian R. "The Rules of Research: Keeping Your Favorite Demonstrations Safe" (page 3). **Gs**

Shmaefsky, Brian R., David Barnes, and Chris Martin. "Demonstrating the Principles of Column Chromatography: An Easy Introduction to a Useful Analytic Technique" (page 161). **B, C**

Shmaefsky, Brian R., Timothy D. Shmaefsky, and Kathleen M. Shmaefsky. "A Vivid Demonstration of Fall Leaf Color Changes: Assessing the Environmental Factors That Affect Plant Metabolism" (page 69). **B**

Shmaefsky, Brian R., Timothy D. Shmaefsky, and Kathleen M. Shmaefsky. "The Roles of Different Mobile Phases in Liquid Chromatography: A Moving Demonstration of Chemical Interactions" (page 165). **B, C**

Shmaefsky, Brian R., and Mary Jo Smith. "Using Fluorescent Dyes to Demonstrate Solution-Mixing Techniques: How to Bring Sample-Preparation Skills up to Speed" (page 13). **B, C**

Tarino, Janet Z. "A Limiting Reactant Demonstration: Making a Stoichiometric Concept Visible for Beginning Students" (page 169). **B, C**

Weldon, Sharon L., and Marjorie A. Jones. "An Interactive Classroom Method to Demonstrate DNA Structure: Teaching Polymerization by Real-Life Participation" (page 73). **B**

Zuehlke, Kathryn Hajek. "An Interactive, Fiery Model of Genetic Complementation: Shedding Light on a Conceptually Difficult Biological Topic" (page 43). **B**

# Safety Guidelines for Conducting Demonstrations

Safe working conditions in the laboratory cannot be stressed enough in contemporary science teaching. It is imperative that teachers not expose their students to undue risks in their quest for science knowledge. That holds true not only for laboratory lessons; safety also applies to classroom demonstrations.

The popular "Favorite Demonstration" column in the *Journal of College Science Teaching* promotes demonstrations and activities that are safe to conduct as well as pedagogically sound. Demonstrations conducted before the 1990s were not required to address laboratory safety issues. It was assumed that all instructors were prudent when carrying out demonstrations. However, a host of unfortunate incidents that harmed students and instructors resulted in tighter safety precautions being imposed on science classrooms.

Safety considerations appear repeatedly in this book—in the following guidelines for conducting demonstrations, in the article "The Rules of Research: Keeping Your Favorite Demonstrations Safe" (page 3), and in most of the demonstration articles themselves. Use the following recommendations and the safety advice found in the article on page 3 before conducting any of the demonstrations in this compilation:

1. Do not perform any demonstrations that may risk the health of students.
   a. No uncontrollable explosions.
   b. No pyrotechnics.
   c. No tasting of laboratory chemicals.
   d. No exposure of potentially hazardous chemicals to the skin.
   e. No production of fumes without proper ventilation.
   f. No loud sounds or bright light emitting reactions without providing students with protection.
   g. No beta and gamma radiation emitting displays.
2. Keep a written procedure of each demonstration.
3. Be aware of all hazards associated with the activities, chemicals, and equipment associated with the demonstration.
4. Have information about using the chemicals and equipment readily available.
5. Have appropriate emergency and safety equipment nearby.
6. Wear approved personal protection equipment when handling chemicals or operating equipment.
7. Provide students with approved personal protection equipment if they are close to the demonstration.
8. Dispose of used materials properly.
9. Apply the following principles of safety found in E. Scott Geller's noted *The Psychology of Safety Handbook* (New York: CRC/Lewis Publishers, 2001).

*"Safety is not a priority, it is a value."*
*"Safety should be an unwritten rule, a social norm, that workers should follow regardless of the situation."*
*"It should be a value that is never questioned—never compromised."*

How can you and your students avoid searching hundreds of science Web sites to locate the best sources of information on a given topic? SciLinks, created and maintained by the National Science Teachers Association (NSTA), has the answer.

In a SciLinked text, such as this one, you'll find a logo and keyword near a concept your class is studying, a URL (*www.scilinks.org*), and a keyword code. Simply go to the SciLinks Web site, type in the code, and receive an annotated listing of as many as 15 Web pages—all of which have gone through an extensive review process conducted by a team of science educators.

Need more information? Take a tour—*www.scilinks.org/tour.*

# safety

# The Rules of Research

## Keeping Your Favorite Demonstrations Safe

Brian R. Shmaefsky

Demonstrations are wonderful educational strategies for reinforcing and stimulating learning. They are highly instructional as well as entertaining if suitably incorporated into lectures and laboratory sessions. This is not a biased, unsubstantiated opinion, but rather the reflection of a 20-year investigation of the role of demonstrations in college science teaching. Unfortunately, the educational value of demonstrations may be clouded by an ignoble side. Many faculty members fail to recognize that demonstrations used in biology, chemistry, and physics have equivalent hazards as laboratory activities.

Any demonstration using chemical or physical reactions should be carried out with the same alacrity and precautions used when conducting instructional laboratories. Of the utmost importance is avoiding hazardous situations by doing demonstrations that are not dangerous. Instructors must consider the learning value of using explosions, incendiaries, fuming reactions, or projectiles before planning demonstrations. Several questions should be considered: Do the potential risks of the demonstration justify the gain in educational outcomes? Can the same concept be presented using another demonstration? Would the demonstration have equal impact using a multimedia presentation? Can the activity be modeled more safely in a microscale laboratory or by using virtual laboratory software?

Faculty members who are not fully familiar with demonstration safety precautions will benefit from Internet resources. I find the following sites to be especially helpful:

- Laboratory Safety Institute, online at *www.labsafety.org*. This Web site contains many useful safety hints for conducting demonstrations and teaching laboratory sessions. Included are safety workshop opportunities and access to laboratory safety discussion lists. Safety books and fact sheets are also available on the site.
- Science Inquiry, online at *www.science inquiry.com*. This Web resource is predominantly directed at K–12 educators. However,

much of the information is pertinent for introductory-level college science instruction. Included in the site are demonstration ideas and lists of books and literature references on inquiry teaching.

If the demonstration is deemed appropriate, then it is imperative to observe all safety precautions outlined in the instruction manuals and Material Safety Data Sheets (MSDS) for the equipment and chemicals used. Any people carrying out the demonstration must be outfitted with appropriate personal protective equipment (PPE). Information can be obtained from the instructional manual and the MSDS. Students or spectators should also be provided with protection or PPE. Isolation of spectators using barriers or a safe distance zone is acceptable if it is not practical to provide the whole audience with PPE.

Appropriate PPE for many science demonstrations include:

- Body protection—chemical- and water-resistant aprons, gowns, or coveralls
- Ear protection—ear covers or disposable ear plugs
- Eye protection—full-wrap, splash-proof, impact-resistant goggles, or face shields
- Foot protection—fully covered shoes or boots
- Hand protection—chemical-, heat-, or impact-resistant gloves
- Respiratory protection—chemical- or dust-blocking masks or respirators (with proper ventilation)

Faculty as well as any students directly involved in demonstrations must be using PPE.

**Topic: safety in the science classroom**
Go to: *www.scilinks.org*
Code: JCSTC4

Emergency response measures should be in place before doing any demonstration with potential hazards for the faculty or students. Graduate students and assistants helping with the demonstration must do the following:

- Alert the laboratory coordinator or safety officer that the demonstration is being done.
- Have a plan for calmly, quickly, and safely evacuating students from the room.
- Have ready access to ample supplies of PPE.
- Know the locations of the nearest emergency exits.
- Have ready access to emergency telephone numbers for emergency responders, first-aid care, or campus police.
- Know the locations of the nearest fire alarm or emergency call boxes.
- Have a cart equipped with materials for cleaning up after an accident.
- Know the locations and conditions of the nearest fire extinguishers.
- Know the location of first-aid equipment.
- Be familiar with the location of MSDS for chemicals used in the demonstration. Check your board of education or college rules regarding the use of chemicals and banned chemicals.
- Be familiar with the location of the instruction manuals for any equipment used in the demonstration.
- Know how to expeditiously dispose of any hazardous wastes resulting from the demonstration in an appropriate manner. Check your board of education or college rules regarding chemical pickup by Hazmat.

This list may be posted or incorporated into a checklist for use before any demonstration. Copies should be available to all faculty members conducting favorite demonstrations. The safe use of demonstrations is a fundamental issue echoed in the safety statements required before any presenter can perform a session at a National Science Teachers Association convention.

Laboratory coordinators or safety officers benefit from a demonstration safety checklist. Industrial research labs use such checklists before a potentially hazardous laboratory procedure or production operation can be implemented. In the classroom, a checklist would require that certain information be completed before and after the demonstration. It could be tailored to individual needs or institutional requirements. Sample checklists are shown in Figure 1. By following these commonsense procedures, educators can confidently present demonstrations and keep learning a vibrant and enjoyable activity for science students.

---

**figure 1** Sample checklists to be completed before and after performing demonstrations

**Before the demonstration:**

Date

Person(s) conducting the demonstration

Building

Room number

Office phone or extension

Approximate number of students observing

Type of demonstration: biology, chemistry, geology, or physics

Process description (describe what is being done)

Protocol steps or copy of activity

List of hazardous materials

Potential hazards or risks

Personal protective equipment for demonstrators

Personal protective equipment for spectators

Location of instruction manuals or MSDS

Safety precautions being taken

Emergency or accident procedures in place

**After the demonstration:**

Methods of waste disposal

Locations of used equipment

Modifications done not listed in protocols

List of unexpected incidents

Comments for next demonstration

---

# general science
## principles

# A Bright Idea: Reinforcing Logico-Deductive Reasoning

Jan Benjamin and Brian R. Shmaefsky

Many students in freshman- and sophomore-level science courses have little experience formulating testable hypotheses. Their typical high school and college education includes little more than a lecture on the scientific method replete with examples of experimental design. Most students also take part in conjecturing hypotheses associated with narrowly delineated laboratory activities. Teachers of large lecture sections, in particular, devote little time to guiding students' hypothesis testing.

However, an accurate comprehension of the scientific method is critical for understanding experimental design and for the success of science majors in upper-level courses and graduate programs. The typical approach to teaching the scientific method entails presenting a series of steps meant to make the logic behind the scientific method more intelligible. Unfortunately, this alone does not fully instill an understanding of testable-hypothesis generation. Students need step-by-step interaction with the scientific

 **figure 1** Touch lamp theory

Touch lamps operate by monitoring the discontinuity of an alternating current (AC) flowing throughout the body of the lamp. The touch lamp circuit pulses a small electrical charge into and out of the lamp body. This electrical charge is continuously monitored by a silicon chip. The chip activates a switch when the charge changes and exceeds a certain value. Apparently, the body's conductivity provides a disruption in the current that exceeds a set value for operating the switch. The switch used in the lamp is known as a flip-flop memory bit. It flips back and forth between an on and off position to operate the lamp. Many of the touch lamps use a three-way light that permits the lamp to go from dim to bright. The circuitry in the three-way lights is the same as in an ordinary touch lamp, except that the chip operates a three-way lamp switch (MadSci Network 1998).

method to get a thorough appreciation of the logico-deductive foundations of scientific inquiry (Paul and Elder 2002).

The following activity was designed to reinforce the teaching of the scientific method in large lecture sections of introductory science courses. This strategy is applicable to college-level biology, chemistry, engineering, and physics courses. Its success at boosting comprehension is well documented in the educational research on active or participatory learning (Cross 2003).

## Materials

The materials for this demonstration are inexpensive and simple to obtain—it generally requires only one touch lamp to be purchased. Touch lamps lack a standard on-and-off switch, so users can touch any surface of the lamp to turn on or off the lamp (see Figure 1 for details). The touch lamp used in this activity was purchased for $10 at a national discount store chain, and almost all discount stores and furniture retailers sell inexpensive touch lamps.

This demonstration requires the following materials to be readily available:

- Touch lamp
- Overhead projector or LCD device for displaying written student responses
- Objects for touch lamp switch variables, including a piece of cloth, piece of paper, steel paper clip, aluminum can, copper coin, plastic ruler, and rubber tube
- Objects for touch lamp conclusion, including a surgical glove and salad oil

## Procedure

Topic: scientific method
Go to: *www.scilinks.org*
Code: JCSTC10

Teachers can begin by giving an in-class lecture on the scientific method, with examples pertinent to the field of study being taught, and then introduce students to the touch lamp. It can be introduced as a scientific curiosity purchased while shopping. We like to tell students that we found an interesting lamp that has no switch. Then, we show the class how touching the lamp on the tip of the lamp shade turns on and off the light. We explain that the lamp shade is made of metal and sits in proximity to the lightbulb.

Teachers can then ask students to predict if touching any other part of the lamp will activate the switch. Each student who volunteers an answer should provide a written explanation for his or her prediction, which will be displayed on the overhead for the class to read.

Once students have had a chance to make predictions, we test the predictions by touching the parts students thought would or would not activate the lamp. We record the results next to the predictions, and it quickly becomes apparent that touching any portion of the touch lamp body will turn on or off the light. However, students should note that touching the cord is ineffective. We follow this up by telling students that we think pressure on the lamp's surface activates the switch. Then, we ask them to come up with a way to test this hypothesis.

After soliciting several hypotheses, we touch the lamp with each of the materials brought in as a switch variable. Students will notice that not all of the objects cause the lamp to turn on or off. They should then come up with another hypothesis for how the lamp switch works.

We immediately announce to the class that we have another hypothesis: It is the skin's electrical conductivity that makes the lamp switch work. The class debates this hypothesis and determines whether the materials can act as a conduit for the skin's conductivity.

Eventually, we tell the class that we have a way to test the new hypothesis. We put on a surgical glove, touch the lamp, and show the class that the lamp continues to switch on and off. We then suggest that the glove may be too thin to cover up the skin's electrical conductivity. So, we announce that we will reduce the skin's conductivity by coating one finger with salad oil. We touch the lamp again and note that the switch does not operate. This is a good time to ask students to summarize how logico-deductive reasoning is used to come up with experimental designs to test hypotheses.

The low cost of touch lamps makes it feasible to design a laboratory activity around them. So, for a further extension of this demonstration, students working in groups of two or three can develop hypotheses about the switch mechanism. Teachers can give the class access to materials they can use to test the lamp's operation.

## Student Evaluation

Student evaluation of the activity shows that the novelty of the activity improves attentiveness. The great focus on the demonstration enhances learning of scientific method applications. Test performance on science method questions is higher for students who participated in this demonstration, as compared to students attending the traditional lecture format. Students taking part in the demonstration scored an 85 average on scientific method multiple-choice and essay questions, as compared to the 70 average scored by those who were not involved in the activity.

## Acknowledgment

*We thank the Kingwood College students enrolled in Biology 1406 and Biology 1408 for their help in evaluating the effectiveness of the touch lamp demonstration.*

## References

Cross, P. K. 2003. *Techniques for Promoting Active Learning*. Phoenix, AZ: League for Innovations in the Community College.

MadSci Network. 1998. *Engineering: How Does a Touch Lamp Work?* Available online at *www.madsci.org/posts/archives/may98/893276774.Eg.r.html*.

Paul, R., and L. Elder. 2002. *How to Improve Student Learning*. Dillon Beach, CA: The Foundation for Critical Thinking.

# Using Fluorescent Dyes to Demonstrate Solution-Mixing Techniques

## How to Bring Sample-Preparation Skills up to Speed

Brian R. Shmaefsky and Mary Jo Smith

Reinforcing proper sample-preparation skills is a critical element of teaching analytical-instrumentation techniques. This entertaining and educationally effective demonstration shows the necessity of using the proper mixing technique when preparing solutions.

In the demonstration described here, the instructor prepares a variety of clear solutions before the class and asks students to judge whether the solutions appear homogeneous or inadequately mixed. The solutions are then induced to fluoresce with ultraviolet light to provide visible evidence of homogeneity or non-homogeneity (Shmaefsky 1993) (Figures 1 and 2).

## Materials

The demonstration requires the following materials:

- 10 mL of 1% (w/v in water) Fluorescent Brightener 28 (Sigma Chemical Company) (*Caution: Do not substitute with Sodium Fluorescein. Fluorescein has superior fluorescent properties in water, but it is classified as a potent carcinogen.*)
- 100 mL of distilled water in a 250 mL Erlenmeyer flask
- 100 mL of 40% (w/v in water) sucrose in a 250 mL Erlenmeyer flask

figure 1 — Instructor mixes the fluorescent brightener with distilled water, resulting in a homogeneous solution with complete coloration.

figure 2 — Mixing the fluorescent brightener with the more viscous sucrose solution produces a swirled pattern of coloration, which indicates the solution is not homogeneous.

- 100 mL of glycerol in a 250 mL Erlenmeyer flask
- Pipette for delivering 3 mL aliquots
- Long-wave ultraviolet light source (360nm–400nm)

## Procedure

Announce to the class that you will be asking them to speculate about the homogeneity of certain solutions following your demonstration of solution preparations.

First, tell the class that you will be adding an aqueous solution of fluorescent dye to distilled water. At this time, add 3 mL of the fluorescent-brightener solution to the flask containing distilled water. Leave the flask undisturbed. Ask the class if the solution is homogeneous (they should emphatically insist "No").

Illuminate the solution with ultraviolet light to see if the students are correct. Homogeneity is indicated by a uniform blue fluorescence (Figure 1). A haze of dark- and light-fluorescent-blue swirls is evidence of inadequate mixing (Figure 2).

Then, gently swirl the solution and pose the same question. Again, illuminate the flask to check for homogeneity.

Repeat these steps for the flasks containing the 40% sucrose and glycerol. The students will note that these more viscous solutions mix differently than the distilled water. It takes more vigorous swirling to ensure proper mixing in the 40% sucrose and glycerol flasks.

The mixtures should be discarded with mixed solvent wastes for standard incineration.

## Alternative Procedures

You may wish to compare the mixing efficacies achieved by different techniques. For example, mixing solutions with a stirring rod can be compared to hand swirling or mechanical shaking. Also, mixing solutions in a flask can be compared to mixing solutions in a test tube or a graduated cylinder.

## Summary

This demonstration has been used effectively in analytical chemistry and biochemistry classes, as well as introductory chemistry classes. The students walk away from this demonstration with a much greater awareness of the variables involved in preparing chemical solutions for qualitative and quantitative analysis.

## Reference

Shmaefsky, B. R. 1993. A method for analyzing the safe handling of chemicals by students. *Journal of College Science Teaching* 23(1): 54–55.

# natural sciences

# Seasonal Size Variations of Martian Polar Caps

## An Interdisciplinary Approach to Planetary Studies

D. Blane Baker, Robert Sproles, and Glenn Good

Mars, whose axial tilt and rotation period are similar to those of the Earth, experiences four distinct "seasons," each lasting approximately six Earth-months (Gianopoulos 1999). In addition, Martian seasons resemble those on the Earth in that while one hemisphere experiences winter, the other hemisphere experiences summer. With the change of seasons, portions of the Martian polar caps, known as seasonal polar caps, exhibit dramatic growth and recession (Fix 1999).

The seasonal caps expand during the respective hemisphere's fall and winter with the formation of dry ice "frost" from atmospheric carbon dioxide (Chaisson and McMillan 1999). During each hemisphere's spring and summer, the seasonal caps shrink (and may eventually disappear) as the poles warm, leaving behind the so-called residual polar caps. Such dramatic variations of the Martian polar caps are clearly evident, even as viewed from Earth-based telescopes (Pasachoff 1999).

To illustrate physical processes occurring on Martian polar regions during the seasonal changes, we use a simple classroom demonstration. The demonstration apparatus consists of a model planet enclosed within a bell jar that is evacuated and filled with carbon dioxide gas (Figure 1). The model planet contains a liquid nitrogen reservoir as a means of lowering its "polar" temperature. As the polar region (a copper sheet on top of the reservoir) cools, atmospheric carbon dioxide undergoes deposition, forming a layer of dry ice "frost." As the polar region warms because of the depletion of the coolant, the polar cap re-

Model of "Mars" showing coolant reservoir, polar region, and general setup

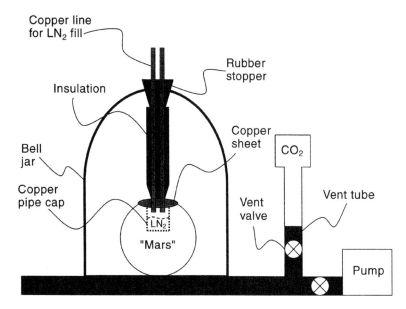

topics including phase transitions, vapor pressure, heat transfer, and Martian atmospheric and surface features. Pedagogically, the demonstration is valuable since it covers a variety of interdisciplinary topics (Caprio et al. 1998) and encourages active student participation (Bunce 1995).

In the future we plan to use interactive teaching (Sokoloff and Thornton 1997) and peer instruction techniques (Mazur 1997) to engage the entire class in the learning activity. In such a scenario the instructor explains the demonstration briefly and then asks students to write down predictions of what they expect to observe. Then the students form small groups and discuss their predictions. In the process of discussion, students maintain, modify, or change their predictions. Once the demonstration is performed, students are asked to summarize their observations and to compare them to their predictions.

cedes (and eventually disappears). As a result, the seasonal processes that occur on Mars are clearly elucidated in the model system.

The primary advantages of this demonstration are its affordability and its simplicity. The approximate cost of the materials (excluding the bell jar and vacuum pump) is less than $40, with most materials available within college science departments. The design of the apparatus is relatively simple; thus the time for assembly is minimal (approximately one hour). In addition to its low cost and simplicity, the demonstration is an ideal active-learning project.

During the classroom demonstration, several student volunteers participate in the following activities: evacuating the bell jar assembly, adding liquid nitrogen to the copper reservoir, admitting carbon dioxide into the bell jar, and monitoring variations of the polar cap. As the students engage in the hands-on activity, the discussion questions (see below) focus on several

## Materials

- Bell jar with opening for insertion of rubber stopper
- Bell jar base for connection to vacuum pump, rubber stopper
- Vacuum pump
- Vacuum hose
- Vacuum grease
- Two sections of 0.64 cm (0.25 in.) OD copper tubing, pipe insulation
- 3.8 cm (1.5 in.) OD copper pipe cap
- Lecture bottle of carbon dioxide gas
- 15.2 cm (6 in.) diameter Styrofoam sphere
- Copper sheet (approximately 0.3 mm thick)
- Liquid nitrogen (approximately 0.5 L)
- Tygon tubing
- Styrofoam cup (or dewar)
- Funnel
- Gloves and goggles

## Construction

Please note that the construction phase of this project, which requires approximately one hour, should be completed prior to the classroom demonstration.

Construct a cylindrical hole in the Styrofoam sphere such that the copper pipe cap fits snugly inside the sphere. Make sure, however, that the pipe cap does not extend beyond the surface of the sphere (and do not insert the pipe cap permanently inside the sphere just yet). Cut a circular section measuring about 6 cm in diameter from the copper sheet, drill two holes near the middle of the circular portion (for insertion of the copper tubing later), and soft-solder the circular sheet to the open end of the copper pipe cap. ("Center" the circular sheet on the cap before soldering.)

Next, insert the copper tubes through the holes in the copper sheet (about 2–3 mm), and soft-solder the two sections of copper tubing in place. (Make sure that the copper tubes are long enough to extend from the planetary model through the opening in the bell jar when the entire setup is complete). Apply pipe insulation around the copper tubes, leaving several centimeters open near their ends for passage of the tubes through the rubber stopper.

Finally, drill two holes in the rubber stopper to allow the copper tubes to pass through as they exit the bell jar. To ensure as tight a seal as possible between the stopper and tubes, drill the holes so that the stopper fits snugly around the tubes. (See Procedure for additional sealing details.)

As an optional course, obtain a Bourdon-type vacuum/pressure gauge and adapt the gauge to accept copper tubing. Then insert the tubing into a third hole bored into the rubber stopper that seals to the bell jar, allowing the gauge to stand upright outside the jar. During the demonstration, monitor the pressure of the system as the polar region warms and cools to show the variation of "atmospheric pressure" as a function of the amount of carbon dioxide gas present.

For informational purposes, the Martian atmospheric pressure varies by as much as 30 percent as a result of the periodic deposition and sublimation of atmospheric carbon dioxide (Chaisson and McMillan 1999). While this variation sounds large, the actual atmospheric pressure on Mars is approximately 0.01 of the atmospheric pressure on the Earth; thus, the 30 percent variation does not amount to a large pressure change.

## Procedure

1. Place the Styrofoam model planet on the base that supports the bell jar and insert the copper pipe cap inside the cylindrical hole in the sphere, allowing the copper lines to stand upright. To give the appearance of a polar region, conform the circular copper sheet to the sphere by gently pressing down on its perimeter.

2. Cover the model planet with the bell jar so that the copper lines extend through the opening in the top of the bell jar.

3. Pass the rubber stopper over the copper lines and seal the stopper to the opening in the bell jar. (Vacuum grease is useful for making reasonably tight vacuum seals around the outside of the rubber stopper and around the copper lines that pass through holes in the stopper.)

4. Close the vent valve on the bell jar assembly, open the valve to the pump, and evacuate the system (i.e., the bell jar and its connection to the vacuum pump). Then close the valve to the pump.

5. While the system is under vacuum, fill the coolant reservoir with liquid nitrogen, using a funnel to carefully transfer liquid nitrogen from a small Styrofoam cup (or dewar) into one of the copper lines. (The other line serves as an exhaust.) **Wear explosion- and splash-resistant safety goggles in addition to surgical gloves for safety**. Note that since the vacuum region of the bell jar must remain isolated from the internal portion of the coolant reservoir, the soft-solder joints must be leak-tight.

6. With the lecture bottle of carbon dioxide in a secure location, attach a section of Tygon tubing to the control valve on the bottle and purge the tubing. Then attach the free end of the tubing to the vent tube on the bell jar assembly, making sure the control valve is closed.

7. Open the vent valve connected to the bell jar base. Then "bleed" just a small amount of carbon dioxide gas into the bell jar through the control valve on the lecture bottle. Observe the accumulation of solid carbon dioxide on the cold copper sheet after a few moments. Later, as the "polar region" warms, observe the disappearance of carbon dioxide through the process of sublimation.

As a pedagogical note, we discuss with the students various aspects of the demonstration while the coolant remains in the reservoir. Liquid nitrogen in our model system lasts approximately 15–20 minutes in the reservoir, allowing ample time for discussion.

## Discussion

The classroom discussion accompanying the demonstration emphasizes aspects of chemistry and physics that relate to the project, as well as aspects of Mars's atmosphere and surface features. In order to encourage student interaction, we present the students with discussion questions at the beginning of class. Samples of those questions and appropriate answers are outlined below. Several additional questions, suggested by one of our reviewers, are listed in the Appendix of this article.

- *Why is it impossible to remove the bell jar from its base after evacuation of the system?* The inability to remove the bell jar from its base results from a pressure difference between the inside and the outside of the jar. Recall that average pressure is the force exerted by a fluid per unit area. Since the pressure inside the evacuated jar is very small, the force required to pull the two apart is essentially the pressure of the atmosphere times the cross-sectional area shared by the bell jar and its base (Serway and Faughn 1995). For cross-sectional areas of the order of our system (0.03 $m^2$) the force required to separate the two is approximately 3000 N.

- *What is the primary method of heat transfer to the liquid nitrogen reservoir?* Heat transfer to the reservoir occurs primarily because of conduction along the copper lines. As heat flows into the reservoir, liquid nitrogen vaporizes and exhausts to the outside of the jar. Once the liquid nitrogen completely vaporizes, the reservoir warms quickly to room temperature due to the high thermal conductivity of copper.

- *Why does solid carbon dioxide disappear as the polar region warms (instead of forming a liquid first)?* Carbon dioxide is a substance that sublimes directly from a solid to a gas (if warmed at any pressure below 5.1 atmospheres) by a process known as sublimation (Ebbing and Gammon 1999). While this process may seem unusual, a number of substances exhibit similar behavior (under appropriate conditions). Even water, which can exist in all three phases over appropriate temperature ranges at 1 atmosphere, sublimes if warmed at a pressure below 0.006 atmosphere (Ebbing and Gammon 1999).

- *How is the pressure of the "atmosphere" affected when carbon dioxide sublimes? Is this similar to the situation on Mars?* Once carbon dioxide begins to sublime to the gas phase, the pressure inside the jar increases. This happens because at any temperature below the triple point temperature (216.6 K), the solid and vapor coexist with one another in thermodynamic equilibrium at a gas pressure called the vapor pressure (Moeller et al. 1980). (Recall that below the triple point there is one and only one pressure at which the solid and vapor coexist in equilibrium with one another at a given temperature.) Subsequently, if the solid's temperature is increased then its vapor pressure increases. As a result, molecules from the solid transform to the vapor phase, thus raising the actual gas pressure to match the vapor pressure.

The situation on Mars is similar. Measurements indicate that the atmospheric pressure varies by as much as 30 percent during the course of a Martian year, due to deposition and sublimation of its major atmospheric component, carbon dioxide (Chaisson and McMillan 1999). While changes in Mars's atmospheric pressure are generally attributed to variations in the number of gas molecules, this explanation is somewhat oversimplified. In addition to an increase or reduction in gas phase molecules, the temperature of the atmosphere also varies with the seasons. In planetary systems, like the Earth, a decrease in temperature is compensated by a reduction in the effective volume of the atmosphere from gravitational effects. Thus, the actual atmospheric pressure is roughly proportional to the number of gas phase species.

• **Is any frozen substance apparent on the cold copper sheet before the introduction of carbon dioxide into the bell jar? What is the substance (most likely)?** On particularly humid days, water condenses and freezes on the cold copper sheet prior to the introduction of carbon dioxide. Small amounts of residual water are most likely present because water has absorbed onto surfaces within the bell jar. In addition, some air (containing water vapor) passes into the bell jar through the vent valve since air remains in the vent tube prior to the introduction of carbon dioxide.

## Conclusion

This demonstration vividly illustrates seasonal size variations of Martian polar caps. It is particularly useful during the astronomy section of our physical science course that follows the chem-

istry and physics sections. Several questions accompanying the demonstration help students to assimilate knowledge covered previously in the course. In addition, the classroom activity is hands-on and encourages inquiry and investigation by students.

As a "favorite demonstration," the planetary model system has several important features: It is relatively simple to assemble, it is interactive and promotes active learning, and it incorporates topics from several disciplines (astronomy, chemistry, and physics).

## Appendix: Additional Discussion Questions

1. *What temperatures do Martian polar regions attain during the winter season?*
2. *At what temperature does solid carbon dioxide form?*
3. *What temperature is liquid nitrogen?*
4. *Why should Martian atmospheric pressures vary by 30 percent over a summer-winter season if the opposing hemisphere's "ice" cap is evaporating? Why don't they compensate each other?*
5. *What is the total atmospheric pressure on Mars? How does it compare to Earth's air pressure?*
6. *How much real pressure change occurs if Mars's pressure lowers by 30 percent? How much real pressure change would occur if Earth's pressure were lowered by 30 percent?*
7. *How do planetary scientists know that the pressure change is due to solidification of polar Martian "ice"? Again, why does the opposing hemisphere not compensate for the winter hemisphere's loss?*
8. *Why does the Earth not experience dramatic seasonal pressure changes when the winter hemisphere accumulates snow and the polar ice caps expand? Does it have something to do with the presence of so much liquid water? Does it have something to do with the composition of the Earth's atmosphere versus the atmosphere of Mars?*
9. *What is the composition of Mars's atmosphere? What is the composition of Earth's atmosphere? Why might they be different?*

## Note

*In addition to using this demonstration in college courses, the authors have introduced it into an Upward Bound Math and Science course funded by the TRIO Program and administered by the U.S. Department of Education.*

## References

Bunce, D. M. 1995. The quiet revolution in science education: Teaching science the way students learn. *Journal of College Science Teaching* 25:169–171.

Caprio, M. W., P. Powers, J. D. Kent, S. Harriman, C. Snelling, P. Harris, and M. Guy. 1998. A path toward integrated science: The first steps. *Journal of College Science Teaching* 27(6):430–434.

Chaisson, E., and S. McMillan. 1999. *Astronomy Today*. 3rd ed. Upper Saddle River, NJ: Prentice Hall.

Ebbing, D. D., and S. D. Gammon. 1999. *General Chemistry*. 6th ed. Boston: Houghton Mifflin Company.

Fix, J. D. 1999. *Astronomy: Journey to the Cosmic Frontier*. 2nd ed. Boston: WCB/McGraw-Hill.

Gianopoulos, A. 1999. Reasons for the seasons. *Astronomy* (27)7:74–77.

Mazur, E. 1997. *Peer Instruction: A User's Manual*. Upper Saddle River, NJ: Prentice Hall.

Moeller, T., J. C. Bailar, Jr., J. Kleinberg, C. O. Guss, M. E. Castellion, and C. Metz. 1980. *Chemistry with Inorganic Qualitative Analysis*. New York: Academic Press, Inc.

Pasachoff, J. M. 1999. *Astronomy: From the Earth to the Universe*. 5th ed. Fort Worth, TX: Saunders College Publishing.

Serway, R. A., and J. S. Faughn. 1995. *College Physics*. 4th ed. Fort Worth, TX: Saunders College Publishing.

Sokoloff, D. R., and R. K. Thornton. 1997. Using interactive lecture demonstrations to create an active learning environment. *The Physics Teacher* 35:340–347.

# The Brine Shrimp as a Model Organism for Biology

## Arthropods Useful in Demonstrating Properties of Organisms

Kimberly Boman and Brian R. Shmaefsky

At the beginning of the semester, college-level general biology classes frequently open with one or two lectures about the properties of living organisms. Overhead transparencies or 35 mm slides supplement the lectures with substantial depictions of various organisms and their properties. Similarly, instructors often deliver their lectures on histology, physiology, and the principles of zoology using visual aids.

Educators, however, are debating the effectiveness of such a passive presentation style. To give lectures full educational value, educators believe, instructors should reinforce biological concepts with tangible examples and laboratory activities.

**Topic: arthropods**
**Go to: www.scilinks.org**
**Code: JCSTC23**

Biology lectures expounding the properties of organisms can easily be enhanced with a living demonstration model organism. A model organism that students often find interesting is the large brine shrimp. These shrimp are representative of many organisms, and instructors can conveniently purchase them from pet shops or biological supply houses.

Instructors can place the shrimp on a microscope slide or petri plate and present them to a large lecture class using a projecting microscope or a microscope attached to a video camera. Computer-integrated microscopes have the added advantage of capturing and animating brine shrimp images.

### Model Organism

Brine shrimp readily model the general structures, physiology, and behaviors of most animals.

And aside from being inexpensive and simple to maintain, they are easy to use for demonstrations in large lecture rooms. The shrimp have clearly visible organ systems and tissues that can be observed with a standard transmission light microscope.

Brine shrimp belong to a subclass of small, free-swimming arthropods that live in both fresh and saltwater bodies. *Daphnia,* which are commonly used as live specimens in the classroom, are in this subclass. Brine shrimp, and other shrimp in the same order, have distinct segmentation and fully developed organ systems that are discernible through their transparent exoskeleton. Students can also observe the digestive tract, musculature, nervous system, and circulatory system unstained in the intact organism. The circulatory system, in particular, is easy to see as the blood visibly flows through the large dorsal and ventral blood vessels. The heart, located dorsally near the tail, pumps the blood cells, or amoebocytes, throughout the body. The amoebocytes are also visible without staining or phase contrast.

## Demonstrations Using Brine Shrimp in the Classroom

### Anatomy and Histology

Brine shrimp represent "typical" animal structures. Their body structures show discernible bilateral symmetry, cephalization, segmentation, and tagmatization. Apart from the excretory system, they have characteristic organ systems. The central nervous system, digestive tract, eye, and vascular system are comparable to those of humans.

Students can observe the tissue types of the organ systems of brine shrimp *in situ* through their transparent bodies. Most of the cell types are clearly visible with the high power lens of a simple transmission microscope. The columnar cells of the digestive tract are evident throughout the length of the body. Skeletal muscles are visible in the appendages and thoracic region of brine shrimp. The muscles clearly reveal striation when the light on the specimen is reduced by using the diaphragm or aperture.

Brine shrimp will tolerate high concentrations of vital stains when kept overnight in test tubes of saltwater and stain. The shrimp can soak up the stains if one or two drops of the organic solvent DMSO (dimethyl sulfoxide) are added to the tube. They will also absorb stains by feeding on stained baker's or brewer's yeast.

### Physiology of Circulation

Students will be able to detect the rate and direction of circulation of blood in shrimp by watching amoebocytes, the equivalent of white blood cells, flowing through the vessels. Like many arthropods, shrimp blood flow slows down to damaged appendages.

The circulatory systems of brine shrimp are highly temperature sensitive and will respond predictably to cool and warm environments. Shifts in pH will also alter their heart rates. Their hearts respond to many cardioactive compounds that alter calcium and sodium flux of cardiac muscle.

### Digestive System and Symbiosis

The brine shrimp is an example of a species with smooth muscle peristalsis. Students will be able to distinguish their intestinal muscles and lining, and if the specimens are fed yeast immediately before the presentation, they will exhibit peristalsis. The instructor can soak the yeast in universal pH indicator to show the pH shifts that occur as materials pass through the digestive tract. Brine shrimp are tolerant of high concentrations of dyes and indicator solutions.

The instructor can stain any intestinal flora to differentiate them from the cells lining the digestive tract. Brine shrimp will eat yeast soaked in an equal volume of 0.5% trypan blue, and the intestinal bacteria will then pick up the stain. The students will be able to see the stained bacteria traveling out of the body with the feces, especially if they are observing them under an oil immersion lens. This is a good time for the instructor to introduce students to the different types of symbiotic relationships between distantly related organisms.

## Behavior, Environmental Physiology, and Toxicology

Brine shrimp exhibit positive phototaxis and respond readily to other physical and chemical changes in the environment. Instructors can facilitate the intake of organic compounds into the bodies of shrimp with DMSO, although metals must be absorbed through their food. Several contemporary studies use brine shrimp to screen for cytotoxins present in plants and wastewater. Cytotoxicity becomes evident with the death of the specimen shrimp or with the loss of a particular organ system function.

Organophosphates and other neuroactive insecticides will alter the ability of the shrimp to respond to environmental stimuli. Brine shrimp will not respond to most herbicides and mild acaricides, insecticides, or nematocides. This observation exemplifies the selective specificity of biocidal agents.

If observed long enough, brine shrimp will reveal their tendency to eat their own casted exoskeletons and the decaying bodies of other brine shrimp. Cannibalism is an excellent example of behavioral adaptation to the need to conserve scarce nutrients.

Brine shrimp are a simple and inexpensive model for living demonstrations in biology classes. Instructors have used them successfully to supplement their lectures in small- and large-class settings.

### Acknowledgments

*The idea behind this demonstration was developed at the Shoestring Biotechnology Workshop held in July 1996 at Montgomery College, Maryland, and the Life Technologies training facilities in Maryland. The Shoestring Biotechnology Project is a National Science Foundation ATE-funded project (DUE 9553720) awarded to the National Association of Biology Teachers in partnership with Life Technologies and Genentech.*

### Background Reading

Freeman, J. A., L. B. Cheshire, and T. H. MacRae. 1992. Epithelial morphogenesis in developing artemia: The role of cell replication, cell shape change, and the cytoskeleton. *Developmental Biology* 152:279–292.

Hegner, R. W., and J. G. Engemann. 1968. *Invertebrate Zoology.* 6th ed. New York: Macmillan.

Russell-Hunter, W. D. 1969. *A Biology of Higher Invertebrates.* New York: Macmillan.

Ward-Booth, D., and M. Reiss. 1988. Organisms for teaching: *Artemia salina:* An easily cultured invertebrate ideally suited for ecology studies. *Junior Biological Education* 22(4): 247–251.

# Demonstrating an Interactive Genetic Drift Exercise

## Examining the Processes of Random Mating and Selection

Ashley J. R. Carter

The phenomenon of genetic drift is a powerful force in molecular evolutionary biology (Kimura 1983). Neutral alleles under the influence of drift, but not selection, likely account for a large part of the widespread levels of genetic polymorphism observed in natural populations. Purely advantageous or disadvantageous alleles would contribute little to polymorphism since these alleles are fixed or lost quickly within populations. Conversely, neutral alleles can drift in frequency for long periods of time before eventually becoming lost or fixed in a population.

Genetic drift is usually presented in very abstract terms in most texts. Many texts present graphs of computer simulation results showing an allele's frequency changing over time, perhaps at different speeds for different population sizes. The graphs are excellent, but they may not have

an impact on a student who learns best using hands-on activities.

In general, students may have a hard time understanding how a frequency can change without selection, or they may not fully appreciate the effects of population size on the dynamics of frequency changes in populations. Supplementing such graphical depictions with a population genetics computer program to simulate drift may not help students because they do not necessarily observe what happens in a potentially "black box" computer program.

The exercise presented here is a hands-on demonstration of the phenomenon of genetic drift in populations. In particular, it reinforces the random nature of drift and demonstrates the effect that population size can have on the mean frequency of an allele over just a few generations. The students will take on the roles of organisms

(with genotypes) and they will choose mates and generate offspring themselves (on note cards). The frequency of each genotype in the population will be recorded over time. From this the allele frequencies for the population can be calculated. The students will see that by simply choosing mates using a random-mating system they will generate allele frequency dynamics.

## Materials

- One note card per student
- One coin per student
- One pen per student

## Procedure

The effects of population size are illustrated by performing the exercise twice, once with the entire class acting as a large, completely mixed population and once with the class partitioned into smaller groups that must "mate" within their own groups. Although the larger population will show some fluctuation in allele frequencies, it should be more stable than some of the smaller populations, at least one of which will hopefully go to fixation/loss of an allele.

To start the exercise, each student is given a note card with an initial genotype printed on it. The genotypes involved are $A_1A_1$, $A_1A_2$, and $A_2A_2$. I suggest creating a starting set of cards designed so that the genotypes are in Hardy-Weinberg equilibrium with equal frequencies of each allele (approximately a 1:2:1 ratio of the genotypes). This way the starting frequency for each allele will be 0.5, the maximum polymorphism possible.

Each generation comprises the following events:

- Each student finds another student to "mate" with. The students are encouraged to mate at random.

- Each student then independently generates a new genotype by randomly selecting an allele from his or her genotype and combining it with a randomly selected allele from the mate. The students can flip coins (e.g., heads for the first allele and tails for the second) or use some other technique. It is important that the technique for randomly choosing between the alleles be well-known and influenced only by chance. This new genotype represents an offspring of the mating between the two genotypes involved. Each student then records his or her new genotype on the note card below the previous genotype. This will be their genotype in the next generation. Each pair of students will mate twice to generate two new offspring, one per student.

- The instructor calls for a show of hands for each genotype and records this data on the board.

While the somewhat chaotic mating period is going on, the instructor can calculate the frequency of each allele from the genotypes and record this information on the board. Alternatively, the class as a whole can do these calculations.

These generations are repeated for an appropriate number of times (at least five or six) or until one allele has been lost or fixed. At the end of the trial, there will be a series of frequency values for each allele. The instructor should do a rough line plot of these values from the starting value of 0.5 to the final value. All fluctuations seen will have resulted purely by chance. Because the students did every step themselves, they will appreciate that there are no mysterious hidden factors that have influenced the allele frequencies. The remainder of the class time can be used to discuss what has just occurred.

## Discussion

The following discussion topics start by reinforcing what the students have seen firsthand in the demonstration and continue on to more advanced concepts. The more advanced ideas are commonly seen scattered throughout texts. By discussing them after the demonstration, the students have a better opportunity to synthesize these ideas because the idea of drift is fresh in their minds. These points address many of the common misconceptions about drift and selection as they pertain to changing the frequencies of alleles in populations. Each point is prefaced by a question that the instructor can pose to the students to initiate discussion.

(1) Did the population size affect how the frequencies changed? Even if all the smaller populations persisted, they should have shown more severe swings in frequency from generation to generation than the larger population.

(2) What do such effects of population size mean for wild populations? Since smaller populations are more likely to lose alleles at a locus, they will more quickly become homozygous for various alleles across their entire complement of distinct loci. This will reduce the pool of variation within the population that facilitates an evolutionary response to new threats or environmental conditions. A smaller population becomes much more vulnerable to extinction than a larger one. This has important ramifications for the conservation of organisms in the wild.

(3) Was the mating truly random? Most students interpret random mating to mean that they should never mate with the same student twice if they can help it. Truly random mating would have many instances of the same students mating. Preferential outbreeding (avoiding all relatives as much as possible) actually acts to increase the frequency of heterozygotes, but has no impact on allele frequency.

(4) If an allele disappears from a population, does that mean it was harmful? If the experiment went well, then at least some of the smaller

groups lost alleles, presumably because of random effects, not because one was consistently bad. The loss of an allele from a population does not imply harmfulness of that allele; it may be lost purely due to chance.

(5) In the converse of (4), does fixation of an allele (it becoming the only allele in the population) prove that it is beneficial? Interestingly, this result means that an allele that is seen to increase in frequency in a population over time need *not* be beneficial. Students may want to provide ideas about how they would test for the possible benefits of a given allele if it is seen to increase in frequency.

(6) What would happen to the allele frequencies if each student with an $A_2$ allele got to mate more often than the students homozygous for the $A_1$ allele? The frequency of $A_2$ would very likely increase over time and the allele would go to fixation, since the starting frequency of the $A_2$ allele is so high that its loss due to random factors (topic 4 above) is remote. However, new beneficial mutations start in single mutant individuals.

(7) What would happen if all members of the population were $A_1A_1$ except for a single $A_1A_2$ mutant? A neutral $A_2$ allele would most likely be lost eventually (25 percent chance of loss in first generation alone if everyone gets to mate as described in this exercise). Even if it were beneficial, there is a real chance of loss for such an allele. Using population genetics theory, the chance of eventual fixation of such a beneficial allele from a single copy is approximately twice the selective advantage of the mutant allele in the heterozygote (e.g., if heterozygotes with the allele have an average of 1 percent more offspring, the allele has a 2 percent chance of becoming fixed in the population as a whole). Kimura (1983) and Gillespie (1998) provide a summary of the relevant mathematics involved. The students may consider how many beneficial mutations have

been lost because of random factors just after their formation by mutation.

Using this hands-on demonstration and these more advanced discussion topics, the instructor has the chance to make students really appreciate the randomness inherent in determining the frequencies of alleles in populations. The students will gain a feel for the processes of random mating and selection that are the cornerstone of much of the modern thinking in evolutionary biology.

## References

Gillespie, J. 1998. *Population Genetics, a Concise Guide*. Baltimore, MD: Johns Hopkins University Press.

Kimura, M. 1983. *The Neutral Theory of Molecular Evolution*. Cambridge: Cambridge University Press.

# Microbe Wars: A Demonstration of Microbial Antagonism

## A Vivid Example of Microorganism Interaction

Marty Fox

Ecology is an integral part of any undergraduate biology curriculum. As such, most instructors incorporate basic ecological principles into their introductory biology courses. Many of these courses employ an ecosystem approach to the study of ecology. This method involves analyzing biotic (living) and abiotic (nonliving) components and establishing the importance of interactions between organisms and their environment (Nebel and Wright 1996).

While instructors stress interactions among and between animals and plants, they often overlook microorganisms, a fundamental component of any ecosystem. This omission is not intentional, but results from a number of factors, foremost of which is that few ecologists are trained in microbiology. A second factor is the rise of the Pure Culture doctrine. This doctrine, which has permeated microbiology over the past century, has been of great benefit to humankind, particularly in the area of disease causation and prevention, but it has also restricted the growth of microbial ecology (Atlas and Bartha 1996). When organisms are isolated and grown in pure culture, they are removed from their natural environment. Segregating the organisms limits the opportunity for studying their interactions with other organisms.

Several years ago, I was invited to teach a course in microbial ecology at the Pymatuning Laboratory of Ecology, a division of the University of Pittsburgh. As I had not taught the course before and had little formal training in the area of ecology, I immersed myself in the literature, sought guidance from several experts in the field, and searched the World Wide Web for appropriate material for the course. While an impres-

sive body of literature devoted to soil, aquatic, and environmental microbiology exists (for reviews see Alef and Nannipieri 1995; Atlas and Bartha 1996; Douglas 1994; Kemp et al. 1993; Levin, Seidler, and Rogul 1992; Metting 1993; Mitchell 1992; Tate 1995), I discovered that this literature is highly technical and contains few exercises that can be easily adapted for an undergraduate biology course.

This article describes an exercise ideal for use in an introductory biology or microbiology class. The exercise requires no specialized equipment and little expertise in microbiology, and it provides a colorful demonstration of a microbial interaction. Furthermore, it serves as an excellent introduction to selective toxicity and antibiotics. The activity explores one aspect of microbial interactions: microbial antagonism. The instructor provides students with three unknown bacteria (A, B, C) and challenges them to discover if one produces a substance that inhibits any of the others.

## Materials

- Cultures of *Bacillus subtilis (BS), Serratia marcescens (SM),* and *Sarcina subflava (SS).* These cultures are usually available on slants, are easy to purchase and maintain, and are used in many introductory biology and microbiology courses. *Escherichia coli* or *Enterobacter aerogenes* may be substituted for *Serratia marcescens.*
- Three tubes of Brain Heart Infusion (BHI) Broth. This will be used to grow up the bacteria immediately prior to plating.
- Three Tryptic Soy Agar (TSA) or Nutrient Agar (NA) plates
- Marker (to mark the location of the streak on the plate)
- Microbial loop or needle

## The Demonstration

The day before the experiment is to be performed, the instructor should seed a separate BHI broth tube with each of the bacteria and incubate the tubes at room temperature. While the optimum growth temperature for *Serratia marcescens (SM)* is around 37°C, *Bacillus subtilis (BS)* and *Sarcina subflava (SS)* prefer it a little cooler, at 30°C and 25°C, respectively.

On the day of the exercise, the instructor provides the students with the cultures and has them determine which of the three unknown bacteria (A, B, or C) produces a substance that is inhibitory to one of the others. While there are a number of ways to perform this task, the easiest is to streak a line of two different bacteria on a plate so that they are perpendicular to one another (see Figure 1), leaving a space of one to two millimeters at the point of intersection to avoid mixing of the organisms. This procedure is similar to Alexander Fleming's approach that demonstrated the action of penicillin (Fleming 1929). The students then incubate the plates at room temperature for one to three days. Each day the students should observe the plates for growth.

The instructors should have the students repeat the plating step (from the same broth cultures) on two consecutive days. This will alleviate any problems caused if the culture is initially too light (giving the bacteria another day to grow in the broth prior to plating).

## Safety

The instructor and students handling the cultures must wear safety goggles that protect from chemical splashes. In addition, it is advisable to wear surgical gloves. Anybody handling the cultures must wash his or her hands with soap and warm water even when wearing gloves. The surface of the plates and the bacteria must not be touched. The instructor must dispose of used cultures by steam sterilization.

## Results and Discussion

While the actual exercise is performed on three separate plates, I have constructed a composite plate containing the three different groups of bacteria to illustrate the types of microbial interactions taking place (see Figure 2). The photograph clearly shows that *Bacillus subtilis,* the white colony streaked horizontally at the top of the gel, secretes a substance that inhibits *Sarcina subflava* (the yellow streak). This inhibitory agent diffuses out of the bacterium and prevents growth at the closest point (where the two bacteria intersect). Note that no *Sarcina subflava* colonies grow within the zone of inhibition that extends outward 10 millimeters from the *Bacillus subtilis* culture. Conversely, *Serratia marcescens* (the red streak) shows no zone of inhibition as the cells grow up against the *Bacillus subtilis* streak.

While the inhibitory substance is not specifically identified, most strains of *Bacillus subtilis* have been shown to produce a polypeptide antibiotic called bacitracin (the name derives from its source, a *Bacillus* isolated from the wound of a girl called Tracy). Bacitracin is used primarily as a topical agent for superficial infections and is effective against a number of gram-positive bacteria including *Sarcina subflava*. Gram-negative organisms, such as *Serratia marcescens, Escherichia coli,* and *Enterobacter aerogenes*, are generally resistant to this compound (Tortora, Funke, and Case 1995).

This activity is a simple, inexpensive, and colorful demonstration of microbial antagonism appropriate for introductory biology and microbiology students. While providing a vivid example of a microbial relationship, the exercise also serves as an excellent introduction to the concept of selective toxicity, a concept upon which modern chemotherapy is based.

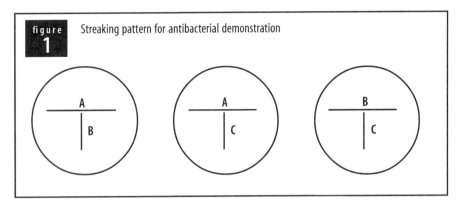

**figure 1** Streaking pattern for antibacterial demonstration

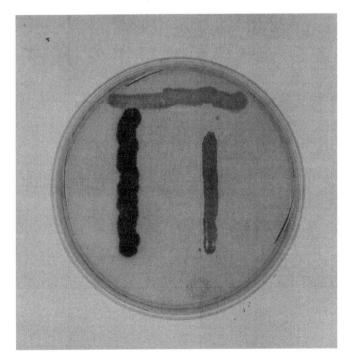

**figure 2** Selective inhibition of *Sarcina subflava* by *Bacillus subtilis.* This photograph shows a composite plate containing all three organisms: *Serratia marcescens* (red colonies) on the left, *Bacillus subtilis* (white colonies) on the top, and *Sarcina subflava* (yellow colonies) on the right.

### Acknowledgment

*The author would like to thank Dr. Craig Van Bell for photographing the bacterial cultures on the composite plate.*

## References

Alef, K., and P. Nannipieri. 1995. *Methods in Applied Soil Microbiology and Biochemistry.* New York: Harcourt Brace.

Atlas, R., and R. Bartha. 1996. *Microbial Ecology: Fundamentals and Applications.* Redwood City, CA: Benjamin Cummings.

Douglas, A. 1994. *Symbiotic Interactions.* Oxford: Oxford University Press.

Fleming, A. 1929. On the antibacterial action of cultures of a *Penicillium,* with special reference to their use in the isolation of *B. influenzae. British Journal of Experimental Pathology* 10:226–236.

Kemp, P., B. Sherr, E. Sherr, and J. Cole. 1993. *Handbook of Methods in Aquatic Microbial Ecology.* Boca Raton, FL: Lewis Publishers.

Levin, M., R. Seidler, and M. Rogul. 1992. *Microbial Ecology. Principles, Methods and Applications.* New York: McGraw-Hill.

Metting, F. 1993. *Soil Microbial Ecology. Applications in Agricultural and Environmental Management.* New York: Marcel Dekker, Inc.

Mitchell, R. 1992. *Environmental Microbiology.* New York: Wiley-Liss.

Nebel B., and R. Wright. 1996. *Environmental Science. The Way the World Works.* 5th ed. Upper Saddle River, NJ: Prentice Hall.

Tate, R. 1995. *Soil Microbiology.* New York: John Wiley and Sons, Inc.

Tortora, G., B. Funke, and C. Case. 1995. *Microbiology: An Introduction.* 5th ed. Redwood City, CA: Benjamin Cummings.

# Floating Spinach Disks: An Uplifting Demonstration of Photosynthesis

Marty Fox, John J. Gaynor, and Judith Shillcock

If questioned about what plants eat, most college students would pause before answering. Their initial confusion is understandable as plants are rarely seen to consume food. Given a few seconds to reflect, however, most students would reach the conclusion that plants synthesize their own food.

A few might also add that the recipe that plants use to make food is remarkably simple: a little light, a few light-absorbing pigments, water, and $CO_2$.

Underlying this simplicity is an extraordinary amount of biochemistry usually covered over a two-week period in introductory biology courses. During lecture, students are introduced to a myriad of metabolic pathways including the Calvin Cycle, Noncyclic and Cyclic Electron Flow, and Crassulacean Acid Metabolism.

**Topic:** photosynthesis
**Go to:** *www.scilinks.org*
**Code:** JCSTC35

The task of helping the students to understand this complex material is facilitated by several excellent laboratory exercises that examine various aspects of the photosynthetic process. The all-important light-absorbing pigments are separated and visualized by paper chromatography (Morgan and Carter 1993).

For more advanced students, the absorption characteristics of the various pigments are determined by spectrophotometry (Skavaril, Finnen, and Lawton 1993). The identification of various end products, such as starch, is accomplished by comparing uncovered vs. covered leaves (Abramoff and Thomson 1991).

These exercises are fine in their own right. They reduce a complicated process to manageable pieces—reductionism at its best. However, they are intellectually less satisfying as they rarely examine the process as a whole or factors that may affect its rate, with one notable exception. Often a simple aquatic plant (*Elodea*) is used to examine the effect of light intensity on photosynthesis (Abramoff and Thomson 1991). While this experimental approach often yields useful data, it is somewhat problematic. A readily available supply of fresh *Elodea* is essential for success. Furthermore, the system must be completely closed so that the oxygen produced by photosynthesis is sufficient to drive a measurable displacement of water.

We would like to share with you an exercise that we believe is ideal for studying the overall process of photosynthesis and the factors that may affect it. The exercise employs disks punched out of a spinach leaf with a hole puncher or cork borer. Initially gases are drawn out of the tiny disks by a brief vacuum infiltration. The gas space is replaced by a bicarbonate solution, increasing the disk density and causing them to sink. As photosynthesis occurs oxygen accumulation decreases the density and causes the disks to refloat.

The refloating of the disks is an extremely visible indication that photosynthesis is taking place. Furthermore, the rate at which the leaf disks refloat can be used as a measure of photosynthetic rate, and the composition of the liquid can be altered to examine various parameters (e.g., pH, heavy metals, $CO_2$ concentration, photosynthesis inhibitors).

A particularly attractive feature of this exercise is that the flexible experimental design provides the opportunity for open-ended, student-directed original inquiry. In this paper we describe the experimental design and results for one parameter that our biology students have studied, $CO_2$ concentration.

## Materials
- Aspirator or vacuum source
- Hole puncher or cork borer (4 mm diameter is ideal)
- Petri plates (glass or plastic)
- Sodium bicarbonate
- 150 W tungsten bulb and apparatus to hold it in place
- Bag of spinach (from local supermarket)
- Four 250 mL side-arm Erlenmeyer flasks
- Beakers
- Forceps

## Methods
1. Several hours before class, wash spinach leaves in cold running water. Allow leaves to soak in the water at 4°C until use.
2. Using a cork borer or hole puncher, cut about 200 leaf disks from a fresh spinach leaf. Cut to either side of but not through large veins.
3. Place 40 disks in each of four 250 mL side-arm flasks. The flasks contain different concentrations of sodium bicarbonate. Flask A: 50 mL of 0.05% (w/v) sodium bicarbonate; Flask B: 50 mL of 0.1% (w/v) sodium bicarbonate; Flask C: 50 mL of 0.2% (w/v) sodium bicarbonate; Flask D: 50 mL of 0.1% (w/v) sodium bicarbonate (dark control).
4. Cork the flasks and hook up to a vacuum source. Turn on vacuum. You should see air bubbles escaping from the edges of the disks.
5. After 30 seconds, break the suction by carefully removing the cork. The disks should sink.
6. Swirl the flask gently.
7. Repeat steps 4 to 6 until most of the disks sink.
8. Pour the contents of each flask into a separate empty beaker. Discard any disks that are floating. Keep the sunken disks away from bright light.
9. Label the bottom of four petri dishes A, B, C, and D.
10. Fill all four dishes with the appropriate concentration of sodium bicarbonate:
    A: 0.05% (w/v) sodium bicarbonate, B: 0.1% (w/v) sodium bicarbonate, C: 0.2% (w/v) sodium bicarbonate, D: 0.1% (w/v) sodium bicarbonate (dark control).
11. With forceps, gently place 20–30 disks into each petri dish. Be sure the disks do not overlap.

figure 1

The floating disk apparatus used by the authors to test the factors that affect the rate of photosynthesis in plants

figure 2

The effect of $HCO_3^-$ concentration on the rate of photosynthesis

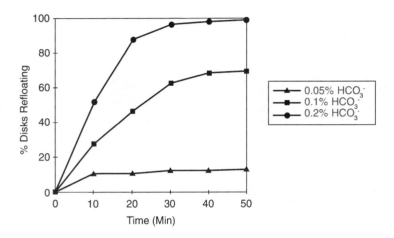

12. Place dishes (A–D) on the base of a ring stand underneath a light. Place a container of water on top of the petri plates to serve as a heat sink as shown in Figure 1. Place dish D in a drawer or cover completely with aluminum foil. This will serve as a control (no light).

13. Turn on the light, and record the number of disks floating in each dish at 10-minute intervals for 90 minutes. (To make a count: turn off the light, remove the container of water from on top of the dishes, uncover the dish and jiggle to free any stuck disks, count the number of floating disks [a disk standing on edge is counted as one-half], wipe off any water that has condensed on the underside of cover, replace the cover and the dish, and turn on the light.)

14. At the conclusion of the experiment, students perform simple statistics and plot the data (see Figure 2).

## Results and Discussion

While several excellent laboratory exercises are available on photosynthesis, they rarely examine the process as a whole or factors that may affect its rate. Floating spinach disks (see Figure 3) provide a simple, inexpensive tool for the study of photosynthesis.

The use of spinach is very appropriate since this organism has historically been the model system for chloroplast isolation and photosynthesis research in higher plants. Despite its simplicity, undergraduates can modify this experiment in the laboratory to investigate various parameters that influence photosynthetic rate in plants.

This laboratory has been field tested in numerous courses including introductory courses for majors and nonmajors, in our Gifted and Talented Program (with students ranging from grades 5 through 12), and with our University Honors Program. In each case students design

**figure 3** The spinach disks after vacuum infiltration (A) and subsequent refloating following exposure to light (B)

an experiment that will examine the influence of some parameter on photosynthetic rate, such as light intensity, light quality (using colored filters to get a crude action spectrum), pH, temperature, sodium chloride, various herbicides (which inhibit chloroplast electron flow), and $CO_2$ concentration. We have exploited this discovery-based laboratory to teach proper experimental design; to introduce methods of data collection, establishing controls, statistical analysis, and graphing; and to encourage students' presentations of their research findings.

Although the experimental design is simple and the success rate high, the following factors may influence the proper functioning of this system:

The most important factor is the "health" or viability of the spinach leaves. We have used fresh spinach purchased from local supermarkets for many years. In the vast majority of cases this has been adequate. It is especially important to allow washed leaves to soak for several hours (preferably at 4°C). This increases turgor pressure and minimizes "limp" or flaccid leaves. (We have used leaves that have been soaking in cold water for up to three days with good results.)

When cutting out leaf disks it is imperative to take from healthy leaf sections (very firm, dark green, with no insect or pathogen damage). Also avoid major veins when cutting disks.

It is also a good idea for students to place cut disks immediately into water or bicarbonate buffer. Disks that are allowed to remain exposed to air desiccate rapidly and show suboptimal performance.

In our experience, disks that are 4 mm in diameter work best for this experiment. Smaller disks work but are less reliable and less consistent; larger disks take longer to vacuum-infiltrate and longer to float.

Do not over vacuum-infiltrate leaf disks. Too little vacuum treatment and the disks do not sink; too much and you may kill the cells in the leaf. You want to apply vacuum just long enough to get the disks to sink. This is ideal because students will be able to see disks floating after a few minutes of light exposures. (Remember that you will not see the disks sink until vacuum is turned off.)

When preparing dark controls, be sure leaf disks are kept away from any light. Dark drawers or foil covers can be used here.

Be sure to use an adequate heat sink between your light source and your petri dishes containing your disks.

A particularly attractive feature of this exercise is that the flexible experimental design provides the opportunity for open-ended, student-directed original inquiry. Even a cursory review of the science curriculum and pedagogical literature indicates that students become more interested and motivated if they are actively engaged in the process of doing science.

Unfortunately, the logistical constraints associated with an introductory biology course have, in many cases, led to a laboratory experience that is less than satisfying. By performing cookbook experiments where the outcome is known beforehand, students are denied the creativity and challenge associated with scientific investigation.

Several studies have shown that open-ended investigations can restore some of the thrill and challenge of scientific investigation and provide a more realistic scientific experience for students (Heady 1993; Ohlhorst 1995; Ortez 1994; Woodhull-McNeal 1989). This "learn-by-doing" philosophy is at the core of recent curriculum reforms that emphasize student-directed original research (AAAS 1990; Project Kaleidoscope 1991). While the philosophy is certainly sound, tools are needed to help science educators convert from instructor-directed outcome-based labs to student-directed inquiry-based ones. Simple, flexible experimental systems, such as floating spinach disks, can provide one of these tools.

## Acknowledgments

*The authors would like to thank Dr. Doug Morrison of Rutgers University (Newark, New Jersey) for originally introducing them to this experiment and Ms. Ellen Belisle, Biology Learning Center, Rutgers University (Newark, New Jersey) for her many helpful suggestions.*

## References

Abramoff, P., and R. Thomson. 1991. *Laboratory Outlines in Biology*. New York: W. H. Freeman and Company.

American Association for the Advancement of Science. 1990. *The Liberal Art of Science*. AAAS Publication 90-12S. Washington, DC: American Association for the Advancement of Science.

Heady, J. 1993. Teaching embryology without lectures and without traditional laboratories. An adventure in innovation. *Journal of College Science Teaching* 23:87–91.

Morgan, J., and M. Carter. 1993. *Investigating Biology: A Laboratory Manual for Biology*. New York: Benjamin Cummings.

Ohlhorst, S. 1995. Successes using open-ended inquiry with college undergraduates and K-12 teachers. Supplement to the *Bulletin of the Ecological Society of America* 76 (#3, part 3):371.

Ortez, R. 1994. Investigative research in nonmajor freshman biology classes. *Journal of College Science Teaching* 23:296–300.

Project Kaleidoscope. 1991. *What Works. Building Natural Science Communities*, vol. 1. Washington, DC: Project Kaleidoscope

Skavaril, R., M. Finnen, and S. Lawton. 1993. *General Biology Laboratory Manual: Investigations into Life's Phenomena*. Fort Worth, TX: Saunders College Publishing.

Woodhull-McNeal, A. 1989. Teaching science as inquiry. *College Teaching* 37:3–7.

# Differential Weathering

## A Delicious Demonstration

Mark Francek

I use the consumption of a Baby Ruth candy bar to nurture students' interest in chemical and physical weathering. The only materials needed are candy bars and granite hand specimens.

After making sure that no student has an allergy to chocolate, caramel, or nuts of any kind, I ask students to place a small piece of a Baby Ruth bar in their mouths, emphasizing that they may suck the candy but not bite it. Then, I begin a 5-minute lecture on the difference between physical and chemical weathering. Again, I remind students not to bite the candy.

When the 5-minute lecture is concluded, only peanuts remain in students' mouths. I give students permission to chew the peanuts and invite one student to the blackboard to list, in progressive order, the ingredients just tasted: chocolate, caramel, and then peanuts. Next to the student list, I write three minerals common in granite in order of increasing resistance to weath-

ering: hornblende, feldspar, and quartz. Finally, we discuss the implications of the demonstration.

Just as in human digestion, water plays an integral role in chemical weathering processes like solution, oxidation, and hydrolysis. In accordance with Bowen's Reaction Series, minerals formed at the highest temperatures and pressures tend to chemically weather first. In this example, the hornblende corresponds to the chocolate, the least resistant ingredient in the candy. In the hand specimen of granite, students then locate the dark minerals. Usually, because of their inferior resistance to chemical weathering, dark minerals like hornblende form tiny weathering pits or depressions on the rock surface.

The next ingredient tasted is the caramel, analogous to the weathering of feldspar in granite. I use this analogy to discuss the relation between weathering and climate—specifically, how chemical weathering is enhanced in wet, tropical climates. High temperatures tend to speed up chemical reactions, and student mouths facilitate the breakdown of caramel. I also mention that weathering rates are high because constant surface runoff and groundwater flow keep weathered ions from saturating the weathering solution. Similarly, salivation and swallowing keep a fresh supply of unsaturated saliva in contact with the caramel.

Finally, we discuss the breakdown of peanuts, analogous to the weathering of quartz. In nature, most solutions lack the strength to chemically break down quartz over the short term. In the mouth, saliva acids lack the strength to dissolve peanuts. Simply circulating peanuts around in the mouth produces little taste because there is little chemical "weathering." In reality, physical weathering, like freeze thaw action, widens joints and increases surface area. In the mouth, chewing widens miniature fissures that exist within the peanut, breaking down the peanut into pieces small enough to be swallowed.

This demonstration can illustrate two additional concepts: the difference between weathering and erosion and the conservation of matter. Students can think of weathering as the dissolving of the chocolate and caramel, and swallowing the peanut fragments as erosion. For the law of conservation of matter, I point out that weathering is a formative as well as destructive process. Primary minerals can change into new forms like clays, just like chocolate, caramel, and peanuts are recycled into new products.

I broaden this activity by manipulating the effects of temperature and time on weathering rates. For temperature and weathering, students place one small piece of Baby Ruth in a clear container filled with 100 mL of water at 20°C and another in a container with 100 mL of water warmed to 60°C. The effect of time on weathering can be gauged by placing a piece of candy in room-temperature water and making observations immediately, hourly, and then after the candy has been exposed to water overnight. Students categorize the degree of cloudiness after each of the experimental conditions.

One limitation of this ordinal classification for cloudiness (high, moderate, or low) is that there is no real way to reconcile the perceptions of students: What is moderate for one student might be "low" for another. This shortcoming is a good opportunity to introduce the advantages of interval level measurement scales, such as those measured by a turbidimeter, which classifies cloudiness using "nephelometric" units. I ask students to name similarities and differences between the results of the temperature-time trials and the taste test.

It is important to point out that weathering is more robust in the taste test because (1) the tongue rotates candy, exposing new weathering surfaces; (2) salivation brings in a fresh supply of "weathering solution"; and (3) swallowing removes saturated solutions allowing weathering rates to remain vigorous. With a little imagination and taste, weathering processes can become clearer to students.

**Topic: weathering/erosion**
**Go to: www.scilinks.org**
**Code: JCSTC42**

# An Interactive, Fiery Model of Genetic Complementation

## Shedding Light on a Conceptually Difficult Biological Topic

Kathryn Hajek Zuehlke

The phenomenon of complementation is not only one of the most important, but also one of the most challenging concepts for undergraduate genetics students to grasp. Complementation occurs when parents with the same mutant trait have offspring that are wild type, that is, designated as the standard characteristic, for the trait.

The underlying mechanism of complementation requires that each parent has a mutation affecting the same phenotype (observable trait), but the mutations lie in different genes. The offspring inherit one mutant and one wild type allele of each gene, with one allele contributed by each parent. The wild type allele of each gene pair directs the synthesis of enough protein to produce a wild type trait and mask the presence of the mutant allele (Hartl 1996).

To predict whether two mutations will complement and give a wild type trait, students must understand how genes are inherited and expressed. The interactive method of teaching complementation that I describe below uses a simple process (lighting a candle) and requires common, inexpensive materials (eight candles, four matchbooks, scissors, and water) to represent a biological process.

Using this demonstration as an analogy is valuable for both students and instructors since it easily illustrates for students the concept of complementation and promotes discussion of related topics in genetics.

Students will better comprehend genetic complementation using candles and matches to represent gene pairs and lighting a candle to demonstrate a biological process.

A) No complementation

Parents

Offspring

B) Complementation occurs

Parents

Offspring

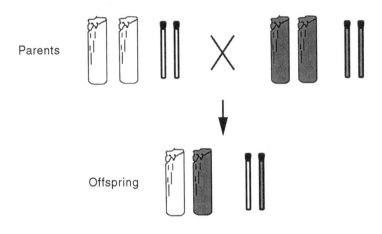

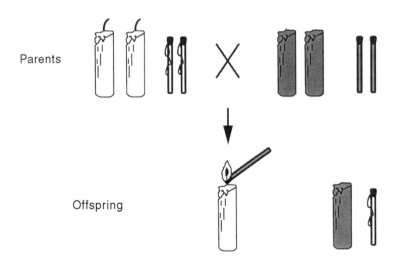

## The Demonstration

In this demonstration, candles and matches represent different gene pairs, and students act as "parents" and "offspring." The instructor, while lighting a candle, explains to the students that the process they are going to study is called "candle lighting." The wild type form of the trait is a lit candle, and only one candle needs to be alight to have a wild type phenotype. The candle and match genes are the only genes involved in the candle-lighting pathway.

The instructor gives two students representing the parental generation two candles and two books of matches (Figures 1A and 1B). Using different colored candles and matchbooks for each parent helps students follow the "inheritance" of the alleles. Students need two of each item because higher organisms have two alleles per gene, called diploidy. The instructor has the students predict their candle-lighting phenotype and test their hypotheses by lighting their candles.

The instructor continues by explaining that geneticists study biological processes using mutagens, such as chemicals or radiation, to generate mutant organisms. In this case, the scissors represent a mutagen, and students produce candle-lighting mutants by cutting the wicks off one of each of the student's candles. The students make the mutations homozygous and represent inbreeding by cutting the wicks off the second candles. Once again, the students predict and test their candle-lighting phenotypes.

Now the students are ready to perform the first complementation test (Figure 1A). The parents segregate their alleles into gametes by giving a candle and a matchbook to each of two additional or "offspring" students (four students total). The offspring fuse the gametes by pairing the candles and matches so that candles and matches from one parent are paired with those from the other parent. The students predict and test whether complementation has occurred.

For the second complementation test, the instructor gives two students each a pair of matchbooks and new candles. Students cut the wicks off one parent's candles and "mutate" the other parent's matchbooks by dunking them in a beaker of water. The water represents any event that produces a mutation. Thus, each parent is homozygous for a distinct mutation affecting the candle-lighting phenotype (Figure 1B).

After segregating the parental alleles into gametes and fusing the gametes to produce offspring, the offspring students hold an intact candle and matchbook as well as a mutant set of each. Since a student needs to hold only one functional set of genes to give the wild type phenotype of one lit candle, the parents should predict that complementation has occurred. The offspring, in turn, test their hypotheses by lighting a candle and explaining why complementation occurred in the second but not the first test.

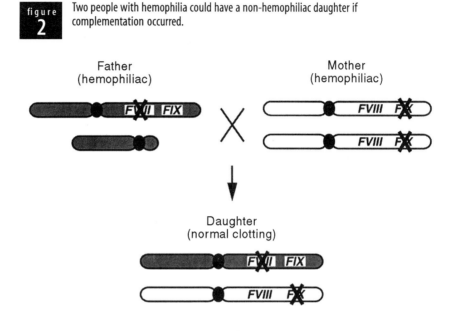

**figure 2** Two people with hemophilia could have a non-hemophiliac daughter if complementation occurred.

## Other Suggested Topics and Hints

This creative demonstration holds the students' attention because it is amusing to watch classmates try to light wickless candles and use soggy matches. But instructors should be forewarned that more persistent students might light their wickless candles by melting the wax away from the wick stub. One strategy for handling this situation is to recut the wick. Alternatively, this could be an opportunity to introduce the concept of leaky mutations.

A second topic that instructors could present is complementation in humans using the example of two hemophiliac parents having a normal daughter (Figure 2). People with hemophilia have blood that clots abnormally because they are unable to synthesize Factor VIII or Factor IX. The genes (*FVIII* and *FIX*) encoding these proteins are located on the X chromosome.

Since men have only one X chromosome, complementation can only occur in women. If a man with a mutation in *FVIII* and a woman with

a homozygous mutation in *FIX* had a daughter, the daughter would inherit a wild type copy of *FIX* from her father and a wild type copy of *FVIII* from her mother. Thus, the daughter would have blood that clots normally.

Other questions and discussions that the demonstration raised in my classroom are as follows:

- Do the wickless candles represent dominant or recessive alleles?
- Why is complementation testing invalid if the mutant alleles are dominant? (Complementation only occurs if the mutant alleles are recessive.)
- Describe an analogy in which the mutant allele would be dominant over the wild type.
- Why do geneticists use parents that are homozygous for a mutation in complementation testing?
- What crosses would a geneticist perform to breed an organism that is homozygous for a

mutation when she currently has only one heterozygous mutant organism?

- What is a complementation group?
- How can complementation testing be used to determine the number of genes in a biological pathway?

This demonstration is an effective pedagogical tool because it uses concrete objects and an easily observable process to help students understand a conceptually difficult biological topic.

## Acknowledgments

*The author thanks Therese Poole for her helpful suggestions and Ann Stapleton for her encouragement and critical reading of the manuscript.*

## Reference

Hartl, D. L. 1996. *Essential Genetics*. Sudbury, MA: Jones and Bartlett Publishers.

# Chemical Evolution as a Body-Language Demonstration

## A Geological Timescale Using Real People

Douglas Hayward

The story of chemical evolution can be told with body measures, depicted as a geological timescale of outstretched arms. It is a human demonstration that was apparently invented by John McPhee, staff writer for *The New Yorker*, and later used to describe the famous Burgess Shale fossil deposit in British Columbia (Lamb 1991).

The timescale demonstration described in this article is extended beyond geohistory to the life span of the universe. Thus, the demonstration audience "gets the feel" of the enormous amounts of time involved in chemical evolution without having to master complex vocabulary. The demonstration may be used with any class when the science content is suitably adjusted.

To conduct your timescale demonstration without equipment, big numbers, and long

Greek names, call for two helpers to stand on either side of you. Spread out your arms, wingtip-to-wingtip, and ask the class to imagine 1 billion years for each of your forearms, upper arms, and body widths from shoulder to shoulder. Together, the three of you represent the 15-billion-year age of the universe (Figure 1).

Now, turn your backs so that you may be read as "A," "B," and "C" from left to right. At A's left is the "big bang" when the universe was formed from energy and at C's right is tomorrow. Your helpers may now step down but their memories will linger with the class.

About 300,000 years after the big bang, at a tenth of a millimeter from the left fingertip of A, the protons and electrons had cooled enough to permit "sticky" collisions and produce neutrons and alpha particles. Chemistry began when

Students and teacher demonstrate the age of the universe. Each person represents 5 billion years of geochemical development.

electrons started circling the positively charged nuclei to make hydrogen and helium atoms. These atoms are transparent, so then there was light. Some of that light is still with us as cosmic background microwave photons that cause about one in every 100 snowflakes on TV screens. The recently discovered ripples in the background radiation grew into galaxies and stars.

Hydrogen and helium attracted each other by gravity and formed stars. As the stars grew, the pressure in their cores increased until they crushed the protons and helium nuclei into the nuclei of carbon, oxygen, and heavier atoms. This process continues today. The stars have so far converted 1 percent of the hydrogen and helium atoms into other chemical elements and filled the periodic table from left to right and top to bottom. More than 90 percent of the atoms in the Sun, Jupiter, and Sat-

urn are hydrogen, and about 600 tons of them are converted to helium every second in the Sun's central region.

Carbon, nitrogen, oxygen, and heavier elements produced in the massive stars were ejected into the Milky Way Galaxy when the stars exploded as supernovas. Some of the stardust was formed into the solar system 4.55 billion years ago on C's left forearm.

On Earth, the oxygen and hydrogen atoms combined into water molecules and rain fell for centuries to fill the oceans. Land appeared above the waters as the continent Pangaea that split up over the ages into our present land masses. The floor of the oceans is still spreading about as fast as a fingernail grows and this pushes the continental plates under each other, creating earthquakes and volcanoes.

Life appeared in the ocean as one-celled bacteria on C's left upper arm 3.6 billion years ago. Bacteria ruled the world for the next 3 billion years and produced the oxygen and nitrogen molecules of the air. Multicelled organisms appeared at the middle of C's right forearm. At the second joint of C's middle finger they became dinosaurs and these evolved into birds and mammals by the first joint of the middle finger. People and all their history are just on the tip of C's fingernail and could be removed with a nail file. Tomorrow begins at the carboxylate group on the C-terminus of the last keratin molecule of the fingernail.

People are 96 percent recycled carbon, hydrogen, oxygen, and nitrogen atoms. Although we are made from stardust, we are each worth only a few cents as coal, air, and water. The calcium and phosphorus in our teeth and bones and the iron in our blood make up the remaining 4 percent of our weight, along with sulfur, sodium, potassium, magnesium, and chlorine (Douglas, McDaniel, and Alexander 1983). The great marvel of the biosphere is not its diversity but its chemical simplicity.

Chemistry has the central role in science and technology and should be taught in elementary schools (Hayward 1990). The periodic table would then provide the scientific foundation for conservation, reuse, and recycling.

As science teachers we can reduce science phobia for our citizens by making demonstrations relevant to their experiences. This demonstration assures the audience of at least one relevant experience: other people.

### References

Douglas, B. E., D. H. McDaniel, and J. J. Alexander. 1983. *Concepts and Models of Inorganic Chemistry.* 2nd ed. New York: Wiley.

Hayward, D. 1990. *Do-It-Yourself Chemistry Experiments for Elementary Schools.* Vancouver, British Columbia, Canada: Department of Chemistry, University of British Columbia.

Lamb, J. 1991. Looking at life half a billion years ago. *The Vancouver Sun,* Vancouver, British Columbia, Canada: August 31, page A9.

# Electrophoresis for under Five Dollars

## How to Do It, Cheap and Easy

Vincent J. Lumetta and Mitchel J. Doktycz

This demonstration describes a procedure essential to biochemical research—electrophoresis—and how it can be conducted easily and inexpensively [using 1994 prices, applicable at the time the article was written] via a simple setup (Figure 1). It requires little more than batteries, food dye, and a sieving medium, such as agarose or gelatin. The procedure is suitable for an undergraduate college laboratory and demonstrates the simplicity of electrophoresis.

The concept of electrophoresis, or the use of electromotive force to transport charged species, has been known and employed since the early 1800s. The procedure is useful in separating ionic species and in characterizing physical constants, such as ionic conductance, and related variables, such as ionic mobilities and equilibrium constants. Its acceptance as a separation technique for biomolecules, however, did not take place until the latter half of the 20th century.

The use of electrophoresis in biochemical research is widespread. Researchers studying nucleic acids use electrophoresis to characterize

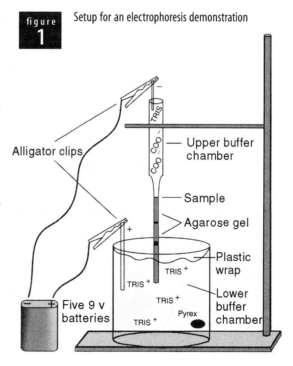

**figure 1** Setup for an electrophoresis demonstration

Alligator clips

Upper buffer chamber

Sample

Agarose gel

Plastic wrap

Lower buffer chamber

Five 9 v batteries

Pyrex

TRIS⁺

the size of the nucleic acid. This information can be used for a variety of purposes. One use is to position the relative location of disease genes on chromosomes. Another is to decipher the nucleotide sequence of a particular gene. The resolution offered by electrophoresis allows separation of nucleic acids differing in size by a single base. This information can be applied to the identification of genetic mutations. Researchers studying proteins use electrophoresis to identify the molecular weight of the protein subunits as well as the net charge of the native molecules. For example, this procedure can be used to identify various mutations in hemoglobin, some of which cause disease.

This introduction of sieving media increased the use of electrophoresis in biochemical research. Sieving media allow separations to be based on size and shape of the macromolecule as well as charge. Commonly used media are gelatin, starch, agarose, and polyacrylamide. The porous structure of these media allows smaller molecules to pass through more easily, while the retarding frictional forces cause larger molecules to migrate more slowly.

The underlying principles of electrophoresis are really quite simple. Typically an electric field is placed across a gel containing buffer ions. The gel is usually contained between glass plates or in a tube. Occasionally the gel is run "open faced," submerged under the buffer. The electrodes are placed in buffer reservoirs connected to either end of the gel.

The buffer provides ions to carry the current that is transported through the gel. The reservoirs are present to prevent depletion of the ions. The buffer ions migrate in the electric field with anions (negatively charged ions) traveling toward the anode (positive electrode) and cations (positively charged ions) traveling toward the cathode (negative electrode). These ions are too small to be retarded by the relatively large pores of the gel while macromolecules such as DNA or proteins are retarded.

*SCI*LINKS.
THE WORLD'S A CLICK AWAY
Topic: electrophoresis
Go to: *www.scilinks.org*
Code: JCSTC52

The differential mobility of biomolecules, which effect the separation, is influenced by a number of factors. One is the gel concentration, such as the weight percent of agarose used, where higher percentages create smaller pores allowing higher resolution of smaller molecules. This is the parameter usually exploited in nucleic acid separations, since nucleic acids of different length have a constant charge-to-mass ratio. Another factor is the buffer type and pH. The amino acid subunits of proteins can possess net negative or positive charges depending on the pH. At a certain pH, the protein may contain a net positive or negative charge or no charge at all. This will cause the protein to migrate either toward the cathode or anode or not at all. For proteins of the same size, a greater net charge will cause a larger electric force to act on the molecule, leading to greater mobility. This is the same phenomenon that effects the separation of the dye molecules in the experiment described below.

## Classroom Electrophoresis for under Five Dollars

My summer goal at Oak Ridge National Laboratory was to use ultra-thin polyacrylamide gels to separate DNA molecules in the process called electrophoresis. In order to optimize the conditions for separation and resolution of DNA fragments, many variables were examined, such as different buffers, ionic strengths of the buffers, and pH. The equipment used to cost several thousand dollars, but the techniques and the chemistry behind electrophoresis are quite simple. An investment of four or five dollars could buy all the equipment necessary to separate protein, dyes, or DNA.

The power source is typically the most expensive piece of equipment needed for electrophoresis. But if a very small amount of agarose medium is used, then five 9 V batteries connected together in series will supply ample power. Acrylamide is toxic and not acceptable in a classroom environment. Agarose medium on the other hand is safe, and so are gelatin and starch (potato flour and water) solutions.

Gel-developing techniques such as ethidium bromide, silver stain, or Stains-All are commonly used for DNA separation studies, but would be difficult to use in the classroom. Therefore, employing simple dyes, like food colors, eliminates the need for staining after the separation and allows the visualization of the separation during electrophoresis. The following lesson plan provides a procedure that is suitable for an undergraduate college laboratory and demonstrates the simplicity of electrophoresis.

## Materials (Per Student Group)

- Five 9 V batteries (Rechargeable batteries or DC power packs can also be used. Low current sources, such as the 45 V power packs described here, present no hazard to students. Power supplies that employ hundreds of volts should be used with proper precautions.)
- Five 9 V battery connecting wires
- Two pieces of thin copper wire
- Two connecting wires with alligator connectors on both ends
- Two 9-in. (23 cm) Pasteur pipettes; they work better than the shorter pipettes
- Parafilm or plastic wrap
- 2% agarose or gelatin solution
- Buffers. (TA) Tris acetate (Sigma). Glacial Acetic Acid, 500 mL (Carolina Biological Supply)
- Ring stand with clamp to hold Pasteur pipette
- Small beaker or paper cup to construct the lower buffer chamber
- Pipette bulbs
- Protein samples, food coloring, or other color dyes

## Procedure

1. Fill a 9-in. (23 cm) Pasteur pipette with 2% agarose solution, in the narrow bore section, 11–12 cm from the tip. Seal the tip with parafilm first.

2. After gelling, layer one drop (0.1 mL) of TA buffer on the agarose gel to prevent dehydration.

3. Load the sample with another Pasteur pipette. Touch the tip of the pipette to the sample (running dye or food coloring) and draw up the sample by capillary action. You need just a small amount of the sample (about 1 micro-liter).

4. Transfer the sample to the top of the gel under the buffer, by using a pipette bulb to expel the sample. Be careful not to form bubbles.

5. Carefully add TA buffer above the sample, without disturbing the sample layer, up to 1 cm from the top of the pipette. This is best accomplished by gently pipetting the buffer down the sides of your Pasteur pipette. (This is called the upper buffer chamber.) An alternative method is to add the buffer first and then underlay it with the sample in a dense medium.

6. Fill a small beaker or a paper cup with TA buffer, using enough to cover at least 1 cm of the tip of the Pasteur pipette. (This is called the lower buffer chamber.)

7. Cover the lower chamber with parafilm or plastic wrap. Place two small holes through the parafilm or plastic wrap and insert the Pasteur pipette into one hole and a piece of copper wire into the other hole. This will be the + (positive) electrode or anode.

8. Cover the top of your Pasteur pipette with parafilm or plastic wrap and insert another piece of copper wire into the upper buffer chamber. This will be the − (negative) electrode or cathode.

9. Connect the wire from the lower buffer chamber to an alligator clip and connect the other end to the positive lead of the batteries.

10. Connect the negative top wire to another alligator clip and connect the other end to the negative lead of the batteries. (Note: If samples are positively charged, place the positive wire in the upper buffer chamber and

the negative wire in the lower buffer chamber.)

11. Note starting point and allow electrophoresis to occur for two–three hours. Place the setup in a safe place away from student contact while the setup is running.

12. Once completed, the dye or sample should move to the tip of the pipette.

## Stock Solutions

### (TA) Tris acetate for buffers

- 50 × concentrated—mix 242 g Tris with 57.1 mL glacial acetic acid, then bring volume up to 1 L with distilled water. (pH should be 8.8.)

- 10 × concentrated—mix 48.4 g Tris with 11.4 mL glacial acetic acid, then bring volume up to 1 L with distilled water. Alternatively, dilute the 50× concentration by mixing 10 mL of the 50× with 40 mL of distilled water.

### 2% agarose in TA (100 mL)

- Take 10 mL of TA (10 × concentration) and mix with 2 g agarose, then bring volume up to 100 mL.

- Cover and heat in microwave one or two minutes or on a hot plate until mixed.

### Alternative to agarose is gelatin

- Follow directions on package to mix with water. Note that gelatin must be kept refrigerated to maintain gel form.

## Some Additional Recommendations

The most difficult part of this exercise is loading the sample onto the gel (you may want to demonstrate this to the class). The density of the sample should be increased by mixing it with sucrose or glycerol, which offers an excellent opportunity to demonstrate different densities and their layering effect. Then load the buffer carefully and slowly, so as to not disturb the sample, and place the TA buffer on top of the sample, about 1 cm from the top of the pipette. Air bubbles will not conduct electricity—if they occur, remove them from the gel and buffer or start over. Finally, the thinner the sample layer the better, since a large volume of sample will take much longer to separate.

The concentration of Tris or TA used in the experiment will affect the rate and/or distance of separation. For example, if you use a 50 times concentration (stock) instead of the normal concentration, then the separation distance of the sample will lengthen. Conversely, as the buffer concentration decreases, the time to move a given distance will decrease. Students could graph time of separation versus concentration of buffer to observe the fact that more ions will carry current, and consequently the sample will run slower.

There are several types of samples that can be used in the experiment. Samples can be dyes or food colors, and plant pigment will also work. You can mix food colors together and get separation on the agarose. For example, mix red, yellow, and green food colors to get brown, then load the brown dye onto the gel and note the separation of colors.

## Safety Concerns

- Long Pasteur pipettes (228 mm long) can break easily; students should handle them with care. Plastic straws can also be used.
- The power supply used (five 9 V batteries) will generate 45 V and micro-amperage. A

small and negligible electrical shock will result if a student touches the wires while the system is running.

- Since glacial acetic acid is caustic, you may want to prepare the buffer and agarose gel before class. After the liquid agarose is prepared, a solid gel will form in 10–15 minutes. This should allow enough time to fill 15–20 Pasteur pipettes. If solidification occurs too soon, simply reheat the gel mix; at 45°C the agarose will then remain liquid. Agarose can be stored, covered and refrigerated, indefinitely. The filled Pasteur pipettes may be stored also, as long as they are kept moist with buffer. Dehydration is best prevented by filling the upper buffer chamber with TA buffer. Store the pipettes upright in the buffer.

- Be careful not to handle the bare wire while the current is running through the system. Also, keep the wires away from metal or electrically conductive surfaces.

# Demonstrating the "Greenhouse Effect"

## Illustrating Variations on an Atmospheric Phenomenon

David P. Martin

**D**id you know that the warming of a greenhouse is not mainly due to the "greenhouse effect"? In 1909 Robert W. Wood performed an experiment that demonstrated this fact very clearly (Fleagle and Businger 1980). Robert Wood's experiment involved constructing two small greenhouses with panes made of different materials. He used panes of glass in one while using panes of polished sodium chloride (table salt) for the other. The glass windows were transparent to visible radiation but not to infrared radiation, whereas the salt windows were transparent to both visible and infrared. Of the two hothouses, the glass one had the characteristics needed for a strong warming from the "greenhouse effect." Yet when the two greenhouses were placed in sunlight they both reached nearly the same temperature.

The greenhouses did warm up, but their warming was not mainly due to the greenhouse effect. The ceiling and walls of each hothouse trapped the warm air in contact with the sunlit

 This diagram depicts an approximate energy balance for the Earth.

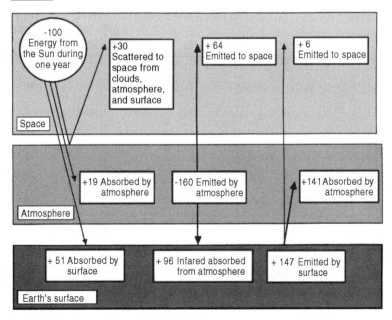

surfaces inside. By containing this air, the ceilings and walls restricted the convective cooling of the inner sunlit surfaces and allowed them to reach a higher equilibrium temperature than if they were not so enclosed. Since both greenhouses restricted convection equally well, they both reached nearly the same temperature.

It was once thought that infrared radiation given off from the sunlit surfaces in a greenhouse was absorbed and then reradiated by the glass panes of its walls and ceiling. This reradiated infrared was thought to warm the inside of the greenhouse in the same way that the atmosphere radiatively warms the Earth's surface. The similarity between the warming of the Earth and the process that was thought to warm a greenhouse may have prompted the name "greenhouse effect" for both warming processes.

Many meteorologists now use the term "atmosphere effect" to describe the warming of a planet as it receives infrared radiation from its atmosphere. This new name properly disassociates the process from that which warms a greenhouse, but it also leaves one without a concrete example for explaining the phenomenon. If a greenhouse is not a good example of a system that warms up by the atmosphere effect, what can we use in its place?

An example as ubiquitous as a greenhouse is, unfortunately, hard to find. However, it is not too difficult to construct a special apparatus that will imitate the atmosphere effect. The purpose of this article is to describe a classroom demonstration of a warming process that really is analogous to the atmosphere effect. Such a demonstration will help students not to confuse the atmosphere effect with other warming processes like the one that warms a greenhouse.

What exactly is "the atmosphere effect"? The diagram in Figure 1 will help us to answer that question. It shows the approximate energy budget for the Earth over the course of one year

**Topic: greenhouse effect**
**Go to:** *www.scilinks.org*
**Code: JCSTC58**

(Ahrens 1991). Since the overall average temperature of the Earth varies little from one year to the next, the Earth can be considered to be at thermal equilibrium over that time. If 100 units of visible light energy arrive at the Earth's outer atmosphere in one year, 30 units are scattered back into space. Of the remaining 70 units entering the Earth's atmosphere, 51 units actually get to the Earth's surface. The Earth's surface absorbs this sunlight and is warmed. It then gives off energy mostly by radiation of infrared. Of the 147 units of ultraviolet light energy given off by the surface only 6 make their way out into space. The rest warms the atmosphere. The atmosphere can also be considered to be at thermal equilibrium over the course of a year. It radiates 96 units toward the Earth's surface and 64 units toward space. These 96 units are responsible for raising the Earth's average temperature about 33°C (Ahrens 1991).

This warming of the Earth is called the atmosphere effect. It is the radiative heating of the planet as it receives infrared from its atmosphere—the atmosphere being heated mainly by the absorption of infrared from the planet's surface.

## A Classroom Demonstration to Illustrate the Atmosphere Effect

A classroom demonstration that illustrates the atmosphere effect will need to deal with at least two problems. The first is that objects in the warm classroom environment radiate more infrared than the Earth's outer space environment. The Earth/atmosphere system radiates to space but receives very little in return, since the average radiating temperature of space is about 3 kelvins. An object in the classroom, however, receives much infrared from its warm surroundings. A net outflow of infrared can only be achieved as the object is warmed to a higher temperature than its environment. Such a warm object immersed in the air of a classroom will then be cooled by convection.

Convection is the second problem for a classroom demonstration of the atmosphere effect. Convective cooling tends to dominate radiative cooling and make variations in radiative cooling due to the atmosphere effect hard to detect.

A diagram for a demonstration apparatus that overcomes these problems and heats up by a process analogous to the atmosphere effect is shown in Figure 2. The "Sun" in the demonstration is an overhead projector. The "Earth" is an aluminum foil sheet that is painted black to absorb visible light. The "atmosphere" is a sheet of material placed around the absorber "Earth." It is constructed with one side open to allow light from the projector to strike the "Earth." The atmosphere effect can be imitated with this apparatus by replacing the atmosphere with one that absorbs and reradiates infrared more effectively.

The demonstration would not work without the salt box. Its job is to solve the convection problem mentioned earlier. It restricts convective cooling of the absorber by trapping the warm air around the absorber, but because it is transparent to infrared and visible it allows radiative transfer to occur. Its airtight construction also makes it possible to monitor the overall temperature of the absorber during the experiment by measuring the pressure of the trapped air inside.

Even with the salt box in place, the measured increase in temperature due to the imitation atmosphere effect is small (about one Celsius degree). This small temperature increase is measured with a liquid barometer that monitors the pressure of the air inside the salt box. A temperature increase of the absorber "Earth" is indicated by a rise in the level of the barometer fluid.

The atmospheres for the demonstration are shown in Figure 3. The first is made of a plastic film that is relatively transparent to infrared (available from Edmund Scientific Company). The second atmosphere is made of aluminum foil painted on both the inside and outside surfaces. The painted surfaces absorb and reradiate infrared energy well. We used black paint but any

**figure 2** This diagram shows the apparatus used to demonstrate the atmosphere effect.

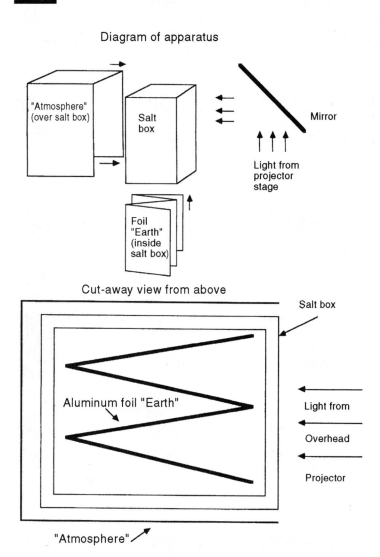

nonmetallic color ought to perform well (Bartels 1990). The third atmosphere is made of aluminum foil painted only on its inside surface. The unpainted surface on the outside reflects infrared and is therefore a poor absorber and emitter of infrared. Thus the third atmosphere radiates better toward the inside than to the outside.

**figure 3**

Three different "atmospheres" produce different results.

**figure 4**

The demonstration apparatus is made up of an overhead projector, a barometer, and the imitation "atmospheres."

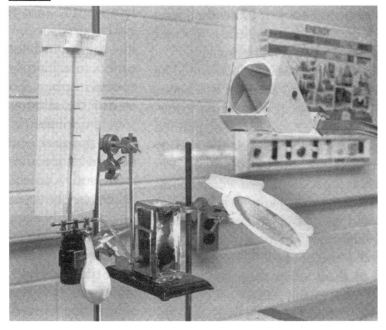

A photograph of the apparatus for the demonstration is shown in Figure 4. The mirror is used to deflect light from the projector to the apparatus. The liquid barometer has a screen behind it to increase the visibility of the indicator fluid. Reference lines are drawn on the screen to help keep track of the level of the indicator fluid during the experiment.

The salt box is connected to the liquid barometer by a length of vinyl aquarium tubing. Figure 5 shows the liquid barometer assembly. An aquarium air valve is used to direct the flow of warmed air during the experiment. The indicator fluid is red power-steering fluid. We did not use water because the salt box will fog in high humidity. In fact, the salt box is stored between uses in a desiccator. Some desiccant is also placed inside the salt box with the foil "Earth." The balloon is used to store the dry air ejected from the salt box as the absorber Earth is warmed. The stored, dry air is put back into the salt box when the absorber cools after the experiment.

The demonstration is prepared by putting the plastic atmosphere in place and illuminating the "Earth" with the projector for about 25 minutes. This is to bring the absorber up to its equilibrium temperature. During this period the valves both to the indicator fluid and balloon are opened. This allows warmed air from the salt box to be caught in the balloon without causing the indicator fluid to rise. (This is needed because the indicator tube is not tall enough to monitor the rise in temperature during the warm-up period.) It is important to use a projector with a high-powered bulb and to place the salt box close to the focus point of the deflected light beam. This helps to achieve the high temperatures needed to perform the demonstration.

After the initial warm-up period, the balloon is carefully squeezed so that barometer fluid is pushed up into the lower part of the indicator tube. When the desired level is reached, the valve to the balloon is closed. The fluid level should be fairly steady or very slowly rising. Students should be asked to predict what will happen to the fluid level when the plastic atmosphere is replaced by the other two foil atmospheres.

The demonstration is performed by marking the fluid level on the screen and then replacing the plastic atmosphere with the one made of painted foil. The fluid level should rise sharply when the second atmosphere is in place. It absorbs infrared from the foil absorber, heats up, and then reradiates infrared back toward the absorber and the classroom environment. We observed a rise of about 3 cm in the indicator fluid when the second atmosphere was put in place.

When the level of the fluid stops rising quickly, its height is marked on the screen again. Then the second atmosphere is replaced with the silver one, which is only painted on the inside surface. Again the fluid level rises to indicate an increase in temperature. We measured an additional 3 cm rise in fluid level.

This third atmosphere mimics the real Earth's atmosphere more closely than the second in that it radiates better back toward the "Earth" than toward its environment. This third atmosphere reaches a higher equilibrium temperature and therefore reradiates more infrared back to the absorber "Earth."

Care should be taken if one wishes to reverse the process. Since the air in and around the salt box gets warmer when the second and third atmospheres are in place, the salt also warms up. This warming of the salt keeps the system from returning quickly to the original temperature when a foil atmosphere is replaced by the plastic, transparent one. In order to re-create the beginning temperature in a timely fashion, the system needs to be cooled to well below the original equilibrium temperature before placing the plastic atmosphere in place. This can be done by leaving the salt box without an atmosphere until the fluid level drops well below the mark made for the first equilibrium temperature. Once the box is sufficiently cooled, the plastic atmosphere can be replaced to achieve the original equilibrium temperature. This process takes several minutes.

The demonstration can be reversed more quickly when the tops of the "atmospheres" are

**figure 5** The atmosphere effect is detected by a rise in the indicator fluid in the barometer assembly.

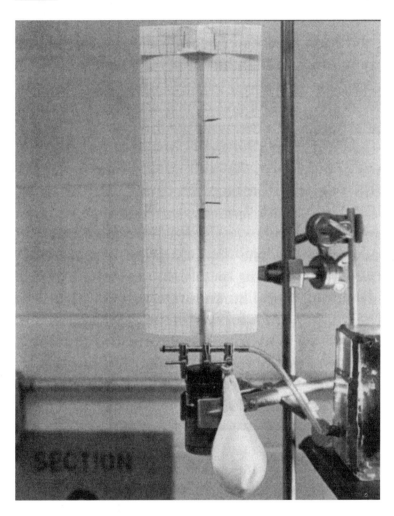

removed and space is allowed for convection between the atmosphere and the salt box. The rise in temperature is slower and less dramatic in this case, however, because the foil "atmospheres" are cooled by convection.

## Construction

The salt box was constructed from eight polished slabs of sodium chloride. These were cleaved from a hand-sized piece of halite purchased from a geological supply company. The pieces were ground and polished using a crystal grinding kit like that sold to polish windows for an infrared spectrophotometer. The pieces varied in size and thickness. They were simply the biggest pieces we could obtain from our sample of halite. The hole for the barometer connection was drilled into the halite with an ordinary metal drill bit.

The salt slabs were glued together with an epoxy glue called "J.B. Weld." Holes in the glue joints were found by forcing dry nitrogen into the box and listening to the hissing sound. The holes were plugged to produce an airtight box. Gloves were worn during the assembly of the salt box to avoid unnecessary exposure of the halite to hand moisture.

## Conclusion

Since a greenhouse is not a good example of a system that warms by the atmosphere effect, another example should be used in our teaching. A demonstration has been described that shows a warming process analogous to the atmosphere effect. It also allows the teacher to vary the nature of the "atmosphere" and show the resulting change to the equilibrium temperature of the system. The teacher should be careful to discuss one variable at a time with the class and then put all the variables together to help students better understand the atmosphere effect.

## Acknowledgment
*Research for this article was partially supported by a grant from the Auburn University at Montgomery Research Grant-in-Aid Program.*

## References
Ahrens, C. D. 1991. *Meteorology Today.* 4th ed. Minneapolis: West Publishing Company.

Bartels, R. A. 1990. Do darker objects really cool faster? *American Journal of Physics* 58(3):244–248.

Fleagle, R. G., and J. A. Businger. 1980. *An Introduction to Atmospheric Physics.* 2nd ed. New York: Academic Press.

# Illustrating Heterochrony and Heterotopy

## Two Developmental Patterns in the Evolution of Organismal Form

Terry O'Brien

Heterochrony, defined as evolutionary change in a lineage in the timing of development, is a topic treated in several popular college textbooks for introductory biology or evolution courses (e.g., Campbell, Reece, and Mitchell 1999; Guttman 1999; Beck et al. 1991; Futuyma 1998; Ridley 1996). One familiar example of a trait due to heterochrony is the large brain size of humans among all primates, which is attributed to an extension of developmental time in the human lineage. The term *heterochrony* was popularized by Gould (1977) and later reaffirmed in numerous works by such biologists as Alberch et al. (1979), Bonner (1988), McKinney and McNamara (1991), Niklas (1994), Raff (1996), McNamara (1997), Schlichting and Pigliucci (1998), and Guralnick and Lindberg (1999).

Heterochrony is one kind of developmental explanation to a basic question in biology: How can two related organisms be quite different in appearance? Other developmental explanations exist—for example, the production of new innovations not present in an immediate ancestor, such as wings or flowers. A third explanation is heterotopy, an evolutionary change in a lineage in the spatial pattern of development (Zelditch and Fink 1996).

One clear example of heterotopy is described by Zelditch and Fink (1996), who demonstrated that the diversity in body forms among piranhas is related primarily to shifts of the spatial arrangement of body landmarks (such as fins, eyes, and gills) during development, not changes in the timing of development (e.g., heterochrony). Heterotopy is increasingly considered among biologists to be of equal importance to heterochrony (Zelditch and Fink 1996; Schlichting and Pigliucci 1998), and the biological literature offers many examples and potential examples of heterotopy, despite the infrequent use of the term (Schlichting and Pigliucci 1998). However, I have not seen any

*SCILINKS.*
THE WORLD'S A CLICK AWAY

Topic: heterochrony
Go to: *www.scilinks.org*
Code: JCSTC63

introductory biology textbooks that address heterotopy.

I have two purposes for this article. First, I want to emphasize to the teaching community in biology that both heterotopy and heterochrony are fundamental processes that deserve inclusion in textbooks and courses. Second, I describe an inexpensive, simple method using balloons to demonstrate heterochrony and heterotopy in the classroom. The method can be used to supplement lectures and assigned readings for a course, especially in cases where heterotopy is not treated in the readings.

**table 1** Explanation of terms used in evolutionary biology

*Acceleration*—in the context of heterochrony, acceleration refers to a peramorphic shift that occurs by speeded development (Figure 1b).

*Allometric growth*—growth at differential rates among an organism's parts, resulting in a change in shape of features as the organism increases in size (illustrated by the inflation of any of the balloons in Figure 1b; see *isometric growth*).

*Heterochrony*—a change in the timing or rate of development of an organism or a structure of an organism, compared with an ancestor (Figure 1b; see *heterotopy*).

*Heterotopy*—a change in the spatial pattern of development of an organism or a structure of an organism, compared with an ancestor (Figure 1c; see *heterochrony*).

*Hypermorphosis*—a peramorphic shift that occurs by late offset (extended time) of development (Figure 1b).

*Isometric growth*—growth at equal rates among an organism's parts, resulting in no change in shape of features as the organism increases in size (illustrated by the inflation of the heterotopy balloon shown in Figure 1c; see *allometric growth*).

*Landmark*—any spatial position of an organism that can be observed during development, whose orientation (distance and direction) can be measured relative to other landmarks (Figure 1c).

*Neoteny*—a paedomorphic shift that occurs by slowed development (Figure 1b).

*Paedomorphosis* (also known as "underdevelopment")—the occurrence of ancestral, juvenile features in an adult as compared with an immediate ancestor (Figure 1b).

*Peramorphosis* (also known as "overdevelopment")—the occurrence of increased development of a structure or organism as compared with an immediate ancestor (Figure 1b).

*Progenesis*—a paedomorphic shift that occurs by early offset (truncation) of development (Figure 1b).

## Materials
- Large, ovoid (egg-shaped) balloons
- Tube (sausage-shaped) balloons
- Black felt-tip markers
- Air supply (desirable, but optional)
- Timer or clock (optional)
- Rulers, calipers, or other devices for measuring distance (optional)

## Procedures
Teachers or students who would like to learn more about heterochrony may wish to first consult Gould (1977), Bonner (1988), McKinney and McNamara (1991), and Futuyma (1998), and for more about heterotopy, compare Zelditch and Fink (1996) and Futuyma (1998). (See Table 1 for definitions of terminology related to these topics.)

The data needed to determine whether heterochrony or heterotopy has occurred in evolution are (1) measurements of size or shape in an organism through time (e.g., development), and (2) comparative data from an ancestor or a near relative that shares a recent common ancestor.

The tube balloons are used to make the reference organism (the sister taxon) and to demonstrate heterochronic changes in development; ovoid balloons are used to demonstrate heterotopy. Before class, determine the best rates to inflate the balloons so that students can easily perceive the differences in timing of inflation. An air supply in the classroom can provide better control over inflation times, but the balloons can also be inflated by mouth.

During class, begin with a statement of the importance of comparing two near relatives (sister taxa; Figure 1a) to infer whether heterochrony or heterotopy is an explanation for the observed differences in the form of a homologous body feature that will be represented by the balloons. Select a tube balloon to serve as the sister taxon and ask students to observe the timing as the balloon is blown to the length of a fully inflated ovoid balloon. To illustrate heterotopy in the following steps, the tube balloon should not exceed the length of an inflated ovoid balloon.

Demonstrate examples of heterochrony with tube balloons by inflating balloons at different rates and to different lengths, as shown in Figure 1b (note that not all types of heterochronic changes are shown; those illustrated in Figure 1 are merely examples). Use the balloon that represents the sister taxon to interpret the type of heterochronic change.

Demonstrate heterotopy with ovoid balloons that are marked with three or more landmarks (Figure 1c) to allow students to observe the spatial pattern of development. It is useful to mark the balloon on only one side so that all landmarks are visible from one perspective. At this step it may be helpful to remind students of the development of the sister taxon balloon by inflating a second sister taxon balloon that is marked with the landmarks corresponding to those on the ovoid balloon. To visualize the effects of heterotopy, ask students to think about how the angles between landmarks differ between the ovoid balloon and the sister taxon tube balloon. Note that for these balloon shapes, changes in distances between landmarks of the sister taxon and taxon X can occur by either heterochrony or heterotopy (not shown in Figure 1).

The procedures are simple, easily repeatable, and can be completed in about 10 minutes during a class period.

## Discussion

The use of balloons to demonstrate heterochrony or heterotopy has a number of benefits for both students and the instructor. Several current textbooks for introductory biology courses include content on the concept and significance of heterochrony, but include no explicit mention of heterotopy. As Raff (1996) has aptly stated, "It's not all heterochrony." This demonstration facilitates the inclusion of heterotopy among course concepts and will complement an instructor's existing methods of active learning in lectures.

**figure 1** Distinguishing heterochrony and heterotopy

a—A phylogenetic tree depicting the relationship between organism X and its closest taxonomic relative, a sister taxon. For simplicity, the sister taxon is assumed to have forms during development like that of the common ancestor.

b and c—Balloon shapes and inflation times to demonstrate the evolution of form differences between taxon X and its sister taxon, due to heterochrony (b) or heterotopy (c). To represent developmental trajectories, balloons are inflated (shown here from left to right), beginning at time $t_0$. In each case, the type of evolutionary change in development is determined by comparing taxon X to the sister taxon. To demonstrate heterotopy, both balloons can be marked with landmarks (shown by squares), each representing a reference point by which to interpret spatial changes in development. Note that among developmental patterns, each time increment (e.g., from $t_0$ to $t_1$ and $t_1$ to $t_2$) is an equal amount of elapsed time, and that the timescales differ. In the case of heterotopy, the timescale of development is unchanged as compared with the ancestor.

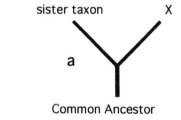

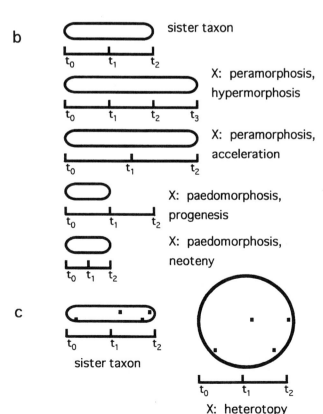

For those who prefer that students experience the activity more directly (e.g., hands-on or inquiry), these procedures can also be adapted so that students investigate heterochrony and heterotopy during laboratories. For students who are visual or tactile learners, or who have difficulty interpreting spatio-temporal relationships, this demonstration may be a preferable alternative to illustrations with graphs and figures.

The discovery of patterns and processes of development in relation to evolution is an important theme of many introductory biology courses. If learning is limited by preconceptions (Committee on Learning Research and Educational Practice 1999), it is important that opposing or complementary views are presented early in students' college experiences so they achieve a more complete understanding by the time they reach advanced studies. The concept of heterotopy is a logical complement to heterochrony and should be included even in introductory courses on evolution and development.

A limitation of the balloon demonstration is that students might be tempted to view heterochrony and heterotopy as mutually exclusive patterns of evolution in development. It can and should be emphasized that both may contribute to the differences between two related organisms, even in the same structure. Thus, heterotopy and heterochrony are endpoints of a continuum, rather than like sides of a coin.

Another concept that describes a change in shape is allometric growth, which can be confused with heterochrony or heterotopy. Allometric growth is disproportionate growth among different parts of an organism that results in a change in the organism's relative proportions as its size changes. A commonly used example of allometry in humans is the relatively large increase in body size relative to head size as one develops from birth to an adult. Unlike heterochrony or heterotopy, the determination that growth is allometric requires only measurements of size and shape of an organism, but no information about developmental time (O'Keefe, Rieppel, and Sander 1999). In the case of heterochrony and heterotopy, it requires information about the time of development (Alberch et al. 1979; Ayers 1989; McKinney and McNamara 1991; Niklas 1994; Godfrey and Sutherland 1995; Zelditch and Fink 1996; Rice 1997; Schlichting and Pigliucci 1998; O'Keefe, Rieppel, and Sander 1999), as well as comparisons to ancestors or near relatives. With respect to the balloons used in this demonstration, tube balloons of different sizes show allometry and ovoid balloons of different sizes show isometry. However, heterochronic shifts (Figure 1b) do not necessitate the occurrence of allometry, as heterotopic shifts (Figure 1c) do not necessitate the occurrence of isometry.

A final point I would like to make is that for most first-year undergraduate students, the terminology included in Figure 1 and Table 1 is unfamiliar and should be used judiciously in the classroom. In my experience, it is better to provide a limited amount of terminology rather than terms specific to each pattern of developmental evolution. The use of some terminology can facilitate students' learning, as terms may function as anchors that students use to identify concepts. In the introductory courses for biology majors that I have taught, I freely use the terms *allometry, heterochrony, heterotopy, paedomorphosis,* and *peramorphosis* to cover the basic patterns of developmental evolution. However, I reserve emphasizing terms that describe finer categories of heterochrony, such as *hypermorphosis, progenesis,* and *neoteny,* for upper-level courses in evolution.

### References

Alberch, P., S. J. Gould, G. F. Oster, and D. B. Wake. 1979. Size and shape in ontogeny and phylogeny. *Paleobiology* 5:296–317.

Ayers, C. 1989. *Process and Pattern in Evolution.* New York: Oxford University Press.

Beck, W. S., K. F. Lien, and G. G. Simpson. 1991. *Life: An Introduction to Biology.* 3rd ed. New York: Harper-Collins.

Bonner, J. T. 1988. *The Evolution of Complexity by Means of Natural Selection*. Princeton: Princeton University Press.

Campbell, N. A., J. B. Reece, and L. G. Mitchell. 1999. *Biology*. 5th ed. Menlo Park, CA: Benjamin Cummings.

Committee on Learning Research and Educational Practice. 1999. *How People Learn: Bridging Research and Practice*. Washington, DC: National Academy Press.

Futuyma, D. J. 1998. *Evolutionary Biology*. 3rd ed. Sunderland, MA: Sinauer Associates.

Godfrey, L. A., and M. R. Sutherland. 1995. Flawed inference: Why size-based tests of heterochronic processes do not work. *Journal of Theoretical Biology* 172:43–61.

Gould, S. J. 1977. *Ontogeny and Phylogeny*. Cambridge: Harvard University Press.

Guralnick, R. P., and D. R. Lindberg. 1999. Integrating developmental evolutionary patterns and mechanisms: A case study using the gastropod radula. *Evolution* 53:447–459.

Guttman, B. S. 1999. *Biology*. Boston: McGraw-Hill.

McKinney, M. L., and K. J. McNamara. 1991. *Heterochrony. The Evolution of Ontogeny*. New York: Plenum Press.

McNamara, K. J. 1997. *Shapes of Time. The Evolution of Growth and Development*. Baltimore: Johns Hopkins University Press.

Niklas, K. J. 1994. *Plant Allometry. The Scaling of Form and Process*. Chicago: University of Chicago Press.

O'Keefe, F. R., O. Rieppel, and P. M. Sander. 1999. Shape dissociation and inferred heterochrony in a clade of pachypleurosaurs (Reptilia, Sauropterygia). *Paleobiology* 25:504–517.

Raff, R. A. 1996. *The Shape of Life*. Chicago: University of Chicago Press.

Rice, S. H. 1997. The analysis of ontogenetic trajectories: When a change in size or shape is not heterochrony. *Proceedings of the National Academy of Sciences of the United States of America* 94:907–912.

Ridley, M. 1996. *Evolution*. 2nd ed. Cambridge, MA: Blackwell Science.

Schlichting, C. D., and M. Pigliucci. 1998. *Phenotypic Evolution. A Reaction Norm Perspective*. Sunderland, MA: Sinauer Associates.

Zelditch, M. L., and W. L. Fink. 1996. Heterochrony and heterotopy: Stability and innovation in the evolution of form. *Paleobiology* 22:241–254.

# A Vivid Demonstration of Fall Leaf Color Changes

## Assessing the Environmental Factors That Affect Plant Metabolism

Brian R. Shmaefsky, Timothy D. Shmaefsky, and Kathleen M. Shmaefsky

In most temperate and subtropical regions, fall is a time when the splendors of nature are unveiled through the transformation of leaf colors. To most people, the color change of leaves is an aesthetic experience, while biologists see it as a set of elaborate biochemical steps worth describing in class.

Most students learn that daylight, temperature, and nutritional variations are factors that initiate the hormonal changes leading to the alteration of colors that is induced by senescence. *Senescence* is best described as the physiological changes leading to tissue death, which in leaves is usually characterized by color change. However, many students do not know that the rate and degree of color change depend on environmental factors before and after senescence.

For example, oak trees in western Oklahoma change color just like the trees in eastern Connecticut. But the rate and degree of color change vary for the same species of oak in these two different environments.

Students can design a large-scale classroom experiment that assesses the factors affecting post-senescence fall leaf color changes. This activity, which is fitting for the fall season, reinforces lectures in ecology, plant physiology, and scientific method. For botany lessons it is a more vivid model of senescence and plant hormones than traditional demonstrations using ethylene to ripen apples or bananas.

### Background

The fall metamorphosis of leaves is the conclusion of a senescence process initiated by a variety of physiological events in the leaf. The amount of average daily sunlight, temperature, and rainfall are some of the environmental factors that govern these events.

Most of the observable color change happens when the leaf loses chlorophyll and the accessory pigments appear more prominent in the leaf. A variety of colors emerges from the predominant accessory pigments. Blue, red, and purple coloration can be due to the unmasking of anthocyanins.

The redness of anthocyanins is enhanced by sugars in the leaf cells.

Different growing conditions can affect the red fall coloration between two trees or within the same tree on different branches. In many leaves, red coloration develops during the decay process. The brown-orange pigment quercetin, common in oaks, is converted to the scarlet pigment pelargondin upon decomposition. Thus, the bright red in oaks is not present until it develops during senescence.

Two commonly masked colors are yellow, which develops from xanthophylls, and orange, which comes from carotenes. Eventually, the accessory pigments decay completely to produce the brown leaf color indicative of dead plant tissue. The rate and degree of senescence are subject to plant factors, such as sugar content of the leaf, and environmental factors such as temperature, humidity, and concentration of leaf litter. These environmental factors are simple to manipulate and can readily be demonstrated to the class using the classroom activity I describe below.

## Materials and Methods

Each student or group of students will need the following materials:

- One plastic sandwich bag with a locking seal
- One assortment of freshly collected fall leaves from deciduous trees (10 small leaves per bag)
- Optional: Apple or banana sections
- Optional: Munsell plant color chart (available in forestry supply and biological supply catalogs)
- Corkboard and walls or table to display the specimens

Students should be refreshed about the scientific method before proceeding with this activity as they need to be involved in the demonstration's experimental design. The role of the instructor is to critique the design and guide revisions made by the students. Before beginning this activity students should provide hypotheses for their experiments and a short justification for their experimental design.

This activity can be conducted during a lecture period. The instructor should begin by dividing the class into groups with each group assigned to a particular research team. Then each team should collect leaves of similar color or type.

Deciduous tree leaves are preferred because of the known series of color changes they experience after senescence. Timothy and Kathleen collected native palm and pine leaves to see if they undergo any observable color transitions.

The instructor should then have students place the leaves in the sealed bags in an area with uniform environmental conditions. The bags must be in a location where students can easily observe the leaves. Adjustments should be made for any variables the students are going to control. For example, they can compare the color change of leaves placed under different environmental situations by varying the humidity, lighting, pH, temperature, or other variables that they believe to affect color change. Leaves can also be treated with plant hormones, such as auxin, to see if they have any influence on color change. Plant hormones are generally applied as a paste and can be placed on the end of the petiole or rubbed on a small area of leaf surface.

Students must observe and record their initial analysis of the leaves' color, which can be compared to a Munsell color chart. They can also develop a standardized color schema using criteria developed by the class. The students should note the nature of the color change and the rate of color loss of the leaves as the experiment progresses.

During lecture any changes in the leaves can be noted by the instructor or individually recorded by the students for later analysis. Variations in leaf color changes are noticeable

**Topic: leaf structure and function**
Go to: *www.scilinks.org*
Code: JCSTC70

within three days after starting the experiment.

The class can apply statistical methods to this experiment by conducting nonparametric tests such as chi-square, Kruskal-Wallis, Mann-Whitney U, and Wilcoxon signed-rank tests. It is crucial that the students record the data in a quantifiable manner. For example, each color can be assigned a value, such as number one for green and number two for yellow. Then using statistics such as the Wilcoxon test, students can statistically determine if there are significant differences in the rate or amount of leaf color change under varying conditions or between two different types of leaves.

## Conclusion

This activity was designed to introduce college students to experimental design. Instructors can integrate the exercise into lectures on plant physiology to show how environmental factors affect plant metabolism, or the exercise can be used for lessons in ecology and thermodynamics.

The demonstration is also practical because it provides simple-to-interpret visual cues. Timothy and Kathleen had no trouble recognizing that leaves from the same tree placed in different environments changed colors at a different rate.

They quickly surmised that this was due to the one variable that they controlled. In addition, they recognized that different trees exhibited differences in leaf color change.

I found in my classes that most students completing general biology are not able to make these types of observations. Many college students are not given enough opportunity to design a preliminary experiment that produces simple data such as that used in this activity. Students are, in many instances, so bogged down with trying to understand the terminology and concepts in an experiment that they are too confused to identify the proper variables and interpret data accurately.

### Background Readings

Garden Gate Magazine: Fall Color. *http://www. gardengatemagazine.com/design/fallcolr.html*

Illinois Department of Natural Resources: Leaf Color. *http://dnr.state.il.us/entice/woodlands/ fallcolors_3to5.htm*

Salisbury. F. B. 1992. *Plant Physiology*. 4th ed. Boston: Wadsworth.

Taiz, L., and E. Zeigler. 1991. *Plant Physiology*. Redwood City, CA: Benjamin/Cummings.

# An Interactive Classroom Method to Demonstrate DNA Structure

## Teaching Polymerization by Real-Life Participation

Sharon L. Weldon and Marjorie A. Jones

As academic biochemists, we are continually challenged to aid students in visualizing biologically functional molecules. The nucleic acids, DNA and RNA, are especially important since they are the compounds that carry genetic information for living things. These molecules are long strings of complex organic units and have multiple levels of structure. We have devised a classroom interactive method to help demonstrate the intricacies of nucleic acid structure as it relates to the biological function of these molecules.

Deoxyribonucleic acid (DNA) is a linear polymer made from monomers of nucleotide units, using phosphodiester bonds. A nucleotide comprises a nitrogenous base, a five carbon sugar (pentose), and one or more covalently attached phosphates. In DNA, the 2' hydroxyl group of the pentose is missing, thus the name deoxyribose (d) sugar. The major nucleotide units used

in the synthesis of DNA are dATP, dGTP, dCTP, and dTTP, all of which have the deoxyribose sugar. Ribose sugar is present in ATP, GTP, CTP, and UTP, which are the nucleotides used in RNA polymers. The ribose or deoxyribose sugars are covalently linked to form the backbond of DNA or RNA connecting the 3' OH of one sugar, via a phosphodiester bond, with the phosphate on the 5' carbon of the next nucleotide.

To protect the genetic information, DNA exists as two polymer strands, the "double helix," with noncovalent bonding stabilizing the interaction between "complementary" nitrogenous bases (purines with pyrimidines). Therefore, the adenine of dAMP complements the thymine in dTMP, while guanine interacts favorably with the cytosine of the complemen-

**SCi LINKS.**
THE WORLD'S A CLICK AWAY

**Topic: DNA**
**Go to:** *www.scilinks.org*
**Code: JCSTC73**

**figure 1**

Early organization involves chaos as students try to recognize who the individual components of the system are and decide how to accomplish the goal of forming double-stranded DNA.

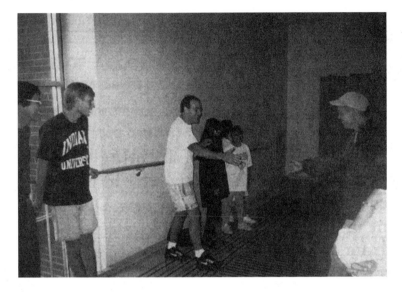

**figure 2**

The formation of the double helix is well under way, and student polymerases are organizing the "growing" end of the polymer.

tary chain. If the noncovalent bonding is disrupted, the two polymer chains of DNA separate, forming parental strands that may serve as blueprints for the synthesis of new DNA or of RNA if ribonucleotides are used in the reactions.

Enzymes that catalyze the covalent linkage of nucleotides are called *polymerases*. DNA polymerases use one DNA or parental chain to direct the formation of its complementary, daughter strand, using nucleotide units. Since the parental DNA dictates the order of the complementary strand, the DNA sequence is conserved through multiple replications and the genetic information is maintained.

To help students better visualize the polymerization process, we have developed the following interactive exercise. The individual components of DNA synthesis were written on slips of paper and students randomly selected their "part" in this activity. In a class with 70 students, about 60 students were designated as the deoxyribose nucleotides (15 each of dAMP, dGMP, dCMP, dTMP).

Each student represented a nucleotide as follows: the left arm served as the phosphate group, which would be involved in the phosphodiester bond between nucleotides; the body symbolized the deoxysugar; the right hand represented the nitrogenous base. Four students acting as DNA polymerase enzymes were instructed to synthesize a molecule of DNA by ordering the nucleotides appropriately. Five students were designated as histones, which are proteins that bind and protect DNA by folding it into tightly packed nucleosomes. One student was designated as a nuclease, an enzyme that can hydrolyze the phosphodiester bond and therefore break the nucleic acid polymer chain. The nuclease was instructed to "break" the phosphodiester bond whenever the lack of histones exposed 2–4 nucleotides to the environment.

After obtaining these brief instructions, the students were "let loose" to build a DNA (Figure 1, Figure 2, Figure 3). The polymerases quickly noticed that they must coordinate their efforts to form a proper type of double-stranded DNA alpha helix. To build DNA, two polymers must be generated and the nitrogenous bases must be paired purine to pyrimidine. A portion of the class (about one-half of the students designated as nucleotides) was instructed to form one polymer of DNA; the student nucleotides were placed next to each other with their left hand on the right shoulder of the individual on their left side in order to form the polymer. The individuals serving as polymerases were instructed to organize the remaining student nucleotides to form the second strand of DNA, again using the left hand on the right shoulder of the next "nucleotide" to form the phosphodiester bond. The polymerases were aided in the task by the ability of each nucleotide's right hand (the nitrogenous base) to shake or "base pair" with the complementary nitrogenous base on the opposite polymer chain.

The joined hands signified the noncovalent hydrogen bonds that strengthened the double helix structure. Once the polymerases recognized that the limiting step was to match complementary bases, they quickly synthesized the two polymer chains that then snaked along the room. After 3–4 nucleotide pairs were added to the growing chains, a histone was positioned to "protect" the phosphodiester bonds from the roaming nuclease. When students recognized the "chaos" that resulted from nuclease digestion of the growing chain, they worked harder to prevent this enzyme from reaching the polymer. They rapidly found that cooperation was very useful.

As shown in the photos from this project, the early DNA was very disorganized, but as the complementary chains "grew," the DNA became very organized. At this point the class discussed how much easier it was to build one polymer first and then use this polymer (with its now specified sequence of nitrogenous bases) as the blueprint to rapidly build the second polymer. The students could readily see the value of such

**figure 3** A substantial length of the DNA polymer has been formed and histones are associated with the chain. A nuclease tries to disrupt the system.

a template. We then briefly discussed what would happen if we added an RNA polymerase (an enzyme that could polymerize ribonucleotides) and how a complementary RNA strand could be built using the sequence information of one of the DNA polymer chains. Finally, we asked what would happen if the double-stranded complementary DNA helix structure was heated. The students quickly noticed that, if the hydrogen bonding between the nitrogenous bases was broken through the increase in kinetic energy, the two DNA chains would no longer associate with each other.

During the interactive project (which lasted about 25 minutes but could take more or less time depending on the level of the students and the questions that an instructor wished to explore), the students enjoyed this activity. Role-playing was obviously appreciated as a supplement, and similar types of activities were suggested by the students. Individuals remarked that they received a much better picture of the dynamics of molecules as well as the many factors that affect polymer formation, folding, and stability.

The scenario described here was performed in an introductory biochemistry course at Illinois State University. However, with sufficient unit preparation, this activity could also be applied to biology classes in high school and middle school. Key elements of DNA structure could even be presented at the elementary school level. Basic concepts such as student monomers joining together in simple, covalent bonds to form the DNA polymer or "conversing" with the corresponding nucleotide in the opposite DNA strand by shaking hands will appear more as rules of the game, but will provide a solid groundwork on which to build. The format allows students to develop group spirit and enjoy the dynamics of the science. The idea that they can picture themselves as interactive molecules in a chaotic environment drives home the complexity of living systems.

# physical sciences

# Chemistry at Work

## Generating Electricity Using Single Displacement Reactions

Barbara A. Burke

**M**etals vary in their ability to replace hydrogen in water. The following abbreviated form of the Activity Series (Whitten, Gailey, and Davis 1992) reflects this variation:

$$Li > Mg > Al > Zn > Fe > Cu$$

Lithium metal is the most reactive and copper the least.

When a metal spontaneously reacts with an acidic or basic aqueous solution, electrons are transferred. These single displacement reactions can be used to generate electricity if they are made part of a circuit. A metal high on the Activity Series liberates more energy than those below it. This will be shown in the demonstration described in this article.

## Reagents, Materials, Equipment
- One 1.5 V motor (attach a paper propeller), 1.5 V buzzer, 2.0 V flashbulb, and socket.

  RadioShack is a source for moderately priced electrical equipment, and old-fashioned flashbulbs and sockets can be purchased at reasonable prices from photography stores. The total cost of all the necessary equipment should be approximately $8.

The motor, buzzer, and flashbulb socket should be attached to a 3" × 12" × 1/2" board and screwed into a clamp removed from an old wooden funnel stand. The entire board should then be clamped onto a ring stand for the demonstration (Figure 1). Note that alligator clamps are soldered to the leads of the motor, buzzer, and flashbulb socket.

- Three pieces, each about 6"–12" in length, of the following: coiled 16-gauge copper wire, coiled magnesium ribbon, coiled zinc strip, and twisted aluminum foil.
- 12 M sulfuric acid ($H_2SO_4$), 6 M sodium hydroxide (NaOH), wash bottle with distilled water, two 150 mL beakers, and one 400 mL beaker. Faculty only should handle the sulfuric acid. Thick butyl gloves designed for strong acids must be worn to prevent harm by the acid. In addition, the teacher should wear a rubber laboratory apron and keep students away from potential acid spillage.

## Safety Precautions
Wear chemical-resistant safety goggles and acid-resistant gloves when performing the demonstration since the sulfuric acid and sodium

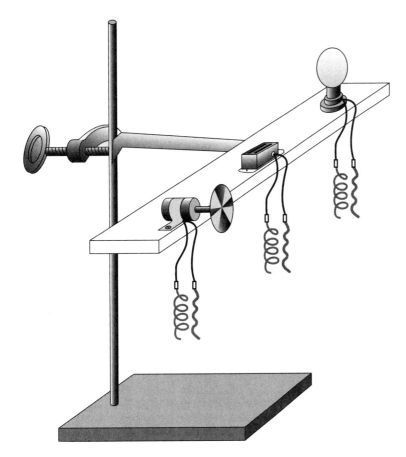

**figure 1** Completed design of the demonstration equipment

nect one alligator clip each to the motor and the buzzer to separate pieces of the copper wire and the magnesium ribbon. Place about 75 mL 12 M sulfuric acid in the 150 mL beaker. In turn, dip the wires connected to the motor, buzzer, and flashbulb socket into the beaker of 12 M sulfuric acid. The motor turns (watch propeller), the buzzer sounds, and the flashbulb goes off. Now rinse off the metal strips with distilled water using the wash bottle (use the 400 mL beaker to catch the wastewater).

Remove the magnesium strips and replace the used flashbulb. Put the twisted aluminum strips in place of the magnesium ones. In turn, dip the wires connected to the motor, the buzzer, and the flashbulb socket into the beaker of 6 M sodium hydroxide. This time only the buzzer should be activated. Rinse the metal strips with distilled water using the wash bottle, again using the 400 mL beaker to catch the wastewater.

Remove the aluminum strips. Replace the aluminum strips with coiled zinc strips. In turn, dip the wires connected to the motor, the buzzer, and the flashbulb socket into the beaker of 12 M sulfuric acid. This time nothing should be activated, even though the zinc metal can be seen to be reacting with the sulfuric acid solution (bubbles of hydrogen gas form).

## Discussion

This demonstration very graphically illustrates the relationships between redox chemical reactions, electricity, chemical energy, and work using simple, single displacement reactions. I perform this demonstration in my third quarter general chemistry classes when discussing electrochemistry. Students enjoy it and discover that they themselves are able to develop explanations about what has occurred. I think they really begin to understand the meaning of free energy (DG), its calculation from E° values, and how it

hydroxide solutions are quite caustic. Also provide students with chemical-resistant goggles. These reagents should be handled with care. If either spills on your clothes or body, rinse immediately with large amounts of water. Work in a well-ventilated area or near a fume hood since hydrogen gas is generated in these reactions.

## The Demonstration

Place a flashbulb in the socket and clamp one alligator clip to the coiled copper wire and the other to the coiled magnesium ribbon. Likewise con-

**Topic:** redox reactions
**Go to:** *www.scilinks.org*
**Code:** JCSTC80

is related to work. These are no longer only theoretical exercises for the students—they have now witnessed the reality of these relationships. Students look up the $E°$ values and discuss what they have observed. I believe that this demonstration helps them gain a deeper understanding of the fundamental chemistry underlying battery operation and design than they otherwise would.

The reaction $Mg(s) + 2 H^+(aq) \rightarrow Mg^{2+}(aq) + H_2(g)$ generates the highest voltage ($> +2.37$) and so activates the motor, the buzzer, and the flashbulb.

The reaction $6 H_2O + 2Al(s) + 2 OH^-(aq) \rightarrow 2 [Al(OH)_4]^- + 3 H_2(g)$ generates the next highest voltage ($> +1.66$) and activates both the flashbulb and the buzzer, but not the motor. This reaction does not activate the motor because the amperage is not high enough to start the motor.

The reaction $Zn(s) + 2 H^+(aq) \rightarrow Zn^{2+}(aq) + H_2(g)$ generates the lowest voltage ($> +0.763$), which does not liberate enough energy to activate any of these.

I developed this demonstration from one by Fidel Villarreal (1969), using a coiled magnesium strip and copper in 6 N sulfuric acid solution to activate a flashbulb.

## References

Villarreal, F. 1969. Electricity by chemical reaction. In *Tested Demonstrations in Chemistry*, eds. H. N. Alyea and F. B. Dutton. Easton, PA: Journal of Chemical Education.

Whitten, K. W., K. D. Gailey, and R. E. Davis. 4th ed. 1992. *General Chemistry with Qualitative Analysis*. New York: Saunders College Publishing.

# Simple "Jack in the Box" Demonstrations for Physical Sciences Courses
## Five Easy Demos

Theodor C. H. Cole

Our Introduction to Physical Science is a lecture course (nonlab) for nonscience majors, offered to evening students who are expecting a stimulating class after a hard day's work. The passive character of straight lecturing—supported by films, slides, and videos—makes it difficult to keep the students' attention. Because real interest in science comes from active involvement, it is important—also in lecture courses—to include student-assisted demonstrations, weekend field trips, and student projects.

In our overseas setting (Germany), laboratories are mostly not available and classes are held at different sites throughout Europe. Demonstrations thus must rely on simple, "portable" activities. The necessarily simple designs of these demonstrations convey to the student another very important message: It is possible to enjoy science even without the sophisticated and expensive equipment used in professional research.

The course has sections in physics, chemistry, geology, and astronomy. The student should receive a general overview of each field and understand the interdisciplinary character of the natural sciences…and be stimulated to take further courses. The demonstrations presented here relate to everyday life, address interdisciplinary aspects, and have implications for the life sciences.

## Physics: Electricity Calculations

Conservation is one of our major resources. To realize where energy can be saved, it is necessary to be able to calculate the energy consumption of electric appliances. This project shows the relationship between electricity use, energy resources and technologies, and air pollution. After an introduction to mechanics, basic electricity, and

Topic: electrolysis
Go to: www.scilinks.org
Code: JCSTC83

power-plant design, students solve the problems in the box below:

---

1. Find the power rating of an electric appliance, in watts (W).
2. Determine how long the appliance is used, in hours (h).
3. Calculate the electricity (energy = work), in kWh (kilowatt times hours) from the formula: $w = p \times t$ (work equals power times time) with $w$ = work = energy = electricity; $p$ = power; $t$ = time.
4. Calculate the price of electricity consumption based on the local utility company's base rate per kWh.
5. Determine how much coal the power plant burns in order to supply this amount of electricity. (Take into account the efficiency of the power plant and the total energy content of the coal.)
6. Determine how much air pollution is generated by burning the amount of coal determined in #5.

**Example:** Computer and monitor are left on overnight!
1. The computer is rated at 250 W, the monitor at 150 W.
2. Overnight time is 16 h (× 30 days per month).
3. Calculate: $p$ = 250 W + 150 W = 400 W
   $t$ = 16 h × 30 = 480 h
   $w = p \times t$
   $w$ = 400 W × 480 h = 192,000 Wh
   = 192 kWh
4. Consider: 12 cents per kilowatt hour
   Calculate: 192 kWh × 12 cents/kWh = $23.04
5. Consider: power plant efficiency of 30% and bituminous coal at 8 kWh/kg
   Calculate: 30% of 8 kWh/kg = 2.4 kWh/kg
   192 kWh divided by 2.4 kWh/kg = 80 kg
6. Consider: 2% $SO_2$ for bituminous coal
   Calculate: 2% of 80 kg = 1.6 kg

---

The permissive exposure level (PEL) set by the Occupational Safety and Health Administration (OSHA) for sulfur dioxide is 5 ppm (12.5 mg/m³); thus, 1.6 kg of $SO_2$ pollute at least 128,000 m³ of air.

Environmental concern has led to new legislation demanding that power plants install antipollution devices. The consumer pays the bill, as reflected by the steady price increase per kilowatt hour. So, it pays to turn the computer…off!

## Astronomy

This project follows a discussion of the Earth's rotation and revolution; sidereal/solar day, year, and seasons; and zodiac, ecliptic, and star charts. The exercise uses a formula to determine solar time (24 hours) from sidereal time (full rotation of the Earth—23 hr. 56 min.) and position of the Earth on its orbit around the Sun (2 hr. per month); that is, the stars seem to make two full rotations around Polaris in the course of one year.

Let's assume we were lost at night without a watch and wanted to know the solar time. Here's how we would determine it (Figure 1):

1. Look for the "Big Dipper" (Ursa Major); stretch out your hand and with your index and middle fingers measure the distance between the two outermost "pointer stars"; go five of these distances in the same line as the "pointer stars" and locate the North Star (Polaris) of the "Little Dipper" (Ursa Minor).
2. Facing north, imagine a clock dial centered on Polaris (north 6 o'clock, south 12 o'clock).
3. The clock's hand is pointed from Polaris toward the two "pointer stars" of the Big Dipper.
4. Read apparent time from the direction of this pointer.
5. Calculate using the formula:
   24 (or 48)* - $(h + M) \times 2$
   $h$ = apparent hour from stars
   $M$ = number of months as of November 7

*If result is negative or greater than 24, subtract from 48.*

figure
**1**
The apparent time as read from the stars is 4 o'clock; the date is November 7. Inserting into the formula tells us the actual solar time: 0 o'clock, that is, 12 o'clock midnight.

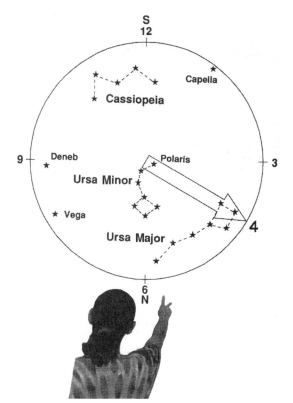

figure
**2**
Schematic of water electrolysis setup

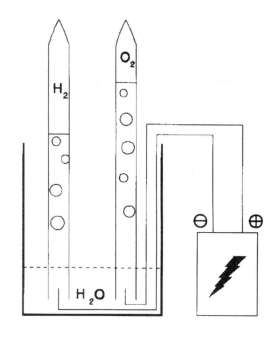

figure
**3**
Water electrolysis apparatus

## General Chemistry: Electrolysis

This is the classical demonstration of the breakdown of a compound into its elements. The experiment supplements the discussion of elements/compounds, mixtures/pure substances, the physical states of matter, the "fingerprint" uniqueness of melting and boiling points for every substance, the general aspects of chemical reactions, and the periodic table.

The experiment will result in gases clearly showing a ratio 2:1 for hydrogen vs. oxygen; due to the relatively small amount of gases and rapid diffusion, it is not possible to "pop" the hydrogen. The equipment easily fits into a coat pocket (Figure 2 and Figure 3).

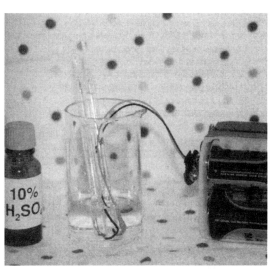

To begin the experiment, take two small conventional glass pipettes (Pasteur pipettes) and weld the tips over a flame or seal with tape. Fill the pipettes with water and place them in a jar with ½-inch water. Prepare two wires (copper wire needs to be protected against oxidation by taping a piece of noncorrosive metal to the positive wire; tape a flattened piece of platinum wire to the negative wire for better hydrogen bubbles).

Insert the electrodes into the pipettes (you can briefly lift the pipettes out; the small diameter and surface tension keep the water inside). Connect one or two 6 V lantern batteries in series.

## Organic Chemistry: Ester Synthesis from Butyric Acid and Pentanol

Two disagreeably smelling chemicals are turned into a pleasant, pear-like odor by means of a classical chemical test-tube reaction. This supplements the discussion of the basic groups of organic chemicals (especially hydrocarbons, alcohols, carboxylic acids, and esters), biochemicals (especially fats), natural products (fruits), organic and aqueous phases—and gives students an opportunity to see and use a simple lab setup. The experiment is performed outdoors (weather allowing) to guarantee sufficient ventilation. It uses a simple setup with a camping-gas burner, tubes, disposable pipettes, forceps, and a water bottle.

The chemicals needed are: butyric acid, pentanol, and sulfuric acid (catalyst). Use 1 part acid, 3–4 parts alcohol, and 3 parts catalyst. Heat slowly and shake well, but don't hesitate to show students what happens if it's not properly agitated! Chemical-resistant goggles must be worn by the instructor and students. Gloves are not needed; however, keep the demonstration in a well-ventilated location away from an open flame that may ignite the hydrogen and oxygen gas.

Though most instructors might hesitate to use butyric acid (*handle carefully—use pipette!*), there are several advantages: Turning this penetrating odor into a pleasant smell is a major surprise to students; the reaction is prompt and complete after a few minutes; the turbid, milky ester phase is clearly visible. A drop of ester on filter paper develops the full bouquet.

## Inorganic Chemistry: Catalysis; Geology: Minerals—Combustion of a Sugar Cube with Cigarette Ashes

The purpose of this demonstration is to show the phenomenon of catalysis by means of metals/heavy metals (minerals) contained in tobacco ashes. By holding a match against a piece of sugar, we notice that the sugar initially melts (phase change: solid-liquid-glass), forming caramel. One match in most cases does not suffice to start the reaction, that is, to produce a flame. After lighting a cigarette and discussing the nature of ashes, you rub the piece of sugar into the ashes. Upon brief contact with a match, the sugar burns.

### Acknowledgment
*Special thanks to the students of Physical Science and Concepts of Biology, Term 5/93.*

# An Eye-Opening Demonstration—The Catalytic Decomposition of Hydrogen Peroxide

## Enhancing a Chemistry Lecture with a Common Eye-Care Product

Brendan R. Flynn

The decomposition of hydrogen peroxide into water and oxygen by manganese dioxide (Alyea and Dutton 1965a, b), iodide ion (Summerlin and Ealy 1985), or the enzyme catalase found in potatoes (Summerlin, Borgford, and Ealy 1987) and blood (Alyea and Dutton 1965c) serve as classic examples to illustrate the phenomena of homogeneous and heterogeneous catalysis to students.

A variation on these processes is to use a readily available platinum-coated plastic disk, originally patented (Gaglia 1975) and designed to be used as a catalyst with 3% $H_2O_2$ to

disinfect soft contact lenses. [At the time this article was originally published (1994), the disk was manufactured by CIBA Vision Corporation and identified as the AODISC® Neutralizer.] The disk removes residual $H_2O_2$ from contact lenses after sterilization, thus preventing eye irritation. While the disk may be purchased at grocery stores and pharmacies, we have found that each year one or more students use this lens cleaning system and willingly donate old disks.

The catalysis is easily presented by simply placing the disk in 3% $H_2O_2$ in a small beaker, which is then passed around the room or shown on an overhead projector. The production of bubbles of oxygen gas is quite visible (Figure 1). The process is very safe and no precautions should be necessary. The demonstration can be

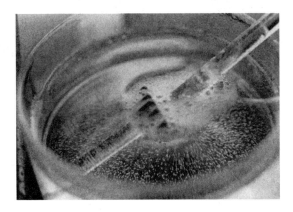

figure
1
When placed in an $H_2O_2$ solution of any concentration, the AODISC's platinum coating stimulates the solution's decomposition into oxygen and water. Here, the AODISC is stabilized with a glass stirring rod to show the reaction more clearly.

used as a focal point to discuss various theoretical concepts and to show some practical applications of chemistry and chemical technology. The information contained in the patent (Gaglia 1975) further provides a wealth of material for class discussion.

## Background: Thermodynamics and Kinetics

Hydrogen peroxide is thermodynamically highly unstable with respect to decomposition to water and oxygen. The reaction is quite exothermic, is accompanied by a large entropy change, and is theoretically spontaneous at all temperatures. Indeed, as a safety measure, 30% $H_2O_2$ is stored in vented polyethylene bottles (no catalytic surfaces) to prevent pressure buildup.

$$2\ H_2O_2\ (1) \rightarrow 2\ H_2O\ (1) + O_2\ (g)$$

*Per Mole $H_2O_2$ at 298K*

| | |
|---|---|
| $\Delta H^\circ$ rxn | -98.6 kJ |
| $\Delta S^\circ$ rxn | 62.9 J/K |
| $\Delta G^\circ$ rxn | -117.0 kJ |

However, despite of the favorable thermodynamics, the thermal (uncatalyzed) reaction does not readily occur, due to the high activation energy. While the decomposition of $H_2O_2$ is known to be extremely sensitive to catalysis by a variety of substances (Evans and Upton 1985) including the surface of the reaction vessel, it has been estimated that at 100°C the half-life of the thermal reaction is of the order of ten million years (Giguere and Liu 1957). More recently, a value of 76 kJ has been quoted for the activation energy of the thermal reaction (Kotz and Purcell 1991).

Thus we have a simple illustration of the concept that for a spontaneous reaction to occur at a reasonable rate, both thermodynamic and kinetic requirements must be satisfied.

## Further Observations and Discussion

The disk, when new, has a shiny metallic luster and is shaped like a mechanical gear to provide a large surface area for catalysis (Figure 2). Evolution of bubbles from 10% or 30% $H_2O_2$ is markedly more rapid than from the 3% solution, illustrating the effect of concentration on reaction rate. The platinum coating eventually disappears, particularly when using the more concentrated solutions.

The AODISC is shaped like a mechanical gear to provide as much surface area for catalysis as possible.

A very dramatic effect may be seen if the disk is floated on the surface of 30% $H_2O_2$ contained in a 100 mL graduated cylinder. The solution bubbles very vigorously, becomes quite hot, and steam is generated due to the heat produced by this very exothermic reaction. *Caution should be exercised, as 30% $H_2O_2$ is very corrosive and is a strong oxidant. Those using it should wear rubber gloves and safety goggles, and should avoid contact with any oxidizable materials.*

In the patent itself, the inventor (Gaglia 1975) discusses the polymeric materials used to prepare contact lenses, which are hydrophilic and must be biocompatible. The need for isotonic buffered saline solutions as a rinsing medium is also presented, as is the necessity for sterilization of the contact lens with a disinfectant and the removal of excess $H_2O_2$ from the lens. Finally, various experiments that describe the actual preparation of the platinum surface by electrolytic reduction are presented in some detail.

Here we have a simple, dependable demonstration that uses materials readily available to teachers and illustrates an important phenomenon. But, equally as important, the demonstration can lead to open-ended discussions of many of the concepts presented in beginning chemistry courses. Should the instructor wish, the demonstration can also be used as an introduction to the patent literature.

## Acknowledgment

*The author wishes to thank Dr. Paul Nicholson, CIBA Vision Corporation, Atlanta, Georgia, for his assistance in the preparation of this manuscript. AODISC is a registered trademark of CIBA Vision Corporation.*

## References

Alyea, H. N., and F. B. Dutton. 1965. Tested Demonstrations in Chemistry. Easton, PA: *Journal of Chemical Education.* (a) 7; (b) 152; (c) 48.

Evans, D. F., and M. W. Upton. 1985. *Journal of the Chemical Society-Dalton Transactions.* 2516–2529.

Gaglia, C. A. 1975. U.S. Patent 3,912,451.

Giguere, P. A., and J. D. Liu. 1957. *Canadian Journal of Chemistry* 35:283–285.

Kotz, J. C. and K. F. Purcell. 1991. *Chemistry and Chemical Reactivity.* Philadelphia: Saunders College Publishing. 643.

Summerlin, L. R., and J. L. Ealy. 1985. *Chemical Demonstrations—A Sourcebook for Teachers*, vol. 1. Washington, DC: American Chemical Society.

Summerlin, L .R., C. L. Borgford, and J. L. Ealy. 1987. *Chemical Demonstrations—A Sourcebook for Teachers*, vol. 2. Washington, DC: American Chemical Society. 150–151.

# The Ammonia Lava Lamp

## A Colorful Demonstration of Diffusion

Marty Fox, John J. Gaynor, and Judith Shillcock

The perfume section of a major department store is a wonderful place to experience diffusion. Enthusiastic salespeople armed with an arsenal of fragrance-dispensing weapons unwittingly educate unsuspecting shoppers about the movement of particles. With the air reeking of at least a hundred scents, I am always astounded when they ask me, "What do you think of *this particular product?*" Perhaps they need a brief refresher course on diffusion.

Students usually encounter the topic of diffusion in their introductory biology sequence, where it is defined as the movement of substances from an area of higher concentration to an area of lower concentration as a result of the random spontaneous movements of individual particles. At this early stage, they begin to appreciate that living organisms depend heavily on this process for life. For unicellular organisms, diffusion is the major mechanism for the import of nutrients and the export of

**SCILINKS.**
THE WORLD'S A CLICK AWAY

Topic: diffusion
Go to: www.scilinks.org
Code: JCSTC91

waste products. For multicellular organisms, diffusion is responsible for the transport of many important substances, such as oxygen transport into the blood cells within our lungs.

Currently, there are many excellent exercises on diffusion in print. The movement of NaCl out of a dialysis bag (Abramoff and Thomson 1991), the diffusion of various dyes through agar (Abramoff and Thomson 1991), and the diffusion of water into a bag containing molasses or starch (Skavaril, Finnen, and Lawton 1993) are but a few that we have used in the past. Each is relatively easy to perform and provides a measurable indication that diffusion has taken place.

Yet, each of these demonstrations lacks a key ingredient: an element of visual excitement that will help the students remember the exercise long after it is over. We would like to share a highly visual diffusion exercise that is sure to make an impression on students. The exercise is loosely based on a general chemistry laboratory employing an "ammonia fountain" to demonstrate the solubility of a gas (Summerlin and Ealy 1988). This is an introductory demonstration that can be performed in less than 15 minutes. Included is an exercise that examines the effect of temperature on rate of diffusion.

## Materials

When designing this experiment, we chose equipment and reagents that are readily available, relatively inexpensive, safe for student use, and easily disposed of by flushing down the sink. The use of supermarket ammonia water, which does not require special storage or handling, and rubbing alcohol are intentional consequences of this decision. As with all chemical experiments, protective eyewear should be worn.

- Test tubes (22 mm diameter, 78 mL total volume)
- Test tube rack
- Dialysis tubing (Carolina Biological, 1¾" wide)
- Rubber bands
- Tape (2" wide, clear) or a clamp
- Ammonia (a fresh unopened bottle can be purchased at a supermarket. An MSDS for ammonia can be obtained online through a Web search.)
- Rubbing alcohol
- Phenolphthalein (J.T. Baker Chemicals, 1.0% [w/v] in rubbing alcohol)
- Sheet of white paper
- White vinegar or dilute acetic acid

## Demonstration

- Conduct this demonstration in a well-ventilated room.
- Add 1.0 mL of 1.0% (w/v) phenolphthalein and 999 mL distilled water to a large, *clean* beaker, and stir until mixed. We have found that it is easier to make a large quantity of water containing phenolphthalein than it is to add the indicator to individual test tubes at a later date. If the solution turns pink, then the pH is too high. This could be caused either by a basic residue on the inside of the beaker or by the water itself. If this happens, discard the solution, clean the beaker, and try again. If the problem continues to occur, a few drops of dilute acetic acid or white vinegar should solve the problem.

- Fill a test tube with the water/phenolphthalein solution. Test tubes that have a "lip" are easier to stack and are recommended for these exercises.
- Cut a piece of dialysis tubing large enough to cover the opening of your test tube. The tubing should be cut along an unopened side and presoaked in distilled water for a few minutes. After presoaking, the piece of cut tubing will easily unravel, yielding a single dialysis membrane.
- Gently stretch the cut piece of dialysis tubing over the top of the test tube and fasten with a rubber band. The tubing should be taut, with no creases or wrinkles.
- Fill a second test tube with ammonia water and put it in the test tube rack. The amount of head space at the top of the tube will influence how long it takes to see results.
- Invert the test tube containing the water/indicator and secure over the test tube containing the ammonia water with a piece of clear tape or a clamp.

The ammonia water consists of molecules of ammonia dissolved in water, along with a small amount of $NH_4^+$ and $OH^-$ produced by the ionization of ammonia (Brady and Humiston 1986). As the ammonia diffuses upward, the pH change will cause the indicator in that region to turn a brilliant pinkish-red color. Phenolphthalein changes to this color when the pH of the solution becomes basic in the range 8.2–9.8 (Kotz and Purcell 1987).

The overall visual effect of this demonstration is quite spectacular and not unlike what one experiences when observing a lava lamp (see Figure 1). We recommend placing a sheet of white paper directly behind the test tubes to maximize the effect of this "lava"-like migration.

The ammonia lava lamp apparatus. The upper tube contains phenolphthalein indicator, and the lower tube contains dilute ammonia water solution. The tubes are separated by a single sheet of dialysis membrane. Panel A shows the progress of the ammonia front after about 90 seconds; panel B shows the progress after about 130 seconds.

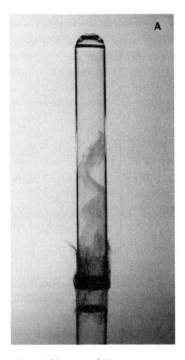

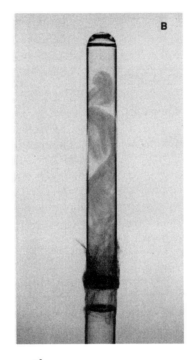

## The Effect of Temperature on the Rate of Diffusion

This exercise uses the time it takes for the color change to travel a certain distance as a measure of the rate of diffusion. The protocol is essentially the same as above, with the following exceptions:

- Prior to adding water/phenolphthalein, the test tubes should be marked at 2 cm intervals from the top or lip with a permanent marker.

- This experiment requires *three* sets of tubes. Each set should be covered with parafilm or plastic wrap and placed at the appropriate temperature for at least 30 minutes. It is a good idea to physically separate the ammonia water tubes from the tubes containing indicator during the incubation period, as

some escaping ammonia vapors could contaminate nearby solutions and prematurely begin the experiment.

- Place Set 1 on ice (approximately 4°C). Set 2 remains at room temperature (20° C). Set 3 should be placed in lukewarm water (36°C). When the temperature of the solutions reaches the desired level, remove the parafilm or wrap and begin the experiment.

- Record the time it takes for the *leading edge* of each of the ammonia waves to migrate a desired distance.

Clamping or taping the tubes together requires a little time and some dexterity. Do not be upset if, while connecting the tubes, you notice a pink wave of color migrating upward. Within a single tube there will be numerous waves of ammonia. The rate of movement of the first four or five waves should be approximately the same for a given tube. Thereafter, the rate of movement of the waves will decrease as the concentration gradient becomes less steep.

The exercise concludes with statistical analysis and graphing of the data. The graph in Figure 2 shows typical results obtained for this exercise. The graph represents the mean value of four independent experiments.

## Conclusion

Considering the importance of diffusion as a transport mechanism, and in light of studies that suggest that most students tend to learn biological concepts better by active participation than by rote memorization (Knott 1992; Sojka 1992),

This graph shows the effect of temperature on the rate of diffusion of ammonia in water/phenolphthalein solution.

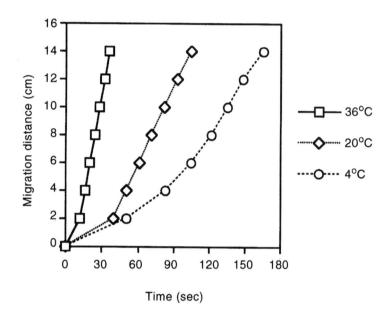

Time (sec)

joy the visual spectacle of the "pink lava" diffusing upward. We hope that your students will enjoy this experiment as much as ours have.

## Acknowledgment

*The authors acknowledge with thanks the assistance of Dave Fogg, associate director of the media center at Montclair State University, for providing photographs of the demonstration apparatus.*

## References

Abramoff, P., and R. Thomson. 1991. *Laboratory Outlines in Biology—V.* New York: W.H. Freeman and Co.

Brady, J., and G. Humiston. 1986. *General Chemistry: Principles and Structure.* 4th ed. New York: John Wiley and Sons.

Knott, R. C. 1992. The kinds of experiences youngsters need to be able to understand ecology. *Association of Southeastern Biologists Bulletin* 39(4):160–164.

Kotz, J., and K. Purcell. 1987. *Chemistry and Chemical Reactivity.* New York: Saunders College Publishing.

Skavaril, R., M. Finnen, and S. Lawton. 1993. *General Biology Laboratory Manual: Investigations into Life's Phenomena.* New York: Saunders College Publishing.

Sojka, F.A. 1992. The need for hands-on science. *Journal of College Science Teaching* 22(1): 4–5.

Summerlin, L., and J. Ealy. 1988. *Chemical Demonstrations: A Sourcebook for Teachers.* Washington, DC: American Chemical Society.

we have attempted to provide our students with a rich and varied hands-on experience of this phenomenon in the classroom. This exercise has proved to be very successful with our general biology and cell biology students. It serves not only as a striking demonstration of diffusion, but also as a "friendly" vehicle to introduce the students to concepts such as acid-base theory, the use of chemical indicators, and introductory statistics. Finally, it is gratifying to watch the students en-

# Stopping a Siphon Action by Reduction of Atmospheric Pressure

## Demonstrating Physics with a Simply Constructed Apparatus

Robert M. Graham

A fascinating sidelight to the study of atmospheric pressure is a discussion and demonstration of the operation of a siphon. Siphon action involves the transfer of a liquid through a tube over an intermediate level to a lower level. This action occurs because of atmospheric pressure. An interesting consequence of this fact is that a siphon could not work on the Moon, where atmospheric pressure is nonexistent.

Siphoning liquid from one container to another is a common demonstration, often used in the study of atmospheric pressure and the barometer. Normal atmospheric pressure, discussed in the context of barometers, is frequently referred to as a 76 cm (30 in., as reported by weather forecasters) column of mercury. Since mercury has a density of 13.6 times that of water, a water barometer would have to be 76 cm × 13.6, or 10.3 m (34 ft.) in height, impractically tall (Hewitt 1989).

Sucking on a soda straw to lift liquid also depends on atmospheric pressure. The sucking action reduces the pressure in the straw, and the liquid is then pushed up the straw by the force of atmospheric pressure on its surface (Wilson 1989). Because atmospheric pressure has a maximum value of 10.3 m (34 ft.) for water, the maximum possible length of a soda straw would necessarily be 10.3 m. Hewitt (1989) notes that "however strong your lungs may be, or whatever device you use to make a vacuum in the straw, at sea level the water could not be pushed up by the atmosphere higher than 10.3 m." Similarly, 10.3 m is the maximum height for siphoning water. "If the liquid is water and the siphon is taller than 34 ft. it will split on top" (Epstein and Hewitt 1981).

Siphoning can be stopped before the normal complete transfer of liquid and takes place when the liquid in the two containers has reached the same level. This is accomplished by changing the

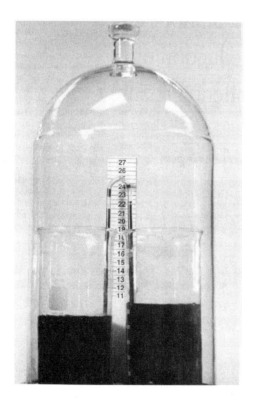

**figure 1** Lowering the atmospheric pressure inside the bell jar causes the siphon between the two beakers to cease. The siphon will start again when pressure is reintroduced.

pressure on the system, a relatively easy task with the proper setup of normal equipment, pictured in Figure 1.

## Setup

Equipment and materials required for this demonstration are as follows: a vacuum pump, a bell jar, two beakers, a glass tube, a centimeter scale, and 950 mL of water with a small amount of potassium permanganate crystals added for visibility.

The vacuum pump is similar to a Sargent-Welch #1401N01. A large bell jar increases visibility. This bell jar is similar to a Cenco #14302-03 with a diameter of 22.2 cm and a height of 42.5 cm. The beakers are Fisher #S30837, 1000 mL, Corning 1060. [The information in this para-graph and other catalog numbers in this article were accurate at the time the article was published in 1995.]

The glass tube depicted in Figure 1 has an inside diameter of approximately 3.8 mm and an outside diameter of 6 mm. It had a length of 52 cm before it was heated and bent with equal amounts of tubing on each side. The radius of the bend is approximately 1 cm. A typical supplier number for the glass tubing is Sargent-Welch #S-40140-E. To hold the tube upright, place a piece of double-faced mounting tape on the upper edge of the empty beaker. Cut the ends of the tube at 45° angles; this makes it unnecessary to raise the tube off the bottom of the beakers. The visible centimeter scale behind the U-tube was created with an Apple MacDraw program, and then mounted on a suitable cardboard support, with the zero end even with the bottom of the beakers.

## Operation of the System

Fill the right beaker nearly full with the potassium permanganate-tinged water. Fill the U-tube with water—this water does not necessarily have to be colored. Holding a finger over the tube end that goes down into the empty beaker, place the other end into the violet liquid. After the end in the empty beaker is approximately 2 cm below the water level of the full beaker, remove your finger from the end in the empty beaker, and the siphon should start.

Attach the U-tube to the double-faced tape. Install the bell jar, and start the vacuum pump. As the pressure gradually drops in the bell jar, a few small bubbles will begin to appear in the tube ("boiling water"). At the beginning of the process, atmospheric pressure is about 1030 cm of water. As the pressure in the bell jar continues to drop, it will eventually reach a point where the water flowing in the U-tube will

**Topic: atmospheric pressure**
**Go to:** *www.scilinks.org*
**Code: JCSTC96**

"break," as in Figure 1, and the flow will stop. As the vacuum pump continues to run, the water will continue to fall in both sides of the U-tube.

At this point, stop the pump. In our case, the pressure in the bell jar needed to be approximately 15 cm of water—1.1 cm of mercury—before the siphon would stop, measured by subtracting the 10 cm liquid level in the right beaker from 25 cm, the height of the top of the U-tube. Gradually allowing the atmospheric pressure in the bell jar to increase will cause the water to rise in the U-tube until it once again joins at the top. Then the water will begin to flow again until the water levels in both beakers are the same.

The key to the success of this process is having a U-tube of small diameter. This slows down the siphoning process, and the pump then has enough time to bring the pressure in the bell jar low enough to stop the siphon before the liquid levels in the beakers have become equal.

### References

Epstein, E., and P. Hewitt. 1981. *Thinking Physics*. San Francisco: Insight Press.

Hewitt, P. 1989. *Conceptual Physics.* 6th ed. New York: Harper Collins College Publishers.

Wilson, J. 1989. *Physics.* 2nd ed. Philadelphia: Saunders College Publishing.

# The Remsen Demonstration: "Nitric Acid Acts upon Copper"

## A Colorful Slice of Chemistry's History

Myra Hauben and Geoff Rayner-Canham

When chemists report on new discoveries, it is customary to trace the previous work in the field. To show the link with the discoverer, we often cite an individual's name, so we have Wilkinson's compound in inorganic chemistry, the Markovnikov addition reaction in organic chemistry, and the Michaelis-Menten equation in biochemistry, to name just a few.

In chemical demonstrations, however, we rarely identify the origin of the experiment. This is unfortunate, not only because the originator is not given due credit, but also because many experiments are forgotten and then "re-invented" by later chemical educators who have failed to review the literature and who, themselves, then reap undue credit.

One excellent demonstration to which a name can be assigned involves the reaction between copper and concentrated nitric acid. This reaction was first described by Glauber in 1648 (Mellor 1967), but we owe its birth as a demonstration to the American chemist Ira Remsen (1846–1927). Hence, this procedure should be called Remsen's demonstration. Remsen's account would have been long forgotten but for the more recent articles by Henry A. Bent (1986) and Richard W. Ramette (1980), both of which acknowledge their source.

## Remsen's Discovery

In his biography (Getman 1980), Remsen describes the experiment he performed at age 12 that changed his life:

*While reading a textbook of chemistry I came upon the statement, "nitric acid acts upon copper." I was tired of reading such absurd stuff and I determined to see what this meant.... Having nitric acid and copper, I had only to learn what the words "act upon" meant. Then the statement, "nitric acid acts upon copper," would be something more than mere words.... In the interest of knowledge, I was even will-*

ing to sacrifice one of the few copper cents then in my possession. I put one of them on the table, opened the bottle marked "nitric acid," poured some of the liquid on the copper, and prepared to make an observation. But what was this wonderful thing which I beheld? The cent was already changed, and it was no small change either. A greenish blue liquid foamed and fumed over the cent and over the table. The air in the neighborhood of the performance became colored dark red. A great colored cloud arose. This was disagreeable and suffocating—how should I stop this? I tried to get rid of the objectionable mess by picking it up and throwing it out the window, which I had meanwhile opened. I learned another fact—nitric acid not only acts upon copper but it acts upon fingers. The pain led to another unpremeditated experiment. I drew my fingers across my trousers and another fact was discovered. Nitric acid acts upon trousers. Taking everything into consideration, that was the most impressive experiment, and, relatively, probably the most costly experiment I have ever performed. I tell it even now with interest.

## Remsen's Fame

It was this simple experiment that was to ultimately aim Remsen toward a career in chemistry. Remsen, in turn, was to have a profound effect on the teaching of chemistry in the United States.

Remsen was born in New York, but he pursued his chemical studies in Germany with the great organic chemistry names of the time: Liebig, Volhard, and Fittig. He returned to the United States in 1872, where he taught at Williams College. His growing reputation led to an offer at the newly founded Johns Hopkins University, and it was there that he revolutionized the teaching of chemistry in the United States by introducing the German ideas of laboratory research into the program (Hannaway 1976).

 The liquid in the beaker is red, and gas production has just started.

 The liquid in the beaker is red, and the gas in the flask is deep brown.

Remsen had a profound effect upon his students, many of whom became the leading American chemists of the next generation (Tarbell, Tarbell, and Joyce 1980), and he was a prolific author of textbooks in general, theoretical, organic, and inorganic chemistry. As well, in the field of organic synthesis, it was Remsen who suggested to Constantine Fahlberg that Fahlberg attempt the synthesis of orthobenzoyl sulfamide. Fahlberg succeeded in the synthesis, noted its intense sweetness, and patented the compound as saccharin without acknowledgment of Remsen's initiation of the project (Kauffman and Priebe 1978).

## The Experiment on an Overhead

As Remsen described, the core of the experiment is the simple addition of nitric acid to copper, and this experiment has since been described by Ramette (1980) as an "exocharmic reaction"—one that is visually impressive. Ramette reads the Remsen quotation while "simultaneously performing the experiment. By putting the cent in a large beaker on an overhead projector, the color changes are prettily and clearly shown. The class reaction is always delightful.... I stop the reaction by adding water before the cent has fully dissolved, and then toss the thin disk back to the audience."

## The Hauben/Rayner-Canham Modified Version

We have extended the experiment as we describe below. The use of a round-bottomed flask with a water-filled beaker to absorb the nitrogen dioxide is an innovation one of the co-authors saw at a chemical education conference; we have been unable to track the originator of this modification. The use of phenolphthalein and ammonia are our own extensions of the experiment.

Fit a 750 mL round-bottomed flask with a delivery tube leading into a 1 L beaker. Fill the beaker with water, and add a few drops of phe-

figure
3

The liquid in the beaker is colorless, and the gas in the flask is deep brown.

figure
4

The contents of the beaker are halfway sucked back; the gas in the flask is brown, and the solution is blue.

nolphthalein and enough dilute sodium hydroxide solution to produce a noticeable red-violet coloration. Add 30 mL of concentrated nitric acid to the flask. Drop in a pre-1982 penny (after that date, pennies have zinc cores) or 3 g of copper sheet, and quickly replace the stopper. Immediately, red-brown gas will start bubbling from the penny surface, spreading through the flask, while the liquid turns from colorless to a deep emerald green (Figures 1 and 2). With the generation of gas, gas bubbles start appearing through the solution in the beaker. Within a few minutes, the phenolphthalein solution will turn colorless (Figure 3).

When the copper is consumed, the gas flow halts and the liquid from the beaker starts sucking back into the flask (Figure 4). As the liquid flows into the flask, the intensity of the brown color decreases until the small volume of gas remaining above the solution is colorless, while the diluted solution becomes a pale blue (Figure 5).

The experiment can be extended by pouring about 200 mL of 50 percent ammonia solution (100 mL of concentrated ammonia plus 100 mL of water) on top. This top layer becomes a deep blue, while the lower layer remains pale blue (Figure 6). At the interface a very thin greenish precipitate can be seen (Figure 7).

## The Interpretation

This experiment is exceedingly colorful, but equally importantly, it illustrates a tremendous range of chemistry. The central reaction is that of copper with concentrated nitric acid, the copper metal being oxidized to the blue copper (II) ion while the nitric acid is reduced to brown nitrogen dioxide:

$$Cu(s) + 4\ HNO_3(l) \rightarrow Cu(NO_3)_2(aq) + 2\ H_2O(l) + 2\ NO_2(g)$$

It is important to use concentrated acid, for more dilute acid results in a reaction to produce colorless nitrogen monoxide gas (Alyea and Dutton 1965).

$$3\ Cu(s) + 8\ HNO_3(aq) \rightarrow$$
$$3\ Cu(NO_3)_2(aq) + 4\ H_2O(l) + 2\ NO(g)$$

The green solution is actually a combination of dissolved brown nitrogen dioxide gas together with the characteristic blue color of the copper (II) complex ions. That the copper (II) complex is actually blue and not green can be shown by repeating the experiment in an open flask (without delivery tube) and then shaking the green solution once the copper metal has all reacted. Clouds of brown nitrogen dioxide are released and the solution changes from green to blue. This initial blue color is probably due to the diaquabis(nitrato)copper (II) ion, $[Cu(OH_2)_2(NO_3)_2]^{2+}$, that is present at high concentrations of nitrate ion (King 1994).

When the nitrogen dioxide produced by the reaction bubbles into the water-filled beaker, there is a rapid reaction to produce a mixture of nitrous and nitric acids:

$$2\ NO_2(g) + H_2O(l) \rightarrow HNO_2(aq) + HNO_3(aq)$$

The change in color of the phenolphthalein shows the increase in acidity. Phenolphthalein is ideal for this purpose, as the resulting acidified solution is colorless and will not affect the solution color in the flask when the indicator solution is drawn back into the flask.

Once the gas flow ceases, the gas remaining in the flask reacts with the water at the mouth of the delivery tube, causing a pressure reduction in the flask. This pressure differential causes the water to flow back into the flask. Fortunately, the dilution of the remaining concentrated nitric acid with the water is much less exothermic than the dilution of sulfuric acid, and this step is quite safe in a Pyrex round-bottomed flask. The blue color of the diluted solution is due to the more common tetraaquacopper (II) complex, $[Cu(OH_2)_4]^{2+}$.

Our second extension of the demonstration is the addition of ammonia solution to the contents of the flask after the water has "sucked back." Ammonia solution is less dense than water (concentrated ammonia has a density of 0.88 g/mL$^{-1}$) and forms an intense blue upper layer. The reaction that produces this color is due to a replacement of the water ligands by ammonia, the nitrogen-donor ammonia being a stronger ligand than the oxygen-donor water molecules.

$$[Cu(OH_2)_4]^{2+}(aq) + 4\ NH_3(aq) \rightarrow$$
$$[Cu(NH_3)_4]^{2+}(aq) + 4\ H_2O(l)$$

At the interface, the greenish layer is copper (II) hydroxide. In this region of low ammonia concentration, the ammonia is acting as a base:

$$NH_3(aq) + H_2O(l) \leftrightarrow NH_4^+(aq) + OH^-(aq)$$

The hydroxide ion then reacts with the copper (II) ion of the lower layer to yield copper (II) hydroxide.

$$Cu^{2+}(aq) + 2\ OH^-(aq) \rightarrow Cu(OH)_2(s)$$

## Safety

The teacher conducting the demonstration must wear chemical-resistant goggles and acid-resistant gloves. It is also advisable to wear a rubber apron and provide goggles for students near the demonstration. This demonstration should be conducted in a well-ventilated room or near a fume hood.

## Applications

This reaction can be used at many different teaching levels in a variety of contexts. It can be used in introductory chemistry as a striking example

The contents of the beaker are fully sucked back; the gas in the flask is colorless, and the solution is blue.

The upper layer of solution is royal blue, and the lower layer is pale blue.

**figure 7** Close-up of the view in Figure 6. A very thin green precipitate has formed between the two layers of solution.

of a chemical change (Webb 1982), not to mention as a reason why concentrated nitric acid should not be poured down sinks having metal pipes! Then the production of nitrogen dioxide and its reaction with water to produce an acid solution (as indicated by the phenolphthalein color change) can be discussed in the context of acid rain.

The reaction is obviously of great use in the discussion of redox reactions, for the nitric acid acts as an oxidizing agent rather than an acid (copper is not oxidized by the hydronium ion of dilute acids, as copper is below hydrogen in the activity series). As well, the reaction of nitrogen dioxide with water is itself an interesting redox reaction as one nitrogen is oxidized from +4 to +5, while another is reduced from +4 to +3.

The demonstration is useful once more in the context of a descriptive inorganic chemistry course (Webb and Rayner-Canham 1982) when discussing transition metal complexes, the oxides of nitrogen, and the oxidizing potential of nitric acid.

## Acknowledgments

*This work was performed during the authors' concurrent sabbatical leaves at the University of York, England, and they acknowledge with appreciation Dr. David Waddington and the Science Education Group for their generous hospitality. As well, the authors acknowledge Kath James for her assistance with the experimental work.*

## References

Alyea, H. N., and F. B. Dutton. 1965. *Tested Demonstrations in Chemistry.* 6th ed. Easton, PA: Journal of Chemical Education.

Bent, H. A. 1986. Remarks at the Dedication of a Chemistry Building at a Liberal Arts College. *Journal of Chemical Education* 63: 54–56.

Getman, F. H. 1980 (reprint). *The Life of Ira Remsen.* New York: Arno Press.

Hannaway, O. 1976. The German model of chemical education in America: Ira Remsen at Johns Hopkins (1876–1913). *Ambix* 23:145–164.

Kauffman, G. B., and P. M. Priebe. 1978. The discovery of saccharin: A centennial retrospect. *Ambix* 25: 191–207.

King, R. B., ed. 1994. *Encyclopedia of Inorganic Chemistry,* vol. 2. Chichester, UK: John Wiley and Sons.

Mellor, J. W. 1967 (reprint). *Comprehensive Treatise on Inorganic and Theoretical Chemistry,* vol. 3. London: Longman.

Ramette, R. W. 1980. Exocharmic reactions. *Journal of Chemical Education* 57:68–69.

Rayner-Canham, G. W. 1993. The conductivity of solutions: Laying the foundations of modern chemical thought. *Journal of College Science Teaching* 23(1):62–64.

Tarbell, D. S., A. T. Tarbell, and R. M. Joyce. 1980. The students of Ira Remsen and Roger Adams. *ISIS* 71:620–626.

Webb, M. J. 1982. Physical and chemical change: What's the difference? *The Science Teacher* 49(3):39–40.

Webb, M. J., and G. W. Rayner-Canham. 1982. Descriptive inorganic chemistry at the second-year level. *Journal of Chemical Education* 59:1012–1013.

# The Johnson DC Electric Motor Recipe

## A New Twist to the Mystery of the Electric Motor

Douglas C. Johnson

The world of electric motors is of great interest to students of all ages. Over the last century, electric motors have played a major role in helping to shape the world we know today. To teach students the basic principles underlying the direct current motor, an instructor needs a model that students can handle during a classroom activity or in a simple demonstration.

### The Random Electric Motor

Many years ago, I ran across a motor that was fun to build and demonstrate, but was not very predictable. The lack of expected results in itself could have provided room for comment and problem solving, but it ended up raising more questions than answers. I recommend that you do not spend much time on this recipe, called the Random Electric Motor, because the recipe that follows it, for the Johnson DC Electric Motor, makes this one obsolete. I first present the Random Electric Motor recipe:

### Materials and Methods

- One ceramic (3/4" diameter × 3/16") magnet
- Two paper clips
- 18" of 30 ga. copper transformer wire
- One "D" size alkaline battery, 1.5 V
- Electrical tape
- Sandpaper
- Wire cutters

The simple and inexpensive Random Electric Motor ("random" because it is uncertain which direction the motor will end up turning) can be constructed from this easy-to-obtain list of materials.

Once you have the necessary supplies, coil the transformer wire around a finger about six turns. Then, loop the ends so they will hold the coil together as they come out of the coil to make an axis for rotation or axle. The result should look like this "-O-"; the "O" is the coil and the "-" are the axles.

SCI LINKS.
THE WORLD'S A CLICK AWAY

Topic: electric motors
Go to: *www.scilinks.org*
Code: JCSTC105

Attach a ceramic magnet to the middle of the battery. Next, bend open the paper clips to an "S" shape and tape them to the ends of the battery so the coils are held by the axles. At the same time, make sure the coil can rotate in the hooked part of the "S" so that the magnet does not get in the way of the coil movement. The magnet needs to be located between the coil and battery. Take the coil and sand off the insulation on the axles. At this point, if you give the coil a turn while in the hooks, the motor will begin to turn in a random direction.

## The Johnson DC Electric Motor

While the above motor opens the activity to problem solving and discussion, the newer motor, the Johnson DC Electric Motor, is much more dependable and easier to follow (Figure 1). Building the motor can be done as a demonstration or assigned as laboratory activity. Below is the recipe to construct the newer and better motor:

## Materials and Methods

- Two 2 $^5/_8$" pieces of 12 ga. copper house wire
- Two 8" pieces of 12 ga. copper house wire
- One strong ceramic (1 $^{13}/_{16}$" × $^{13}/_{16}$" × $^3/_8$") magnet (or) two ceramic ($^3/_4$" diameter $^3/_{16}$") magnets
- 3' of 22 ga. copper magnet wire
- One "D" size alkaline battery, 1.5 V
- Foam block 3" × 5" × 2" (L × W × H)
- Razor blade
- Wire cutters

Take the two 2 $^5/_8$" pieces of 12 ga. copper wire, strip and form them as shown in Figure 2, and place them in the foam block to keep the battery from rolling off the block. Next, take the two 8" 12 ga. copper wires, strip and bend them as shown, and place them in the foam block so the wire touches the battery and the indented end is farthest away from the battery. Place the magnet as shown on the foam block.

Now you are ready to make the coil. Placing two fingers close together, wrap the 22 gauge

The Johnson DC Electric Motor is dependable and easy to construct.

copper wire six times around the fingers. Try to keep the turns even and the center of the coil as symmetrical as possible. Also, wrap the ends of the coil wire so that they will hold the coil together and serve as an axle for rotation, as shown in Figure 2.

Before doing any fine adjustments, hold the coil vertical and place the axle on the edge of a table or hard surface. Take a razor blade and scrape off the top half of the insulation on the axle. Cut the axle 2" long. Do the same thing on the other axle and try not to flatten it by scraping too deeply.

With the coil now as symmetrical as possible, take the coil and place it on the indented area of your motor base and see which side is heaviest. Counterbalance it by placing a small piece of wire about 1" long on the lighter side. Balancing the coil is necessary since there is an extra strand of wire on one side. After the coil is adjusted, balanced, and straightened, it should spin easily in the indented area of your motor base. At this point, check to be sure that enough of the insulation is removed from the coil axle, which allows electricity to flow during half the rotation of the coil. Now you can adjust the balance of the coil and align the axles to provide the minimum amount of force necessary to turn it.

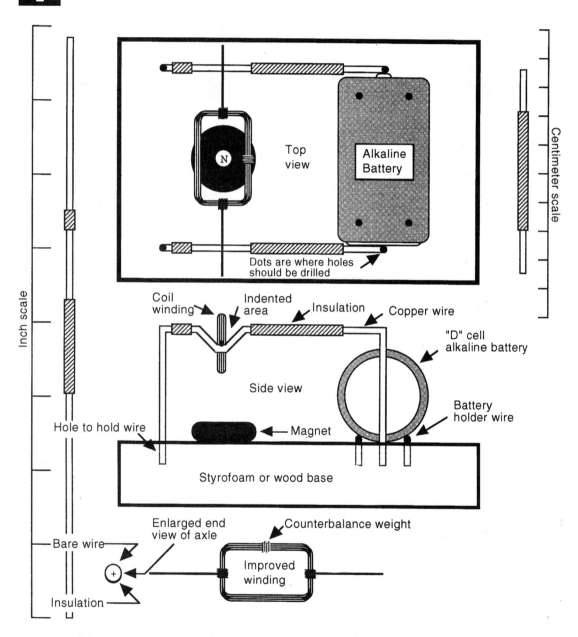

**figure 2** A diagram of the Johnson DC Electric Motor, indicating materials and scale

Put the battery in place between the uprights. Depending on the strength of the magnet, the current flow, and the coil balance, you will find that the coil will really spin fast. If the coil has current flow in the wrong direction, you may have to move the magnet into a different position around the coil to get it to work. With the motor running, try reversing the battery or flipping over the magnet. You will then see the coil stop and reverse direction.

The secret to the motor's dependability lies with the removal of the insulation on the axles to make momentary contact with the battery. This action is similar to a commutator of a direct current motor. In one position, the coil is energized and pushes off the magnetic field, and in the other position, the current flow is stopped, which allows it to continue moving until it is energized again.

Many variations are possible with this motor. You can build coils of different sizes, change the number of turns, and use thinner or thicker wire. I have made a motor using a very fine wire hot glued on a thicker axle, which has run continuously for nine months on one alkaline battery. I have also designed a half-loop motor (unheard of!) that spins quite well. With a strong magnet and a finer coil of wire turned many times, I have successfully run a motor using a solar cell and potato battery. I hope you enjoy this motor as much as I do. It has been a very inexpensive tool for understanding how the electric motor operates.

## Background Reading

Benson, H. 1991. University Physics. *New York: John Wiley & Sons, Inc.*

Carpenter, D. R., Jr., and R. B. Minnix. 1993. The Dick and Rae Physics Demo Notebook. *Lexington, VA: Dick and Rae, Inc.*

# Sulfuric Acid: King of Chemicals

## History, Chemistry, and Some Demonstrations of $H_2SO_4$

George B. Kauffman and Scott D. Pennington

Sulfuric acid ($H_2SO_4$) is the king of chemicals. As the world's most important industrial chemical and the cheapest bulk acid available in every country of the world, it is manufactured on an enormous scale, greater than for any other compound of any element (Chang and Tikkanen 1988; Greenwood and Earnshaw 1984; Kotz and Purcell 1987). Because it is consumed in so many ways in a modern industrial society, its annual production (e.g., 88.56 billion pounds in the United States in 1990) has been used by economists as a reliable indicator of a nation's industrial strength. It has perennially occupied first place in chemicals produced in the United States.

Scholars differ in ascribing a date to the first description of sulfuric acid. It is said to have been mentioned as early as the 10th century by the Persian alchemist and philosopher Abu Bakr Al-Razi (Rhazes) (circa 865–923/932). The "spirit" prepared by strongly heating alum that is mentioned during the 13th century by Geber, Vincent de Beauvais, and Albertus Magnus must have been sulfuric acid (Kopp 1847), but other scholars think that it was unknown until the 16th century (Partington 1960).

In Europe in 1755, Johann Christian Bernhardt was the first to prepare on an industrial scale what was known as "oil of vitriol" by heating "green vitriol" ($FeSO_4 \cdot H_2O$), while in the United States sulfuric acid was one of the first chemicals to be produced commercially—by John Harrison in Philadelphia in 1793. During the 19th and early 20th centuries, it was manufactured by the lead chamber process, which has been rendered obsolete by the more efficient contact process involving the combination of sulfur dioxide (obtained by burning sulfur or roasting sulfide ores) with oxygen at 400–500°C in the presence of a $V_2O_5$ catalyst. The sulfur trioxide ($SO_3$) formed is dissolved in concentrated $H_2SO_4$ to form fuming sulfuric acid or oleum ($H_2S_2O_7$), which on dilution with water yields $H_2SO_4$.

The largest use of sulfur (88 percent) is in the manufacture of sulfuric acid, which in turn has myriad uses. About 60 percent of the $H_2SO_4$ produced in the United States is used in preparing chemical fertilizers such as superphosphates. It is also used in manufacturing detergents, drugs, dyes, pigments, explosives, pulp and paper, textile fibers, petroleum products, alcohols, synthetic resins, metallurgical products, and other chemicals. A familiar use is as the electrolyte in lead storage batteries for automobiles. Space probes have even detected this ubiquitous chemical in the atmosphere of the planet Venus.

Because descriptive chemistry has unfortunately been neglected in today's largely theoretical introductory courses, the king of chemicals makes a particularly appropriate choice for acquainting students with this important but generally overlooked aspect of chemistry. The chemical and physical properties of $H_2SO_4$ may be illustrated by a number of striking but relatively simple lecture demonstrations, a number of which we describe in varying degrees of detail (e.g., Figure 1).

Because $H_2SO_4$ is a strong acid, an oxidizing agent, and a strong dehydrating agent, it should be handled with care by wearing rubber gloves and safety goggles and by carrying out reactions yielding noxious fumes in a hood.

Reactions with fuming acids must always be demonstrated in a well-vented area. It is also advisable to wear a rubber apron when handling the sulfuric acid. Students near the demonstration should be provided with chemical-resistant goggles.

## Strong Acid

Concentrated sulfuric acid (18 $\underline{M}$) is a colorless, viscous liquid of density 1.84 g/mL. Demonstrate its density by having students *carefully* hold a bottle of concentrated $H_2SO_4$ in one hand and a similar bottle filled with water in the other and compare the relative weights. You can make the demonstration more quantitative by weighing the bottles on a platform balance (Arthur 1939).

$H_2SO_4$ is a strong acid; the first stage of ionization:

$$H_2SO_4 \rightarrow H^+ + HSO_4^-$$

is complete, but the second stage:

$$HSO_4^- \rightarrow H^+ + SO_4^{2-} \quad K_a = 1.2 \times 10^{-2}$$

is not.

Add dilute (2 $\underline{M}$) $H_2SO_4$ to various indicators such as litmus, methyl orange, methyl red, or Hydrion paper and note the color change. Add dilute (2 $\underline{M}$) $H_2SO_4$ to small amounts of various metals above hydrogen in the activity series (e.g., Fe, Zn, Mg, etc.) in either a test tube or a petri dish on an opaque projector and observe the evolution of hydrogen gas:

$$Zn + 2H^+ \rightarrow Zn^{2+} + H_2\uparrow$$

Add dilute $H_2SO_4$ to metals below hydrogen in the activity series (for example, Cu). The absence of any reaction shows that cold, dilute $H_2SO_4$ is *not* an oxidizing agent and reacts only with metals above hydrogen in the activity series. Add 2 $\underline{M}$ $H_2SO_4$ to marble chips, chalk ($CaCO_3$), or other carbonates, for example, $Na_2CO_3$, in a test tube and observe the evolution of carbon dioxide, which will extinguish a burning splint or make limewater (saturated $Ca(OH)_2$ solution) turbid (Humphreys 1983a):

$$CaCO_3 + 2H^+ \rightarrow Ca^{2+} + H_2O + CO_2\uparrow$$

Robert Boyle included the dissolving of limestone ($CaCO_3$) with effervescence in his operational definition of an acid. Illustrate the ionic character of $H_2SO_4$ by measuring the conductance of the dilute acid. Demonstrate the presence of $HSO_4^-$ and $SO_4^{2-}$ by adding 1 $\underline{M}$ $BaCl_2$, which produces a readily visible white precipitate of insoluble $BaSO_4$. Demonstrate conductimetric titrations by titrating freshly prepared saturated $Ba(OH)_2$ solution with standard 2 $\underline{M}$ $H_2SO_4$. (The technique of conductimetric titration is discussed in many analytical chemistry texts and laboratory manuals.)

Because concentrated $H_2SO_4$ is relatively nonvolatile (decomposes to $SO_3$ and $H_2O$ at 340°C), other, more volatile acids can be prepared by heating their salts with concentrated $H_2SO_4$ and collecting the desired acid by distillation. For example, carefully heat NaCl with concentrated $H_2SO_4$ in a test tube and detect the HCl formed by observing the white cloud of $NH_4Cl$ smoke produced when a glass stopper from a bottle of concentrated aqueous ammonia is brought close to the mouth of the test tube (Humphreys 1983b). If you substitute $NaC_2H_3O_2 \cdot 3H_2O$ for NaCl, you can detect the $HC_2H_3O_2$ formed by the odor of vinegar (Weisbruch 1951a). In both cases you can demonstrate the acidic nature of the vapors with blue litmus paper. Because thiosulfuric acid rapidly undergoes decomposition:

$$H_2S_2O_3 \rightarrow H_2O + SO_2\uparrow + S\downarrow$$

you can demonstrate that $H_2SO_4$ is a strong acid by adding 2 $\underline{M}$ $H_2SO_4$ to 0.1 $\underline{M}$ $Na_2S_2O_3$ (photographer's "hypo"). The resulting suspension of whitish colloidal sulfur, known as "milk of sulfur," is the basis for various tricks of turning water into milk featured in chemistry sets and magic shows (Davis 1949a; Fowles 1957a; Alyea and Dutton 1965).

## Esterification Catalyst

In the presence of strong acids ($H_2SO_4$, HCl, $BF_3$, or the acid form of a strong acid cation exchange resin) carboxylic acids react with alcohols to yield esters and water (Noller 1965). Some volatile esters have specific fruit odors and have found limited use in synthetic flavors or perfumes, but natural odors and flavors result from highly complex mixtures of organic compounds. Because the odors of some esters are so characteristic and all-pervading, their formation by the $H_2SO_4$-catalyzed esterification makes a convenient lecture demonstration (Davis 1949b).

Into a test tube add 10 drops of the organic acid (acetic, propionic, butyric, or valeric; or about 0.5 g of solid salicylic or anthranilic acid), 20 drops of the alcohol (methyl, ethyl, butyl, *iso*-butyl, or *iso*-amyl), and 5 drops of concentrated $H_2SO_4$, and shake the tube to mix the contents. *Cautiously* heat the tube for about five minutes (Do not overheat; the contents are volatile) and pour the contents into a 25 mL beaker about half-full of ice. (You may have to scrape the methyl salicylate or methyl anthranilate into the ice.) The ice dilutes the $H_2SO_4$, which has partially decomposed to $SO_3$, so that the ester odor can be smelled. Stir and allow your students to note the odor and compare it with the odor of the original acid.

The odors of methyl salicylate, methyl anthranilate, ethyl acetate, butyl butyrate, *iso*-butyl propionate, *iso*-amyl acetate, and *iso*-amyl valerate resemble the odors of wintergreen (the most penetrating of the ester odors), grapes (the esterification reaction is slow and may take 10 minutes or more), nail polish remover, pineapple, rum (it actually smells more like orange "circus peanut" candy), banana, and apple, respectively, while ethyl propionate and butyrate and *iso*-amyl propionate and butyrate have a fruity odor.

## Dehydrating Agent

Concentrated $H_2SO_4$ has a great affinity for water and thus is a good drying agent. Its reaction with water sometimes generates enough heat to raise the temperature to boiling and to cause splattering (Shakhashiri 1983a). Therefore, when the acid is being diluted, it should be added to water to prevent a splash of acid (*never the reverse or acid splashes up as the water is added*) with constant stirring. Acid-resistant gloves, goggles, and an apron must be worn when handling sulfuric acid. When nitric acid is used to prepare nitroglycerin or nitrocellulose (guncotton) from

**figure 1**

The demonstrator fills a beaker with cane sugar (sucrose, $C_{12}H_{22}O_{11}$) and adds an equal volume of concentrated $H_2SO_4$. He then mixes the ingredients *thoroughly* and *quickly* with a thermometer that can be used to measure the rise in temperature...

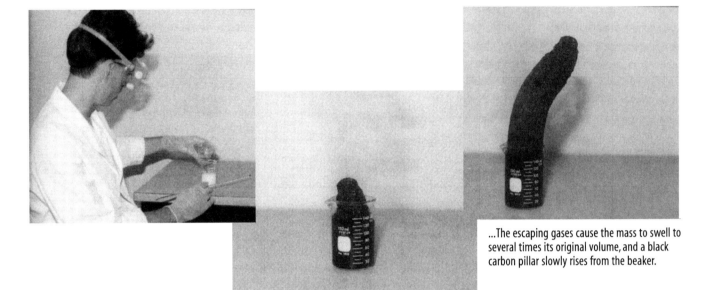

...Within several minutes the sugar begins to char, and steam, $SO_2$, $CO_2$, and $SO_3$ are evolved *(use a hood)*...

...The escaping gases cause the mass to swell to several times its original volume, and a black carbon pillar slowly rises from the beaker.

glycerin or cotton, respectively, it is mixed with concentrated $H_2SO_4$ to react with the water produced in the nitration reaction.

Demonstrate the dehydrating action of concentrated $H_2SO_4$ by adding 10 mL of it to several grams of powdered $CuSO_4 \cdot 5H_2O$ contained in a small flask and warming gently. The blue hydrate slowly changes to the white anhydrous salt (Fowles 1957b). Decant the liquid from the flask, wash the solid residue with water by rapid decantation, and add an equal volume of water. Heat is evolved, and the anhydrous salt reforms the blue hydrate.

The affinity of concentrated $H_2SO_4$ is so great that it can remove the elements of water from organic compounds such as alcohol or especially compounds containing hydrogen and oxygen in the ratio of 2:1 such as carbohydrates. Half fill a 150 mL or larger beaker with cane sugar (sucrose, $C_{12}H_{22}O_{11}$), add an equal volume of concentrated $H_2SO_4$, and mix *thoroughly* and *quickly* with a thermometer that can be used to measure the rise in temperature. Within several minutes the sugar begins to char, and steam, $SO_2$, $CO_2$, and $SO_3$ are evolved *(use a hood)*. The escaping gases cause the mass to swell to several times its original volume, and a black carbon pillar slowly rises from the beaker (see Figure 1). A plate or sheet of aluminum foil will protect the tabletop from any overflow (Arthur 1939; Weisbruch 1951b; Ford 1959; Humphreys 1983c; Shakhashiri 1983b; Ammon et al. 1985; Liem 1987). The readily noticeable odor of $SO_2$ (which can also be detected by the deep blue color produced on moist starch-$KIO_3$ paper placed in the fumes) illustrates that hot concentrated $H_2SO_4$ is an oxidizing agent as well as a dehydrating agent.

## Oxidizing Agent

As we have just seen, $H_2SO_4$ is a strong oxidizing agent, especially when hot and concentrated. Thus, in contrast to the cold, dilute acid, which, as we have seen above under "Strong Acid," does not react with metals below hydrogen in the activity series, hot, concentrated $H_2SO_4$ attacks these metals. For example, heat some copper turnings in a test tube with concentrated $H_2SO_4$ (*use a hood*). As the copper reacts, the liquid becomes greenish and fumes of sulfur dioxide, which can be detected with starch-$KIO_3$ paper or moist, blue litmus paper, is evolved:

$$Cu + 2H_2SO_4 \rightarrow CuSO_4 + SO_2\uparrow + 2H_2O$$

Other substances that can be oxidized by concentrated $H_2SO_4$ include KI, KBr, and $H_2S$. Add concentrated $H_2SO_4$ to solid KI or KBr in a beaker and heat the mixture on a hot plate to about 240°C (*use a hood*). The violet or reddish vapors of iodine or bromine, respectively, become visible, and in the case of KI the odor of rotten eggs is readily detectable:

$$8KI + 9H_2SO_4 \rightarrow 8KHSO_4 + 4I_2\uparrow + H_2S\uparrow + 4H_2O$$

$$2KBr + 3H_2SO_4 \rightarrow 2KHSO_4 + Br_2\uparrow + SO_2\uparrow + 2H_2O$$

Dark purple $I_2$ crystals can be collected by sublimation if the beaker is covered with a watch glass containing an ice cube or ice water.

Concentrated $H_2SO_4$ in the cold acts as an oxidizing agent with the strong reducing agent hydrogen sulfide (Fowles 1957c). Quickly add 1 mL of concentrated $H_2SO_4$ to a stoppered flask filled with hydrogen sulfide (*use a hood*). Roll the acid around the walls of the flask, and a precipitate of sulfur appears, first white but rapidly changing to yellow:

$$H_2SO_4 + 3H_2S \rightarrow 4S\downarrow + 4H_2O$$

Alternatively, you can add concentrated $H_2SO_4$ to 1 M $Na_2S$ contained in a beaker or test tube, but in this case heating is necessary to produce a white colloidal suspension ("milk of sulfur").

## Disposal

The carbon pillar should carefully be crumbled into water using acid-resistant gloves, goggles, and an apron. The dissolved pillar and any excess liquid wastes should be disposed down the drain and diluted with running water until no acids remain in the sink.

### Acknowledgments

*The authors wish to thank Drs. Richard P. Ciula and Stephen A. Rodemeyer for technical assistance.*

### References

Alyea, H. N., and F. B. Dutton. 1965. *Tested Demonstrations in Chemistry*. Easton, PA: Journal of Chemical Education. 41.

Ammon, D., D. Clarke, F. Farrell, R. Schibeci, M. Trotman, and J. Webb. 1985. *Interesting Chemistry Demonstrations*. 3rd ed. Perth, Australia: Science Teachers' Association of Western Australia. 63.

Arthur, P. 1939. *Lecture Demonstrations in General Chemistry*. New York: McGraw-Hill. 219–220.

Chang, R., and W. Tikkanen. 1988. *The Top Fifty Industrial Chemicals*. New York: Random House. 1–6, 187.

Davis, H. M., ed. 1949. *The Chemistry Show Book*. Washington, DC: Science Service. (a) 25; (b) 60–62.

Ford, L. A. 1959. *Chemical Magic*. Minneapolis, MN: T.S. Denison & Co. 18–19.

Fowles, G. 1957. *Lecture Experiments in Chemistry*. 4th rev. ed. London: G. Bell & Sons. (a) 601–602; (b) 215; (c) 196.

Greenwood, N. N., and A. Earnshaw. 1984. *Chemistry of the Elements*. Oxford, England and Elmsford, NY: Pergamon Press. 834, 838–845.

Humphreys, D. A. 1983. *Demonstrating Chemistry: 160 Experiments to Show Your Students.* Hamilton, Ontario, Canada: Chemistry Department, McMaster University. (a) Exp. 76; (b) Exp. 81; (c) Exp. 6.

Kopp, H. 1847. *Geschichte den Chemie,* vol. 3. Braunschweig, Germany: F. Vieweg & Son. 303–309.

Kotz, J. C., and K. F. Purcell. 1987. *Chemistry and Chemical Reactivity*. Philadelphia, PA: Saunders College Publishing. 732, 741, 998–999, 1007–1008, 1086, 1130.

Liem, T. L. 1987. *Invitations to Science Inquiry*. 2nd ed. Lexington, MA: Ginn Press. 135.

Noller, C. R. 1965. *Chemistry of Organic Compounds*. 3rd ed. Philadelphia, PA: W.B. Saunders & Co. 183–184, 193–194, 199.

Partington. J. R. 1960. *A Short History of Chemistry*. 3rd ed. New York: Harper and Brothers. 40, 47.

Shakhashiri, B. Z. 1983. *Chemical Demonstrations: A Handbook for Teachers of Chemistry,* vol. 1. Madison, WI: University of Wisconsin Press. (a) 17–18; (b) 77–78.

Weisbruch, F. T. 1951. *Lecture Demonstration Experiments for High School Chemistry*. St. Louis, MO: Educational Publishers. (a) 277; (b) 185.

# A Colorful Demonstration of Le Châtelier's Principle

## Observing the Effect of Stress on a Solution Containing Iron(III) and Thiocyanate Ions

Arthur M. Last and Peter W. Slade

According to Le Châtelier's principle, when a system at equilibrium is subjected to a stress, the system will respond in such a way that the effect of the stress is minimized (Le Châtelier 1884). Although this is a fairly straightforward concept, some students are initially confused over the meaning of terms such as *system* and *stress*.

A lecture demonstration that illustrates shifts in the position of equilibrium caused by a variety of factors can be of great pedagogical value. Typical experiments that can be used to illustrate Le Châtelier's principle include the addition of acid or base to a solution of chromate or dichromate (e.g., Wynn and Joppich 1987; Frankel and

Li 1989), or the addition of acid or base to an aqueous solution of bromine or iodine (Baker, Gries, and Navidi 1990). However, we feel that the system involving the reaction of iron(III) ion with thiocyanate ion has a number of advantages over these other systems.

The reaction of iron(III) ion with thiocyanate ion (equation 1) is used to illustrate Le Châtelier's principle in a number of commercial laboratory manuals (e.g., Whitten et al. 1988; Slowinski, Wolsey, and Masterton 1989), and is also the reaction upon which some quantitative equilibrium experiments are based (e.g., Baker et al. 1990; Beran 1994). In this reaction, a solution containing iron(III) ion (e.g., iron(III) nitrate) is reacted with a colorless solution containing thiocyanate ion (e.g., potassium thiocyanate) to produce a bloodred solution containing the thiocyanatoiron(III) complex ion, $[Fe(SCN)]^{2+}$ (aq). The reaction is usually represented as in equation 1, although a more precise representation would show this as the conversion of $[Fe(H_2O)_6]^{3+}$ to $[Fe(H_2O)_5SCN]^{2+}$.

> **Equation 1:**
> $Fe^{3+}(aq) + SCN^-(aq) \leftrightarrow [Fe(SCN)]^{2+}(aq)$

The equilibrium constant for this reaction, $K_1$, is $8.9 \times 10^2$ (Dean 1992), indicating that the equilibrium lies well to the right. Note that the bisthiocyanatoiron(III) ion, $Fe(SCN)_2^+$, may also be formed ($K = 2.3 \times 10^3$). We have adapted published procedures in order to use this system for an in-class demonstration of the various ways in which an equilibrium can be shifted. The advantages of using this reaction include the dramatic color change and the fact that the equilibrium is affected by a change in temperature and a wide range of added reagents. We commonly perform this demonstration for classes of 35 students and the quantities of chemicals used in the procedure described below are appropriate for such situations. Instructors teaching larger classes may increase the quantities used without the introduction of any additional safety hazards. As several parts of the demonstration illustrate essentially the same point, we recommend that instructors choose only those parts for which students have sufficient background knowledge to understand the underlying chemistry.

**Topic: factors affecting equilibrium**
**Go to: www.scilinks.org**
**Code: JCSTC116**

## Materials

Some of the materials used in this demonstration are toxic and/or present other safety hazards. The teacher and students handling any of the reagents must wear chemical-resistant goggles and surgical gloves. Student observers should be provided with safety glasses. All used reagents must be disposed of as hazardous wastes.

In order to perform all parts of the experiment, the following solutions are required:
- Silver nitrate (5 mL, 0.1 mol·L⁻¹)
- Sodium hydroxide (5 mL, 4 mol·L⁻¹)
- Iron(III) nitrate (20 mL, 0.2 mol·L⁻¹ in 0.5 mol·L⁻¹ nitric acid)
- Potassium thiocyanate (20 mL, 0.2 mol·L⁻¹)
- Mercury(II) nitrate (5 mL, 0.1 mol·L⁻¹ in 1 mol·L⁻¹ nitric acid)
- Sodium fluoride (10 mL, 0.1 mol·L⁻¹)
- Sodium oxalate (10 mL, 0.1 mol·L⁻¹)

These materials are also required:
- Solid potassium chloride (5 g)
- Ten 100 mL beakers
- Ten stirring rods
- Hot plate

## Procedure

### (a) Preparation of an Equilibrium Mixture

(i) Show the colorless iron(III) and thiocyanate solutions to the class, perhaps pointing out to students that the iron(III) nitrate solution has been made up in nitric acid in order to minimize the hydrolysis of $[Fe(H_2O)_6]^{3+}$ to $[Fe(H_2O)_5OH]^{2+}$. Pour 10 mL of each solution into a 2 L beaker and mix well. The resulting solution has a bloodred color due to the formation of the thiocyanatoiron(III) complex, $[Fe(SCN)]^{2+}$ (aq). Dilute this solution to 1 L so that the intensity of the bloodred color is reduced and small color changes are easier to observe. Transfer 80 mL of the dilute solution to a 100 mL beaker and retain it for comparison purposes.

(ii) If all parts of the demonstration are to be performed, transfer an 80 mL portion of the dilute equilibrium mixture to each of nine 100 mL beakers. These mixtures will be used to show how the position of equilibrium can be changed by applying various "stresses" to the system.

### (b) The Effect of Temperature on the Position of Equilibrium

Heat one of the equilibrium mixtures to 65–70°C on a hot plate while continuing with the rest of the demonstration. The formation of the thiocyanatoiron(III) complex ion is exothermic; thus the equilibrium constant decreases with increasing temperature. Heating the equilibrium mixture causes the thiocyanatoiron(III) ion to dissociate into iron(III) ion and thiocyanate ion, hence the intensity of the bloodred color decreases. Note that excessive heating appears to bring about an irreversible change.

In principle, cooling the equilibrium mixture below room temperature should increase the value of the equilibrium constant and favor the formation of the thiocyanatoiron(III) complex. Thus the intensity of the bloodred color should increase as the mixture is cooled. Although the difference in color between heated and cooled solutions of thiocyanatoiron(III) complex is illustrated in at least one textbook (Gillespie et al. 1986), we found that simply cooling one of our mixtures from room temperature to 0°C fails to produce a perceptible color change.

### (c) Addition of Reactant

(i) Add the remaining 10 mL of the 0.2 mol·L$^{-1}$ potassium thiocyanate solution to one of the equilibrium mixtures. The addition of excess thiocyanate ion causes the equilibrium to shift to the right, intensifying the color of the solution.

(ii) Add the remaining 10 mL of the 0.2 mol·L$^{-1}$ iron(III) nitrate solution to one of the equilibrium mixtures. Again, the addition of one of the reactants causes the equilibrium to shift to the right, intensifying the color of the solution.

### (d) Removal of a Reactant by Precipitation

(i) Add 5 mL of silver nitrate (0.1 mol·L$^{-1}$) solution to one of the equilibrium mixtures. A precipitate of silver thiocyanate ($K_{sp} = 1.0 \times 10^{-12}$)

forms, removing thiocyanate ion from the solution and causing equilibrium (1) to shift to the left with a resulting loss of color.

**Equation 2:**
$$Ag^+(aq) + SCN^-(aq) \leftrightarrow AgSCN(s)$$
$$K_2 = 1.0 \times 10^{12}$$

(ii) Add 5 mL of sodium hydroxide solution (4 mol·L$^{-1}$) to one of the equilibrium mixtures. This has the same overall effect as the addition of silver nitrate in (i), above, except that this time it is the iron(III) ion that is being removed from the equilibrium mixture due to the formation of insoluble iron(III) hydroxide ($K_{sp} = 4.0 \times 10^{-38}$).

**Equation 3:**
$$Fe^{3+}(aq) + 3\ OH^-(aq) \leftrightarrow Fe(OH)_3(s)$$
$$K_3 = 2.5 \times 10^{37}$$

The results of demonstrations d(i) and d(ii) can be interpreted in terms of the relevant equilibrium constants. In d(i), the concentrations of silver ion and iron(III) ion are comparable, and these ions compete for the limited amount of thiocyanate ion present. Because the equilibrium constant for the precipitation of silver thiocyanate (equation 2) is greater than that for the formation of thiocyanatoiron(III) complex (equation 1) by a factor of about $10^9$, the silver ions win the competition, the silver thiocyanate precipitates, and the thiocyanatoiron(III) complex dissociates. Demonstration d(ii) may be interpreted in a similar manner, but here it is the thiocyanate and hydroxide ions that are competing for the limited amount of iron(III) ion.

### (e) Removal of a Reactant by Complex Formation

(i) Add 5 mL of mercury(II) nitrate solution (0.1 mol·L$^{-1}$) to one of the equilibrium mixtures. The mercury(II) ion forms complexes with thiocyanate ion according to the following equations:

**Equation 4:**
$Hg^{2+}(aq) + 2\ SCN^-(aq) \leftrightarrow [Hg(SCN)_2](aq)$
$K_4 = 3.0 \times 10^{17}$

**Equation 5:**
$Hg^{2+}(aq) + 4\ SCN^-(aq) \leftrightarrow [Hg(SCN)_4]^{2-}(aq)$
$K_5 = 1.7 \times 10^{21}$

The magnitude of these equilibrium constants indicate that mercury(II) ion has a far greater affinity for thiocyanate ion than does iron(III) ion. The two metal ions compete for thiocyanate ions, and mercury(II) wins. Thiocyanate ion is thus removed from the original equilibrium mixture, causing a shift to the left and the accompanying loss of color.

(ii) Add 5 g of solid potassium chloride to the equilibrium mixture. The added chloride ion can form a number of complex ions with iron(III) ion, for example:

**Equation 6:**
$Fe^{3+}(aq) + Cl^-(aq) \leftrightarrow [FeCl]^{2+}(aq)$
$K_6 = 3.0 \times 10^1$

**Equation 7:**
$Fe^{3+}(aq) + 2\ Cl^-(aq) \leftrightarrow [FeCl_2]^+(aq)$
$K_7 = 1.3 \times 10^2$

**Equation 8:**
$Fe^{3+}(aq) + 3\ Cl^-(aq) \leftrightarrow [FeCl_3](aq)$
$K_8 = 9.8 \times 10^1$

**Equation 9:**
$Fe^{3+}(aq) + 4\ Cl^-(aq) \leftrightarrow [FeCl_4]^-(aq)$
$K_9 = 1.0$

The formation constants of these complex ions are less than that of the thiocyanatoiron(III) ion. However, the added chloride ion is present in a much greater concentration than the thiocyanate ion, thus the former successfully competes with the latter to form a complex with the iron(III) ion. The original equilibrium shifts left,

leaving an intense yellow-orange solution that is often attributed to the tetrachloroferrate(III) ion (Muir, Diaz, and Figueroa 1978; Toon and Ellis 1973), although given the magnitude of the formation constants, the dichloroiron(III) ion seems more likely.

(iii) Add 10 mL of 0.1 mol·L⁻¹ sodium fluoride solution to one of the equilibrium mixtures. As in (ii), above, the added anion complexes with the iron(III) ion, this time to form colorless ions of the type $[FeF]^{2+}$ ($K = 1.9 \times 10^5$), $[FeF_2]^+$ ($K = 2.0 \times 10^9$), etc. The authors of one lab text (Muir et al. 1978) suggest that the hexafluoroferrate(III) ion, $[FeF_6]^{3-}$, is formed in this reaction. However, other sources (e.g., Cotton and Wilkinson 1980) indicate that this ion, although known in the solid state, is not formed in aqueous solution.

(iv) Add 10 mL of 0.1 mol·L⁻¹ sodium oxalate solution to the remaining equilibrium mixture. The oxalate complexes with the iron(III) ion, shifting equilibrium (1) to the left and causing the color of the solution to change to pale yellow.

**Equation 10:**
$3\ C_2O_4^{2-}(aq) + Fe^{3+}(aq) \leftrightarrow Fe(C_2O_4)_3^{3-}(aq)$
$K_{10} = 1.6 \times 10^{20}$

## An Alternative Perspective

Although it is not a topic that would normally be discussed with freshman students, the concept of Hard and Soft Acids and Bases (HSAB) could be used to explain the results of the demonstrations described in parts (d) and (e), hence these demonstrations could be used when introducing the HSAB concept at the sophomore level. According to HSAB theory, acids and bases may be classified as being hard, soft, or borderline (Pearson 1963). Hard acids prefer to combine with hard bases, and soft acids prefer to combine with soft bases. Of the anions and cations utilized in demonstrations (d) and (e), iron(III), hydroxide, chloride, and fluoride are hard, and silver, mercury(II), and thiocyanate are soft. Thus, in demonstration d(i), the soft-soft combination of silver and thiocyanate is preferred to the hard-soft combination of iron(III) and thiocyanate. This results in the precipitation of silver thiocyanate when silver ion is added to the iron(III)/thiocyanate/thiocyanatoiron(III) equilibrium mixture. Note, however, that attempts to use formation constants of complex ions to quantify HSAB behavior in aqueous solution have not been particularly successful (Hancock and Martell 1996).

## Follow-up Activities

The formation of the thiocyanatoiron(III) complex has long been used as a test for iron(III) in qualitative analysis. However, it could also be used to test for the presence of thiocyanate ion. A novel activity involving the detection of thiocyanate ion in saliva through the addition of a $0.1 \ mol \cdot L^{-1}$ solution of iron(III) chloride has been published (De Roo 1996). The addition of this activity to the foregoing reactions will make this demonstration one that your students will long remember.

### Acknowledgment
*The authors wish to thank one of their colleagues, Nigel Dance, for pointing out the possible application of the HSAB theory to the systems discussed in this article.*

### References
Baker, A.D., L.F. Gries, and M.H. Navidi. 1990. *Laboratory Manual to Accompany Chemistry.* St. Paul, MN: West

Beran, J. A. 1994. *Laboratory Manual for Principles of General Chemistry.* 5th ed. New York: Wiley.

Cotton, F. A., and G. Wilkinson. 1980. *Advanced Inorganic Chemistry.* 4th ed. New York: Wiley.

Dean, J. A 1992. *Lange's Handbook of Chemistry.* 14th ed. New York: McGraw-Hill.

De Roo, I. 1996. Thiocyanate in saliva. *Chem 13 News* 249:10–11.

Frankel, A., and J. Li. 1989. *Chemistry: A Second Course: Laboratory Manual.* Don Mills, Ontario: Addison Wesley.

Gillespie, R. J., D. A. Humphreys, N. C. Baird, and E. A. Robinson. 1986. *Chemistry.* Boston: Allyn and Bacon.

Hancock, R. D., and A. E. Martell. 1996. Hard and soft acid-base behavior in aqueous solution. *Journal of Chemical Education* 73: 654–661.

Le Châtelier, H. 1884. Comptes rendus Hebdomadaires de l'Academie des Sciences. *Paris* 99:786–789.

Muir, M. M., J. A. Diaz, and N. C. Figueroa. 1978. *Laboratory Manual to Accompany Moore/Davies/Collins Chemistry.* New York: McGraw-Hill.

Pearson, R. G. 1963. Hard and soft acids and bases. *Journal of the American Chemical Society* 85: 3533–3539.

Slowinski, E.J., C. W. Wolsey, and W. L. Masterton. 1989. *Chemical Principles in the Laboratory.* 5th ed. Philadelphia: Saunders.

Toon, E. R., and G. L. Ellis. 1973. *Laboratory Experiments for Foundations of Chemistry.* New York: Holt Rinehart Winston.

Whitten, K. W., K. D. Gailey, C. B. Bishop, and M. B. Bishop. 1988. *Experiments in General Chemistry.* Philadelphia: Saunders.

Wynn, C. M., and G. A. Joppich. 1987. *Laboratory Experiments for Chemistry: A Basic Introduction.* 4th ed. Belmont, CA: Wadsworth.

# From Lodestone to Neodymium: Demonstrating Lenz's Law

## An Innovative Approach to Teaching Magnetic Properties

James H. Larson

E instein was enthralled, so the story goes, when a compass was presented to him as a child, and his fascination triggered an interest in science. For me, there was magic in magnets. I vividly remember being given two tiny dogs (Scotties, I believe) mounted on small bar magnets. How fascinated I was by their repulsion and movement as I moved them along on a smooth surface!

Now, decades later, my fascination remains. I share this interest with many others who have had a love affair with magnetism in its many incarnations, from lodestone to neodymium magnets with no end in sight. What is amazing is that despite this rapt attention, magnetism, like gravity, has yet to yield all of its secrets, even though we talk more intelligently about magnetic domains, the Curie point, the Meissner effect, and the prospect of rapid transit through magnetic levitation.

I find that enthusiasm for magnets is still present in young people. We should take advantage of it. One magnetic demonstration that "blows them away" is still not widely utilized by teachers of science even at the collegiate level. I refer to an application of Lenz's law involving a strong magnet falling through a nonferrous metal tube.

SCi LINKS.
THE WORLD'S A CLICK AWAY

Topic: magnetic fields
Go to: www.scilinks.org
Code: JCSTC121

The demonstration apparatus is made up of a 64"-long copper tube through which small magnets are dropped. Depicted above the tube are a "cow magnet" and a disk magnet.

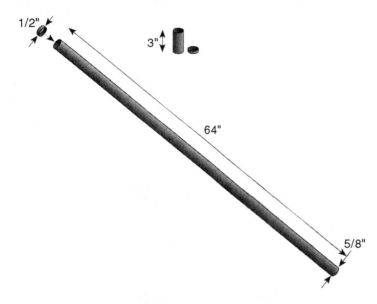

## The Demonstration

*Turning the World Inside Out* by Robert Ehrlich (1990) describes a demonstration wherein a strong magnet is dropped down a nonferrous tube, such as one made of copper or aluminum. The magnet produces eddy currents and associated magnetic fields in the tube that interact with and impede the magnet's transit through the tube. Pasco Scientific markets a commercial form of this equipment. Central Scientific also markets a version, which is only about 13" long.

Because science teachers (especially those of us who teach methods courses) are always looking for inexpensive demonstrations, I decided to try my own version. I obtained a copper tube from our maintenance shop, the type used in home water plumbing. It measured 64" long with a 5/8" diameter (wall thicknesses vary).

Since this demonstration requires fairly strong magnets, and our college is in the heart of dairy country, I purchased two "cow magnets." Urban students have generally never heard of such a creature. But farm students know that

these 3" × ½" cylindrical magnets are forced down the throat of the cow where they lodge in the cow's rumen. Their purpose is to immobilize iron debris that the cow may swallow while foraging. This prevents sharp objects from perforating the digestive tract.

Armed with the copper tube and the cow magnets (Figure 1), I was ready for a test. When I dropped the magnet down the tube, I noted a two-second delay. That wasn't bad, I thought. A magnet dropped outside the tube clearly confirmed the time delay contrasted to a freely falling object.

Then I remembered that I had two small, disc-shaped neodymium magnets, also available from Central Scientific, Arbor Scientific, Edmund Scientific, and presumably elsewhere. My magnets were rated at 37 mega-gauss. They fit just right in the tube I had cut. So I decided to drop them through. To my amazement, they didn't come through, and didn't come through, and I thought, "Uh-oh! Stuck!" But after 17 seconds, the magnet emerged. I tried again…17 seconds again. What a delay! A triple check and I was ready to pronounce the reliability of my data. A quick check of $S = \frac{1}{2} gt^2$ for a falling body (without air friction) shows that a 17-second fall would traverse 4,624 feet, no small difference from my 64" tube. It was immediately apparent to me that I had the germ of an interesting phenomenon that could be used in eliciting possible explanations from novice observers.

## Hypothesis Formation

After performing this demonstration for my physical science and physics students, I asked them to propose possible hypotheses to explain the observed behavior. Since most students seem to have never heard of Lenz's law, or have long since forgotten it, it is seldom given as a reason. Most students postulate explanations of air friction, air pressure, sliding friction, and sometimes other, rather bizarre, ideas. But at least they try. This is especially true when you show them that the magnet is not attracted to the copper tube. I also drop a nonmagnetic iron piece down the tube to illustrate its unimpeded progress.

The demonstration never fails to interest people of all ages. I have also been astounded to note that many of my nonphysics-oriented colleagues (even some in science) have never seen this demonstration. Invariably, most do not recall Lenz's law and fail to invoke the idea.

Lenz's law states that an induced current occurs in a direction such that it opposes the change that produces it. The eddy currents pro-

duced in the copper tube, along with their associated magnetic field, interact with the falling magnet and cause the time lag.

This is an inexpensive, provocative, and counterintuitive demonstration guaranteed to get the mental wheels of hypothesis formulation rolling. It is loads of fun. Try it!

### Reference

Ehrlich, R. 1990. *Turning the World Inside Out.* Princeton, NJ: Princeton University Press.

# Visualizing Chemical Reactions with the Pop-It Bead Model

## Modeling the Dynamic Nature of Chemical Equilibrium (Part One of Two Parts)

John Luoma and Susan Yochum

Chemistry is a central science (Brown, LeMay, and Burstein 1994) that provides conceptual support to many other areas of science (Yoesten et al. 1991). General chemistry is the most challenging of all first-year college courses in the physical sciences. From the first day of instruction, chemistry students must be able to build mental images of submicroscopic atoms, molecules, and ions.

Chemical science provides students with conceptual tools to understand the structure of matter and the changes that matter exhibits when undergoing a chemical reaction. Chemical equilibrium is the culmination of such a reaction. All first-year college chemistry courses cover chemical equilibrium and several of its applications, such as treatments of strong and weak acids and bases, precipitation, complexation, the concentration effect in electrochemistry, and chemical spontaneity.

## Definition of Equilibrium

The equilibrium state appears, to a macroscopic observer in a laboratory, to be a static state. Chemistry teaches that this state is actually a "dynamic" state. In this dynamic state, the rate of this forward reaction is equal to the rate of the reverse reaction. Furthermore, at equilibrium the forward and reverse reactions are occurring simultaneously. Le Châtelier's principle demands this dynamic model of chemical equilibrium. This experimentally verified and accepted principle predicts that the equilibrium will dynamically shift to relieve a stress applied to the equilibrium state.

## Instructional Method

Our instructional method is to provide students with the opportunity to form mental images of the concepts involved in chemical equilibrium.

We have found the following hierarchy of concepts to be an effective teaching scheme:
- Atoms (molecules and ions)
- Kinetic motion
- Bond formation (collisions)
  - Proper orientation
  - Sufficient energy
- Bond breaking
- Concentration
- Reaction rate
  - Production formation
  - Reactant formation
- Competing processes
- Quantification and interpretation
- Applications

## Part One: The Pop-It Bead Model

The concept of dynamic chemical equilibrium is a challenge for many students because they are required to visualize molecular components and processes that they cannot see. Many first-year chemistry students prefer concrete rather than abstract models. Thus, students can benefit from a model that makes atoms and molecules visible, tangible, and dynamic.

The model we describe here meets this need, and also renders concrete, visible, and dynamic a chemical reaction in which new bonds are formed and reactants are reformed by bond breaking. Our model uses readily available materials and requires little lecture time—approximately 15 minutes. It is easy to conduct and it involves student participation. We have found that this demonstration is an effective teaching tool (see the Student Response section below) for students enrolled in mainstream and honors general chemistry courses, as well as nonmajor introductory chemistry courses, at both small and large colleges.

Topic: factors affecting equilibrium
Go to: *www.scilinks.org*
Code: JCSTC116

 Representation of the equilibrium systems used in the demonstration

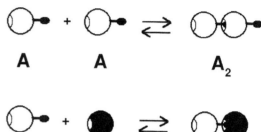

## Materials

- The popular pop-it beads are used as models for atoms. We use two-way 12-mm beads. (Beads, of various colors, are available from Carolina Biological Supply Company. They can be purchased in bags of 250 for a reasonable price.) The two-way beads are used for species $A$ and one-way beads are used for species $B$. The one-way beads, or $B$s, are made by removing the prong on the two-way beads.
- A cardboard box, 8.5" × 11.5" × 3.0" (22.0 cm × 29.2 cm × 7.6 cm), is used as a reaction vessel. (Any comparable size box is adequate.)
- Time is measured with a stopwatch or timing device.
- Two blindfolds may be improvised by inserting paper lenses into safety goggles (or taping the paper to the outside of the goggles).

## Reaction for Study

The representations of the two systems or reactions that are discussed in this demonstration are shown in Figure 1.

## Procedure

As many as five students participate in this demonstration. Each student can play one of the following roles:

- The "Forward Reaction" student—who wears a blindfold—finds two reactants and snaps them together to form a product molecule.
- The "Reverse Reaction" student—who also wears a blindfold—searches for product molecules and unsnaps or breaks the bonds to form reactants.
- The "Agitator" agitates or shakes the reaction vessel to simulate the constant, random kinetic motion of the atoms and molecules.
- One student serves as the "Timer."
- The last student serves as the "Recorder" and records the data on the board.

This demonstration can easily be extended to a class activity whereby the entire class is divided into teams.

## System $A + A \rightarrow A_2$

Place 100 $A$ beads in the reaction vessel. The Agitator begins shaking the reaction vessel. The Timer signals to the Forward Reaction and Reverse Reaction students to begin. Allow the reaction to proceed for one minute. Stop and carefully count the number of products, $A_2$s. The number of unreacted $A$s equals the initial number of $A$s minus twice the number of $A_2$s

The Recorder records the number of $A$s and $A_2$s on the board. Leave all $A_2$s intact and repeat the process until equilibrium is established. Equilibrium is usually obtained in four to eight trials.

## System $A + B \rightarrow AB$

Place 100 $A$s and 100 $B$s in the reaction vessel. The Forward Reaction student forms the product $AB$ only. Continue the procedure as in the $A + A \rightarrow A_2$ system.

## Calculations

Students can observe from the data that a consistent or a fixed number of reactants and products persist for a system that has reached equilibrium. The instructor may choose to have students write the equilibrium expression and

**table 1** — The results and calculations for $A + A \rightarrow A_2$.

| Trail | Time (minutes) | #A | #A$_2$ |
|---|---|---|---|
| 0 | 0 | 100 | 0 |
| 1 | 1 | 76 | 12 |
| 2 | 2 | 80 | 20 |
| 3 | 3 | 68 | 16 |
| 4 | 4 | 64 | 18 |
| 5 | 5 | 68 | 16 |
| 6 | 6 | 68 | 16 |

*Calculations:*
1. Equilibrium expression: $K_c = [A_2/\text{volume}]/[\#A/\text{volume}]$
2. $K_c = [\#A_2/\text{volume}]/[\#A/\text{volume}]^2$
$K_c = (16\ A_2/4.9\ \text{L})/(68\ A/4.9\ \text{L})^2$
$K_c = [3.3]/[14]^2$
$K_c = 1.7 \times 10^{-2}$

*Notes:*
1. [] defined as number concentration or # particles/volume.
2. Volume = length x width x height of the box.
3. We recommend teacher discretion in the use of units for the final $K_c$ value.

**table 2** — The results and calculations for $A + B \rightarrow AB$.

*Data:*

| Trial | Time (minutes) | #A | #B | #AB |
|---|---|---|---|---|
| 0 | 0 | 100 | 100 | 0 |
| 1 | 1 | 92 | 92 | 8 |
| 2 | 2 | 91 | 91 | 9 |
| 3 | 3 | 87 | 87 | 13 |
| 4 | 4 | 87 | 87 | 13 |
| 5 | 5 | 87 | 87 | 13 |

*Calculations:*
1. Equilibrium expression: $K_c = [AB]/([A][B])$
2. $K_c = [\#AB/\text{volume}]/([\#A/\text{volume}][\#B/\text{volume}])$
$K_c = (13\ AB/4.9\ \text{L})/\{(87\ A/4.9\ \text{L})(87\ B/4.9\ \text{L})\}$
$K_c = [2.7]/[18]^2$
$K_c = 8.3 \times 10^3$

calculate the equilibrium constant for each system. Sample data and calculations are shown in Tables 1 and 2.

## Class Discussion

The class is asked to discuss the concepts that are modeled or brought forth in the demonstration. A lively discussion generally ensues, resulting in the following list of observations:

- In order for a bond to form between two atoms, a "successful" collision must occur. A "successful" collision means that the two atoms must collide with *sufficient energy* and with the *proper orientation*. (The Forward Reaction students will discover that some attempted bonds or "snaps" are "unsuccessful" and the beads need to be returned to the vessel.)
- Energy is required to break a bond.
- In an equilibrium system, the forward and reverse reactions occur *simultaneously* and at the *same rate*.
- At equilibrium, reactions are still taking place.
- At equilibrium, the concentrations of reactants and products remain constant.
- Atoms and molecules are in constant, random motion.

## Student Response

We have found that the entire class is attentive to the activity and frequently cheers for the Forward Reaction and Reverse Reaction students. In addition, we asked our honors students to evaluate this demonstration regarding its effectiveness as a model for equilibrium and as a learning aid. Here are some of their responses:

- "This demonstration was fun and brought out a good class discussion."
- "This was very beneficial! It really reinforced the two requirements of sufficient energy and proper orientation."
- "Not only informative but fun as well!"

- "It was really good because the model was almost a perfect illustration of what is really going on and everyone got involved."
- "Helped in focusing in on what would be happening in an actual reaction."
- "Being a visual learner, I found the model very helpful for me to understand."

## Instructional Support

Each pop-it bead represents an atom or a molecule. The shaking of the box by the student Agitator represents the microscopic kinetic motion of molecules. The number of beads in the box represents the number-concentration of those particles and is symbolized by the square brackets, $[A]$. The expression for the rate of the forward reaction $(R_f)$ is equal to the specific rate constant $(k_f)$ times the concentration raised to the proper power. The rate of the reverse reaction is equal to $R_r = k_r [Product]$.

For the two modeled elementary processes, the specific rate constants ($k$s) represent the students' characteristic speeds of making bonds (finding and snapping two beads together) and breaking bonds (finding and unsnapping two connected beads). In short, students have individual methods and levels of dexterity for making and breaking bonds. At equilibrium these two rates are equal and we write

$$R_f = k_f [A][B] = k_r [AB] = R_r$$

This equation can be rearranged such that

$$(k_f/k_r) = [AB]/([A][B])$$

Here we see that the ratio of the specific rate constant of the forward reaction divided by the specific rate constant for the reverse reaction is a constant called the equilibrium constant, $K_c$. The other side of the equation yields

$$K_c = [AB]_c/([A]_c[B]_c)$$

where the $_c$ subscript refers to the equilibrium concentration of that species.

We have found it difficult to compare equilibrium constants for these two types of reactions. It has been suggested that $K_c$ for $A + A \rightarrow A_2$ would be greater than the $K_c$ for $A + B \rightarrow AB$ since it may seem that it would be easier to form $A_2$ than $AB$. We have conducted this activity numerous times and only about half of the runs agree with this prediction.

Another limitation has to do with the size of our model system. Macroscopic chemical approaches to equilibrium occur among billions and trillions of molecules. We have carried out modeling of chemical approaches to equilibrium for these two systems with bead numbers from 50 to 200 and have found that variations due to sample size and to human factors prohibit quantitative interpretation of the equilibrium constants.

## Conclusion

Students have proclaimed this demonstration to be superior in enhancing their ability to build the dynamic mental images of chemical equilibrium. These images satisfy the first seven of the nine conceptual images listed in the Instructional Method section. The equilibrium in this demonstration is established quickly, making it an efficient and effective lecture demonstration.

## References

Brown, T. L., H. E. LeMay, and B. E. Burstein. 1994. *Chemistry: The Central Science.* Englewood Cliffs, NJ: Prentice Hall.

Yoesten, M. D. et al. 1991. *World of Chemistry.* Philadelphia: Saunders College Publishing.

# Demonstrating Chemical Processes with the Transfer-Tube Model

## Modeling the Dynamic Nature of Chemical Equilibrium *(Part Two of Two Parts)*

John Luoma and Susan Yochum

In part one of this set of demonstrations (pgs. 125–129), we noted the centrality of chemistry to other sciences and also noted the uniqueness of the concept of chemical equilibrium to chemical science. The pop-it bead model served very well to illustrate six concepts in our hierarchy for an effective teaching scheme. The pop-it bead model is effective in modeling the component particles, the kinetic motion of the particles, bond formation, bond breaking, reaction rate, and competing processes. This model is effective in modeling the qualitative microscopic and dynamic aspects of chemical equilibrium, and thus is an excellent lecture demonstration. However, the pop-it bead model is less effective in modeling concentration effects and is less effective in quantification and applications of chemical equilibrium.

Here in part two we present another method for modeling dynamic chemical equilibrium that we call the transfer-tube method. This method is not as effective in the earlier portion of our teaching hierarchy, but it is much more effective in modeling concentration effects, reaction rate, competing processes, and quantification. Thus the transfer-tube method complements the pop-it bead method. The transfer-tube method is much easier to quantify than the pop-it bead method; thus, it is also is an excellent lecture demonstration.

## Part Two: The Transfer-Tube Model

The concept of dynamic chemical equilibrium is a challenge for most students because they are required to visualize competing molecular-level processes that take place on too small a scale to actually be seen. Many freshman chemistry students prefer concrete rather than abstract models. Thus, our students benefit from models that make concrete the dynamic competing processes that yield an apparent macroscopic "static" condition called chemical equilibrium. We have found that the transfer-tube model is an effective teaching tool (see the Student Response section below) for students enrolled in mainstream and honors general chemistry courses as well as nonmajor introductory chemistry courses at both small and large colleges.

**Topic: factors affecting equilibrium**
Go to: *www.scilinks.org*
Code: JCSTC116

Other educators (Kauffman 1959; Schaff and Westmeyer 1968) employed qualitative lecture demonstrations of chemical equilibrium. These included two students dipping water from two beakers with different-sized dippers, and two students syringing water from two beakers with different-sized syringes. In these two models, equilibrium is established quickly with the apparatus of the proper size, a characteristic that qualifies these activities as effective lecture demonstrations.

Here we describe the transfer-tube method, which can be considered an extension of the earlier demonstrations (Carmody 1960). This method illustrates the dynamic aspects of chemical equilibrium and further illustrates the measurement of the equilibrium constant.

## Materials and Setup

- Two matched (same diameter) 50.0 mL graduated cylinders
- The transfer tubes are two glass tubes of different diameters that are fire-polished at each end. The lengths of the tubes are such that

The double tube apparatus

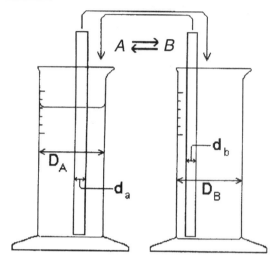

The student at left is performing a double tube transfer.

each tube protrudes 5–10 cm above each graduated cylinder when they rest inside the cylinders.
- The fluid to be transferred is water, which may contain food coloring to enhance its visibility.
- Two 10.0 mL graduated cylinders
- A ruler or Vernier caliper

Figure 1 shows the apparatus. Arrows suggest the transfers.

## Procedures

We suggest that the experiment be conducted by teams of two students each. However, the demonstration can be undertaken by individual students, who can perform the transfers and also record the volumes.

## Double Tube Transfer Procedure

Label the left cylinder *A* and the right one *B*. Place transfer tube *a* into cylinder *A* and a different transfer tube, *b*, into cylinder *B*. Add water to cylinder *A* until the volume reads no more than 50.0 mL. Record on the data sheet, next to transfer number 0, the volume of water in cylinder *A* (e.g., 50.0 mL) and the volume of water in cylinder *B* (e.g., 0.0 mL).

Using a finger from each hand, seal both transfer tubes. Remove the tubes from their respective cylinders and place them in the other cylinders. Release the trapped water. Figure 2 shows the dexterity required!

Return the empty transfer tubes to their original cylinders. Read the volumes of water in both cylinders and record these volumes next to transfer number 1.

Continue the transfers and recordings until the water levels in the cylinders remain the same (within experimental error) for four successive transfers. At this point, equilibrium has been established.

Perform one last transfer, but this time the destination of the contents of each transfer tube should be the small graduated cylinders. Record the volumes of the water in the two small graduated cylinders. Measure and record in millimeters the inner diameters of the two cylinders and the two transfer tubes. See Figure 3.

Reverse the positions of the transfer tubes and repeat this procedure.

## Le Châtelier's Principle and the Perturbation Procedure

After an equilibrium has been established in a double tube transfer experiment, introduce a perturbation by adding more water to cylinder *B,* the product cylinder. Carry out double tube transfers and recordings until a new equilibrium is attained. After establishing the new equilibrium, deliver one more transfer to the small graduated cylinders. Record the volume of the water in these small cylinders.

## Data Presentation

The double tube transfer exercises should be presented on a single sheet of graph paper. The ordinate or *y*-axis should be labeled as "Volume in mL." The abscissa or the *x*-axis should be labeled as "Transfer Number." The transfer number is interpreted as elapsed time for this exercise.

Plot volumes from the data sheet at their respective transfer numbers. Colored pencils work well to distinguish the plot of transfer tube *a* from that of *b*. The data from the two transfer tubes should be identified on the graph. See Figure 4.

Figure 1, with transfer tube *a* (large diameter) and tube *b* (small diameter), is the arrangement that yielded the data identified with squares in Figure 4. Reversing the starting positions of the transfer tubes will yield the triangle data in Figure 4.

For the perturbation data, the relative weights of the product species (the diamond symbol in Figure 5) and the relative weights of reactant species (the triangle symbols in Figure 5) are plotted on a sheet of graph paper oriented as in the original procedure.

## Calculations

Figure 6 shows primary measurements to be made during the activity; Figure 7 shows the calculations to be performed afterward. These calculations show that the transfer-tube model of chemical equilibrium for $A \leftrightarrow B$ yields very nice data. The volume measured equilibrium constants, $K_{eq}(1)$ and $K_{eq}(2)$, agree very well with the geometrically derived equilibrium constants. Compare 1a with 1b, and 2a with 2b. $K_{eq}(1)$ should be equal to $1/K_{eq}(2)$, and we see that 2.21

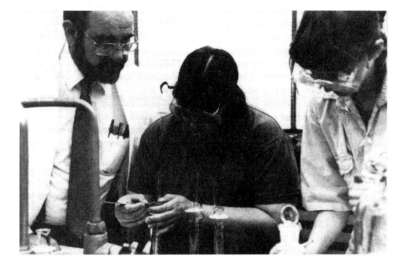

A chemistry student, supervised by author John Luoma, measures the inner diameter of a graduated cylinder.

is very close to 1 /0.44 = 2.27. In all three cases, the small graduated cylinder readings indicated that equal amounts of water were being transferred at equilibrium.

In the perturbation study, the system had a pre-perturbation $K_{eq}$ of 5.45. After the perturbation was applied, Le Châtelier's principle swings into action while the perturbed system shifts to relieve the stress and establish a new equilibrium. The $K_{eq}$ for this state is measured to be 5.42, virtually identical with the initial equilibrium constant.

## Student Response

Student exit surveys yielded approximately 70 percent positive response to the transfer-tube activity. Some of the responses were as follows:

"I refer to this experiment often when I try to visualize chemical equilibrium and reaction rates."

"I really enjoyed these! At first I couldn't understand the principle behind the exercise, but actually performing the transfers and seeing the trends in the data, I really began to understand. This was very helpful."

figure 4 Plots for double tube transfer data

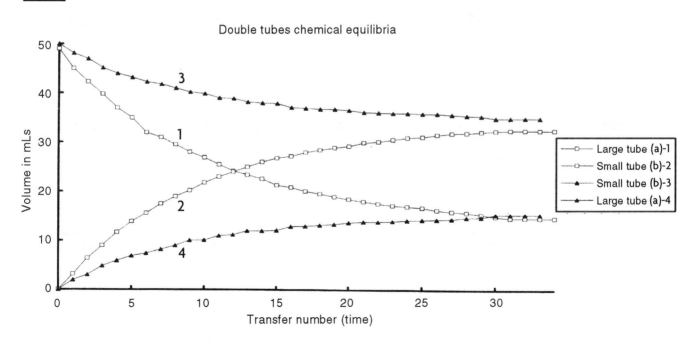

Double tubes chemical equilibria

Legend:
- Large tube (a)-1
- Small tube (b)-2
- Small tube (b)-3
- Large tube (a)-4

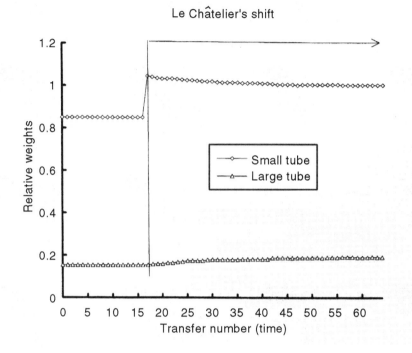

figure 5 Plot for perturbation data

Le Châtelier's shift

figure 6 Primary Measurements

1. Double tube data
   a. Equilibrium volume for cylinder *A*
   b. Equilibrium volume for cylinder *B*
   c. Small graduated cylinder volume for tube *a*
   d. Small graduated cylinder volume for tube *b*
2. Repeat above measurements for reversed transfer tubes
3. Perturbation data
   a. Equilibrium relative volume of cylinder *B* before perturbation
   b. Equilibrium relative volume of cylinder *A* before perturbation
   c. Volume of perturbation
   d. Equilibrium relative volume of cylinder *B* after perturbation
   e. Equilibrium relative volume of cylinder *A* after perturbation
   f. Small graduated cylinder volume of tube *b*
   g. Small graduated cylinder volume of tube *a*
4. Radii
   a. Inner diameter in millimeters of cylinder *B*
   b. Inner diameter in millimeters of cylinder *A*
   c. Inner diameter in millimeters of tube *b*
   d. Inner diameter in millimeters of tube *a*

"Some things are difficult to visualize and the hands-on experience made it easier to understand."

"I never quite figured out exactly what we were trying to do, but I enjoyed the results."

## Instructional Support

The chemical equilibrium that is modeled here is $A \leftrightarrow B$. This equilibrium occurs within the solution (50 mL). This model places the reactants in cylinder *A* and the products in cylinder *B*. The volume of the water in cylinder *A* represents the concentration of *A* in the combined solution. Likewise, the volume of *B* represents the concentration of the product in the reaction volume. The rate of reaction of *A* is determined by size (diameter) of transfer tube *a*, and the rate of formation of the reactants from the products is determined by the size of transfer tube *b*. At equi-librium, the rate of the forward reaction is equal to the rate of the reverse reaction for elementary processes.

In our model, the amount of water removed from cylinder *A* is equal to the amount of water removed from cylinder *B*. Thus, the identical volume reading of the small graduated cylinders convinces the student that equilibrium has been reached. The student senses this because successive transfers have resulted in no changes in the volume of water in either cylinder. Thus, this activity is especially effective in visibly modeling the dynamic steady state that is established at equilibrium.

A common student misconception is that the equilibrium state is that state when the volume curves of cylinders *A* and *B* intersect. This exercise easily defeats this misconception.

**figure**
**7**  Calculations

1. Data of Figure 4 Squares
   a. Equilibrium volume of $B$ ÷ equilibrium volume of $A = 32.5$ mL/14.7 mL $= 2.21 = K_{eq}(1)$
   b. $K_{eq}(1) = (6.0$ mm$)^2 / (4.0$ mm$)^2 = 2.25$
   c. Volume small cylinder for tube $a = 1.0$ mL $=$ Volume small cylinder for tube $b$
2. Data of Figure 4 Triangles
   a. Equilibrium volume of $B$ ÷ equilibrium volume of $A = 15.4$ mL/35.0 mL $= 0.44 = K_{eq}(2)$
   b. $K_{eq}(2) = (4.0$ mm$)^2 / (6.0$ mm$)^2 = 0.44$
   c. Volume small cylinder for tube $a = 1.0$ mL $=$ Volume small cylinder for tube $b$
3. Data for Figure 5 Perturbation
   a. Equilibrium relative volume of $B$ ÷ equilibrium relative volume of $A = K_{eq}(3)$
      $K_{eq}(3) = 0.845/0.155 = 5.45$ before perturbation
   b. Equilibrium relative volume of $B$ ÷ equilibrium relative volume of $A = K_{eq}(4)$
      $K_{eq}(4) = 1.03/0.19 = 5.42$ after 10.0 mL perturbation to 50.0 mL system
   c. Volume small cylinder for tube $a = 1.5$ mL $=$ Volume small cylinder for tube $b$

Quantification can be further enhanced by weighing the cylinders, transfer tubes, and water. Weighing the net amount of water in each cylinder is much more accurate than reading the volumes from the graduated cylinders. The smoothness of the data in Figure 5 illustrates these more accurate measurements.

## Conclusion

Like the pop-it bead activity, this activity enhances students' ability to build the dynamic mental images of chemical equilibrium. Thus, these two methods of modeling dynamic chemical equilibrium span the topics in our hierarchy of concepts employed to effectively teach chemical equilibrium through lecture demonstrations. The quantitative aspects of this demonstration lend themselves very naturally to a laboratory activity or an independent study project.

## References

Carmody, W. R. 1960. *Journal of Chemical Education* 37:312.

Kauffman, G. B. 1959. *Journal of Chemical Education* 36:150.

Schaff, J. F., and P. Westmeyer. 1968. *Chemistry* 41:7, 48.

# Does Black Paint Radiate Heat Better Than White Paint?

## Demonstrating Differences in Emission of Infrared Radiation

David P. Martin and Randy D. Russell

**D**oes a house painted white radiate less heat and thus stay appreciably warmer in the winter? Does a living room radiator painted black radiate more efficiently? Here is a classroom demonstration that will help students answer these questions for themselves.

As noted by Bartels (1990), there is a misconception about the radiation of heat that says that dark-colored objects radiate better than light-colored ones. In reality, our perception of an object's color has only to do with how well that object absorbs and reflects *visible* wavelengths. Dark-colored objects can absorb (and emit) *visible* light well; light-colored objects cannot. Objects that are cooler than "red hot," however, are not warm enough to emit *visible* wavelengths. Rather they radiate heat energy in the *infrared* region of the electromagnetic spectrum. Thus, the ability of an object at room temperature to radiate heat is indicated by its absorption and reflection of *infrared* radiation, not visible light. An object that reflects or absorbs much visible light can act very differently at infrared wavelengths.

Most nonmetallic surfaces radiate infrared quite well regardless of their color (Bartels 1990). Therefore, painted surfaces of any color are generally good absorbers and emitters of infrared radiation, making them good heat radiators at room temperature. This is confirmed in Figure 1, which shows an infrared reflection spectrum for a white-painted surface and a black-painted surface. It is apparent that both surfaces reflect little infrared radiation; thus, they both can absorb and emit infrared well.

The fraction of incident radiation absorbed by the surface is called the *absorptivity* of the surface. According to Kirchoff's law, the emissivity of a surface is equal to its absorptivity at the same wavelength. An ideal radiator (absorber) would have an emissivity of one at all wavelengths. However, the white-painted surface is a selective absorber and emitter of radiation; it has a high emissivity at infrared wavelengths even though it absorbs little visible light.

## Classroom Demonstration

It can be instructive to demonstrate for students that white- and black-painted surfaces both emit infrared well. A photograph and diagrams of an apparatus to illustrate this in the classroom are shown in Figures 2, 3, and 4. One side of a metal can is painted black and illuminated with light from an overhead projector. The nonilluminated vertical surface of the can is covered by three differently painted layers of aluminum foil. The can is allowed to heat up until it reaches its equilibrium temperature, which depends partly on the emissivity of the can's outer surface. As layers of foil are stripped from the can, part of its radiating surface changes. If the foil surface underneath has a lower emissivity than the first, the equilibrium temperature of the can will rise.

The reason for the rise in temperature can be seen more clearly with the following equation, which holds when the can is at its equilibrium temperature.

Power Absorbed at Visible Wavelengths = Net Rate of Loss by Infrared Radiation + Rate of Loss by Convection

$$P_v = \sigma\varepsilon A\,(T^4 - T_c^{\,4}) + hA(T - T_c)^{5/4}$$

$P_v$ is the power absorbed at visible wavelengths

$\sigma$ is the Stefan-Boltzmann constant

$\varepsilon$ is the effective infrared emissivity of the can's surface

A is the surface area of the can

T is the average temperature of the can's surface at equilibrium

$T_c$ is the temperature of the environment

h is the convection coefficient

The approximation for the convection term is given by Sears, Zemansky, and Young (1991). Since $P_v$ remains essentially constant during the experiment, a decrease in infrared emissivity ($\varepsilon$) will produce an increase in equilibrium temperature (T). This must be the case if the losses due to infrared radiation and convection are still to balance $P_v$.

## Measuring the Temperature Change

A good classroom demonstration should be visible to a large group; therefore, the method of displaying the temperature change should meet this criterion. In addition, the temperature to be measured in this experiment is not that of one location on the surface of the container, but rather that of the container as a whole. This condition can be met by making the can itself a temperature sensor.

The can contains a simple liquid barometer tightly sealed inside so that it monitors the gauge pressure of the enclosed air (see Figure 4). We used a plastic tube having an inside diameter of about 3 mm for the barometer tube, and water with food coloring as the barometer liquid. For the bowl of the barometer we used a Styrofoam cup so that the liquid was insulated from the can, allowing the temperature of the can to change rapidly.

The temperature of the air inside the container can be assumed to be closely related to the average temperature of the device as a whole. An increase in the temperature of the inside air results in an increase in its pressure, which in turn forces fluid high into the tube of the barometer. This rise in the fluid level can be related to the temperature rise.

The change in pressure ($\Delta P$) of air inside the can may be related to change in air temperature ($\Delta T$) using the ideal gas equation, which may be approximated by $\dfrac{\Delta P}{P} + \dfrac{\Delta V}{V} = \dfrac{\Delta T}{T}$

where P is the pressure of the air in the can, T is the air temperature inside the can, V is the volume of air inside the can, and $\Delta V$ is the small change in volume created by the movement of indicator fluid inside the barometer tube.

We note that $\Delta V = A\,\Delta h$, where A is the cross-sectional area of the barometer tube and $\Delta h$ is the change in the height of the fluid column. In addition, we note that $\Delta P = \rho\,g\,\Delta h$, where $\rho$ is the density of the indicator fluid and g is the acceleration of gravity. We may assume that the pressure inside the can is not too different from atmospheric pressure ($P \approx P_{atm}$) and that the volume of air inside the can is approximately equal to that when no fluid is present in the barometer tube ($V \approx V_0$). With these substitutions into the ideal gas equation, we have $\left[\dfrac{\rho g}{P_{atm}} + \dfrac{A}{V_0}\right]\Delta h = \dfrac{\Delta T}{T}$

Letting h be the length of the barometer tube, our equation finally becomes $\left[\dfrac{\rho g h}{P_{atm}} + \dfrac{V_{tube}}{V_0}\right]\dfrac{\Delta h}{h} = \dfrac{\Delta T}{T}$ where we have made use of the fact that the volume of the barometer tube is given by $V_{tube} = Ah$.

Approximate values for the apparatus constructed by the authors are $\rho = 1 \times 10^3\,\mathrm{kg/m^3}$, h = 0.3 m, $V_{tube} = 2 \times 10^{-6}\,\mathrm{m^3}$, and $V_0 = 2 \times 10^{-3}\,\mathrm{m^3}$. In addition, $P_{atm} \approx 10^5$ Pa and g = 9.8 m/s². Substituting these values into the above equation gives $(0.03 + 0.001)\dfrac{\Delta h}{h} = \dfrac{\Delta T}{T}$

$$\dfrac{\Delta h}{h} \approx 30\,\dfrac{\Delta T}{T}$$

Such a device is sensitive to very small changes in temperature. In our version, a change in temperature of about 1°C will produce a corresponding change of about 3 cm in the height of the barometer fluid.

**figure 1** Infrared radiation spectra are different for surfaces covered with black paint and those painted white.

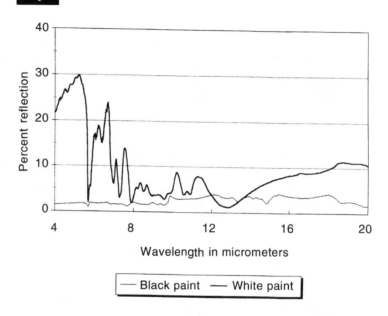

**figure 2** The demonstration apparatus can easily be seen by all members of the class.

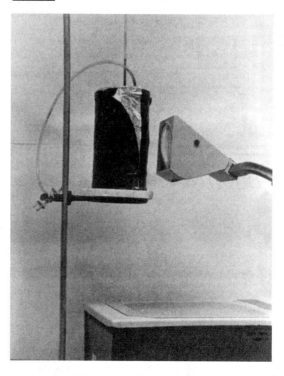

**figure 3**

A top view of the demonstration apparatus

**figure 4**

A cross-section of the demonstration apparatus

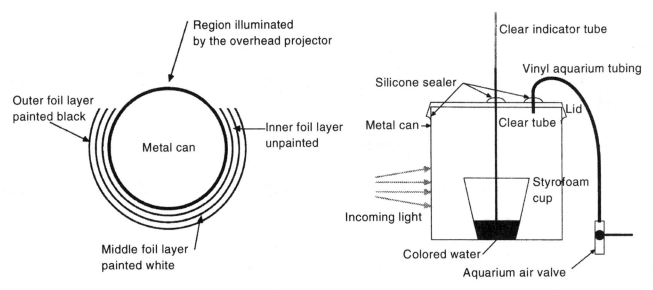

Region illuminated by the overhead projector

Outer foil layer painted black

Metal can

Inner foil layer unpainted

Middle foil layer painted white

Clear indicator tube

Vinyl aquarium tubing

Silicone sealer

Lid

Metal can

Clear tube

Styrofoam cup

Incoming light

Colored water

Aquarium air valve

**figure 5**

Even the different sides of the unpainted aluminum foil demonstrate different infrared radiation spectra.

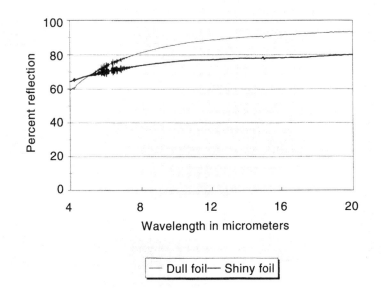

Percent reflection

Wavelength in micrometers

— Dull foil— Shiny foil

## Performing the Demonstration

Prior to the demonstration, most of the can (that part that will not be exposed to light from the projector) is closely covered with three layers of aluminum foil (see Figure 3). The inner layer is left unpainted. The second and middle layer of foil is painted white on the side that faces away from the can. The outer layer is made of foil painted black on the outward facing surface.

The apparatus is placed just in front of the projection lens of the overhead projector, where the light is highly concentrated, for about 40 minutes. This is to ensure that the can is thoroughly heated and has reached its equilibrium temperature. Next, the level of water in the indicator tube is raised by blowing carefully into the pressure regulation valve. The valve is closed when the fluid has risen to the middle of the barometer tube.

Before actually doing the experiment, students should at least be aware of how the level of the fluid in the indicator tube shows temperature and how the equilibrium temperature of the can is related to its emissivity.

The demonstration is performed by exposing a portion of the middle (white) layer of foil to the students and asking them to predict the resulting change in equilibrium temperature of the can when the black outer layer of foil is removed. Next, the outer black foil is removed. No change in equilibrium temperature is observed. This result should be confirmed by watching the temperature for a minute or two. The conclusion to draw from this is that the infrared emissivities of the black and white foils are nearly the same.

The next step is to have students predict the temperature change when the white foil is removed. A few seconds after the shiny inner layer is exposed, the indicator fluid begins to rise, indicating an increase in temperature. Our apparatus showed a rise of 7 cm two minutes after the white foil jacket was removed. The conclusion to draw from this is that the infrared emissivity of the unpainted foil is lower than that of the painted foils. The equilibrium temperature rises until the container is again at thermal equilibrium.

Our conclusion is supported by the infrared reflection spectrum (taken at 45°) for the unpainted aluminum foil shown in Figure 5. Interestingly, the dull side of the foil has a lower emissivity (at 45°) than the shiny side. Both sides, however, show an emissivity much lower (higher reflectivity) than that of the black- or white-painted foil.

## Conclusion

The ability of surfaces to emit infrared radiation can be very different from their ability to absorb and emit visible light. Such differences in infrared emissivities can be demonstrated visibly in the classroom using the apparatus described. The demonstration shows that black- and white-painted surfaces have similar infrared emissivities.

The demonstration also shows that unpainted aluminum foil has a lower emissivity than the white- or black-painted foil. The infrared reflection spectra shown in Figures 1 and 5 substantiate this finding.

### Acknowledgment

*The research for this manuscript was partially supported by a grant from the Auburn University at Montgomery Research Grant-in-Aid Program.*

### References

Bartels, R. A. 1990. Do darker objects really cool faster? *American Journal of Physics* 58(3): 244–248.

Sears, F. W., M. W. Zemansky, and H. D. Young. 1991. *College Physics*. 7th ed. Reading, MA: Addison-Wesley.

# Demonstrating Allotropic Modifications of Sulfur

## Re-creating Io's Volcanic Surface

Jillian L. McCarty and Veljko Dragojlovic

Io, Jupiter's closest Galilean satellite, is one of that planet's 28 known satellites. In 1979, *Voyager 1* discovered active volcanoes on Io's surface. The tidal forces from Jupiter's immense gravity generate enough heat on Io to sustain vigorous volcanic activity, including sulfur volcanic eruptions, sulfur lava fountains, and sulfur geysers.

In fact, Io spews sulfur with such ferocity that it is by far the most volcanically active body known in the solar system, with eruptions releasing plumes hundreds of kilometers above its surface.

*Galileo,* which has been orbiting Jupiter since 1996, photographed many of the same hot spots on Io observed by *Voyager 1* in 1979. *Galileo* also found that Io has a metallic core and that the surface is made of silicate rock, sulfur, and frozen sulfur dioxide. Oxygen, sulfur, and sulfur dioxide, which result from volcanic outgassing, make up Io's thin atmosphere. Photographs of the satellite show high-temperature areas of black-colored viscous sulfur, somewhat lower-temperature areas with flows of molten red and yellow sulfur, and large low-temperature areas of solid yellow sulfur, leading astronomers to name it the "pizza moon" (Goldsmith 1991).

In the classroom, the astrochemistry of Io is sometimes used to illustrate the allotropic modifications of sulfur. Another discussion of Io centers on the conclusions that were drawn about the composition and temperature of its surface from *Voyager 1* photographs. Sometimes students express surprise or disbelief that conclusions about Io were made from what they consider to be scant evidence. A common demonstration that consists of slowly heating sulfur powder in a test tube to illustrate sulfur's allotropic modifications can convince students otherwise. We have developed such a demonstration that more closely simulates Io's surface and validates scientists' conclusions about this satellite of Jupiter.

## The Demonstration

To begin, students make aluminum cups by wrapping aluminum foil around a 100–400 mL beaker. They then fill the cups 1 to 2 cm deep with sulfur and heat them on a hot plate until the sulfur melts. Temperature of the molten sulfur should be carefully monitored. If it becomes too high, sulfur will acquire a dark coloration and retain it for a long time. Dark plates do not adequately reproduce colors of Io's surface. Even when the temperature of sulfur is carefully controlled, plates with some dark areas can result.

To simplify the procedure, and to ensure that the plate has the desired pale yellow color, we covered the surface of molten sulfur with fresh sulfur powder. The powder adheres to the surface, giving it a pale yellow hue. After cooling, students dust off the excess powder and remove the aluminum foil. Alternatively, if dark plates are obtained, they can be left standing until the dark coloration disappears, which may take as long as several weeks. However, such plates are very brittle and can shatter easily. On the positive side, changes in the color and brittleness of sulfur are another point to discuss in the class. It takes about 10 minutes to prepare each plate. (Usually students prepare the plates in advance of the experiment. Sometimes, to save time and avoid the hazards associated with students working with molten sulfur, the instructors prepare the plates.)

The instructor heats the surface of a sulfur plate to the desired temperature (usually a few seconds) by focusing sunlight on the plate using a Fresnel lens (18 × 25 cm or 9 × 13 cm). Since sulfur can ignite, students should have a water-filled beaker ready to extinguish any flames. If sulfur ignites and is allowed to burn for some time, a significant amount of sulfur dioxide will be produced. Sulfur dioxide is an irritant and may induce an asthma attack. Usual safety precautions, such as wearing nonflammable gloves and appropriate eye protection (i.e., full-wrap, splash-proof goggles), should be observed. If this experiment is run as a student laboratory exercise, we recommend the small-size Fresnel lens (9 × 13 cm). Students should not hold the lenses while waiting to conduct the experiment. Lenses should be kept on the table and handled only when needed. This way the students will avoid inadvertently focusing sunlight on their skin, clothing, laboratory notebook, or some other flammable material.

On the same sulfur cake, our students obtained areas of different temperatures. (Color photographs of the results our students obtained and a recent photograph of Io in true color [JPL 2001] may be viewed at *www.nsta.org/gateway&j=jcst&n=46104*). The sulfur retained the black coloration for several months after cooling. The same phenomenon was observed on Io's surface.

## Safety

Instructors handling the chemicals when preparing and conducting this demonstration must wear chemical-resistant goggles, surgical gloves, and a rubber apron. The demonstration should be carried out in a well-ventilated area. In addition, students should be provided with safety goggles. Dispose of used reagents in an appropriate hazardous waste receptacle.

## Sulfur's Allotropic Modifications

Different colors and viscosity correspond to different allotropic modifications of sulfur (Cotton et al. 1999). Common yellow sulfur consists of $S_8$ molecules where eight sulfur atoms are connected in a crown-shaped ring (Figure 1–a). Upon heating, sulfur melts to provide a yellow liquid that flows readily. As the temperature increases, the color of sulfur changes to red and eventually darkens further. The color is caused by the presence of a small amount of red $S_3$ and $S_4$ molecules (Figure 1–b). At about 160–195°C the color of sulfur becomes dark red and its viscosity sharply increases (by a factor of 10,000).

**SCILINKS.**
THE WORLD'S A CLICK AWAY

Topic: sulfur
Go to: *www.scilinks.org*
Code: JCSTC144

The reason for such a high viscosity is that sulfur rings open and combine to form long polymeric chains with more than 500,000–800,000 sulfur atoms per chain (Figure 1–c). Such long polymer chains become entangled, resulting in a dramatic increase in viscosity. As a result of the increase in viscosity, the molten sulfur stops flowing. This phenomenon can be easily observed when melting sulfur in a test tube. Thus, molten sulfur, which flows readily at a lower temperature, will stop flowing and the test tube can be turned upside down without spilling any sulfur.

Above 200°C, as the polymer chains begin to fragment into smaller pieces (Figure 1–d), the viscosity again decreases, and the sulfur, now dark brown to black, begins to flow again. At this point, students can discuss why longer chains are more viscous than the shorter ones. Sulfur chains form helical fibers (Figure 1–e) that can be stretched, giving sulfur rubbery or "plastic" properties. At 445°C the black liquid boils to emit a pale yellow vapor that is composed of $S_n$ molecules ($n = 2$–10, mostly 8).

This demonstration illustrates the importance of teaching descriptive chemistry and is suitable for a general science class as well as introductory chemistry, astronomy, or physics classes. Alternatively, the above demonstration can be adapted as a discovery-based laboratory experiment for students in those classes. For example, after giving students several photographs of Io, invite them to speculate on the chemical composition of its crust and origin of its color. (Photographs are available from JPL's Web site, *photojournal.jpl.nasa.gov*. Additional information, such as samples or photographs of elements, in particular nonmetals such as sulfur, phosphorus, and iodine, and compounds [colored metal oxides] are also provided on the site.)

Advise students to arrive at the simplest possible hypothesis. Students should be able to detect active volcanoes in the photographs and conclude that there are large variations in Io's surface temperature. Working in groups, students

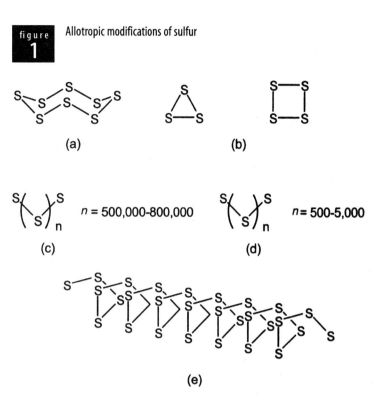

**figure 1** Allotropic modifications of sulfur

(a)

(b)

(c)    $n = 500{,}000\text{–}800{,}000$

(d)    $n = 500\text{–}5{,}000$

(e)

develop a hypothesis about the composition of Io's surface. Photographs of Io from a distance show it as a red disc, which may lead students to speculate that it is composed mainly of iron oxides (since Mars is red and most students know that the color is due to iron oxides). At room temperature, sulfur is yellow, and that may lead students to speculate that red and black colors are caused by the presence of allotropic modifications of phosphorus. Last, after performing the above demonstration, students can write formal reports that confirm, reject, or modify their original hypotheses.

## References

Cotton F. A., G. Wilkinson, C. A. Murillo, and M. Bochmann. 1999. *Advanced Inorganic Chemistry.* 6th ed. New York: Wiley.

Goldsmith, D. 1991. *The Astronomers.* New York: St. Martin's Press.

Jet Propulsion Laboratory (JPL). 2001. Web site: *photojournal.jpl.nasa.gov.*

# Demonstrating a Thermodynamics Fountain

## Heating Up the Classroom with an Energy Transfer Exercise

Miodrag Micic and Roger M. Leblanc

Cryogenic materials, mainly liquefied and solidified gases, are probably the most fascinating materials to use for demonstrating chemical reactions to introductory college students. A popular series of articles (Blachley 1997; Coppola, Hovick, and Daniels 1994; Haub 2001; Hughes and Haworth 1992; Stamm and Franz 1992) has been published presenting very effective and attractive demonstrations using liquefied gases (mostly liquid $N_2$). These articles introduce several basic concepts in chemistry, particularly in thermodynamics and kinetics, while simultaneously bringing excitement to the classroom.

For example, Blachley (1997) and Coppola, Hovick, and Daniels (1994) describe several interesting demonstrations using liquid nitrogen in which the most entertaining one has as its end product an edible "ice cream." Here, however, we take cryogenic material demonstrations to another level. We describe two versions of a straightforward demonstration that illustrates the concepts of energy/heat flow and conversion of heat to mechanical work. It uses a water fountain powered by the expansion of liquid nitrogen or dry ice.

Chemical thermodynamics is one of the most abstract and confusing topics in the general chemistry curriculum. Demonstrations with simple and easy-to-follow instructions can make the concept of energy transfer from hotter to colder bodies in the form of gas understandable even to nonscience majors.

**SCILINKS**
THE WORLD'S A CLICK AWAY

Topic: thermodynamics
Go to: *www.scilinks.org*
Code: JCSTC147

At room temperature, liquid nitrogen will rapidly evaporate while dry ice will sublimate to a gaseous phase. The volume of the gaseous aggregate state is much greater than the volume of the same mass of solid or liquid. The heat required for sublimation in the case of dry ice, or for evaporation in the case of liquid nitrogen, comes from the surrounding environment—we use water in our demonstration. When a small piece of dry ice or a small quantity of liquid nitrogen is added to a large quantity of water at room temperature, the substance will gain energy for rapid sublimation or evaporation from the surrounding water. Energy transfer thereby occurs, with energy flowing from the hot component of the system (water) to the cold component (liquid nitrogen or dry ice). During the energy transfer, water will cool while the nitrogen or $CO_2$ becomes hotter. The heat will be used for the phase transition from liquid to gas phase in the case of liquid nitrogen, or from the solid to the gas phase in the case of dry ice.

As the gas expands and pushes the water into a fountain spray, work is performed against the atmospheric pressure and gravity. If the water is in a closed vessel at constant volume (isochoric conditions), the result will be increasing pressure inside the vessel, with no work performed. In this demonstration, however, the thermal energy of the surrounding water is used by the expanding gas against the atmosphere and the potential energy of the gravitational field of Earth, creating the fountain water flow, also known as the isobaric process.

## Materials

- One washing bottle (~250 mL)
- Tap water
- One cork
- One glass pipe or piece of straw
- Dry ice (~1–2 g)
- Liquid nitrogen (>10 mL)

- Optional: one glass pipe with tap

## Procedure

The simplest version of this demonstration can be performed using a washing bottle (~250 mL) with a vertical position outlet pipe. After the bottle is half filled with water, a few pieces of dry ice (~1–2 g) or a volume (>10 mL) of liquid nitrogen is placed inside. Once the bottle is closed and the cap tightened, a strong stream of water surges up like a fountain (Figure 1). The stream will continue to flow until all the water is used or until all the liquefied or solidified gases are expanded.

In a more "sophisticated" version of this fountain, use a washing bottle or round bottom flask. Close the container with a cork attached with a short pipe and a valve to turn on and off the fountain stream (Figure 2). Also attach a long pipe or straw to produce a well-formed fountain stream. This version of the fountain is much more convenient to operate because the demonstrator can control the fountain stream by opening and closing the valve or tap.

After filling the flask to approximately half of its volume with water (~150 mL), add a few pieces of dry ice (~2 g) and close the flask with the cork. The valve on the short pipe should be kept open while closing the flask. Once the flask is closed with the cork, shut off the valve and the water will start to flow in a fountain stream from the pipe. Closing the valve results in increasing the pressure inside the bottle because of the expansion of gaseous $CO_2$ or $N_2$. The water stream can be impressive in size and intensity depending on the amount of liquid nitrogen or dry ice added to the bottle. The liquid nitrogen causes much more intense streams than the dry ice.

## Safety

If this demonstration is carried out in a classroom, special care needs to be taken when handling liquid nitrogen, and we recommend that only the instructor perform this demonstration. If the dry

After dry ice or liquid nitrogen is added to the water in the washing bottle, the water will surge up like a fountain.

 In this version of the experiment, a cork top attached with a short pipe and valve to control the fountain stream are used.

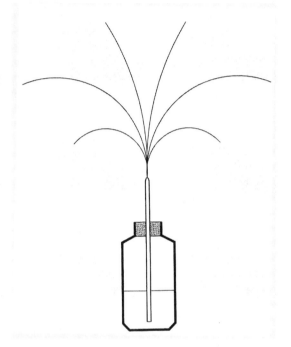

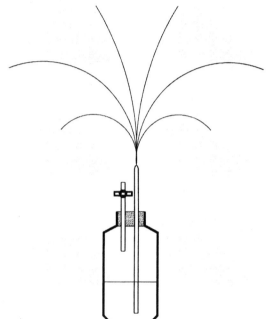

ice is used, however, because it is a much less hazardous material, the demonstration could be done by students provided that it is performed in the laboratory setting, not as a classroom demonstration.

As a matter of precaution, students and instructor should wear both safety goggles and gloves. The fountain outlet pipe should never be pointed toward another person because the water stream can contain small pieces of dry ice or droplets of liquid nitrogen, which can cause injury. While this fountain is a fascinating demonstration, in the case of liquid nitrogen use, it should always be performed by an instructor or qualified demonstrator.

## References

Blachley, R. C. 1997. The joys of liquid nitrogen. *Journal of Chemical Education* 74:616.

Coppola, B. D., J. W. Hovick, and D. S. Daniels. 1994. I scream, you scream. . . : A new twist on the liquid nitrogen demonstrations. *Journal of Chemical Education* 71:1080–1082.

Haub, E. K. 2001. Disappearing-reappearing rabbit trick: A new twist to an old liquid nitrogen demonstration. *Journal of Chemical Education* 78:46–47.

Hughes, E., Jr., and D. T. Haworth. 1992. A demonstration of the molar volume of nitrogen gas. *Journal of Chemical Education* 69:763–764.

Stamm, D. M., and D. A. Franz. 1992. Hot and cold running methane. *Journal of Chemical Education* 69:762–763.

# The Conductivity of Solutions

## Laying the Foundation of Modern Chemical Thought

Geoff Rayner-Canham

O f the many potential demonstrations that can be used in a chemistry course, there is one that lays the foundation of modern chemical thought. It is not only a very simple experiment; it can be done time and time again, with increasing levels of complexity of theory. It is also an experiment that generates a great deal of interest among the students.

*[Caution: The standard lightbulb conductivity tester is connected to the 110 V power supply. Thus it is critical to take specific safety precautions during the performance of these demonstrations. For example, the tester must be disconnected while changing the solutions that are being examined. There should also be a sleeve around each electrode to minimize the possibility of electrocution (see Figure 1)].*

The conductivity-of-solutions basic experiment involves the insertion of a standard lightbulb conductivity tester into a beaker of deionized water (see Figure 1). The bulb does not light, but when some salt is stirred into the water, it does light (Alyea and Dutton 1965).

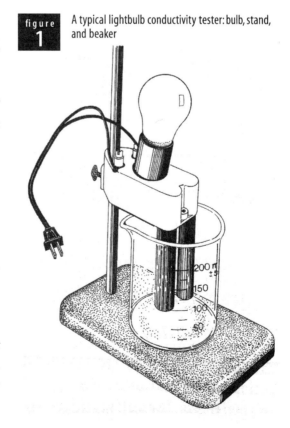

figure 1

A typical lightbulb conductivity tester: bulb, stand, and beaker

## Historical Background to the Experiment

The experiment outlined above is one of the most pivotal in the history of chemistry. Svante Arrhenius in 1884 proposed its modern explanation. At the time, hardly anyone accepted his theory of electrolytic dissociation. In fact, his thesis dissertation on the subject was given a low grade in view of the unacceptability of his conclusions (Jaffe 1976).

But by 1891, general support had grown for his argument that the particles in salt solutions dissociated into ions. In 1903, when the science community finally recognized the significance of his work, Arrhenius was nominated to share in both the chemistry and physics Nobel Prizes that year. Physicists blocked Arrhenius from receiving the physics award, but he did win the 1903 Nobel Prize in Chemistry (Crawford 1984). And significantly, his research into the presence of ions in solution led to the founding of the research school of the Ionists.

Although we ridicule in hindsight those who opposed Arrhenius, the opposition at the time was quite understandable. Then, the scientific community was divided between those who believed in atoms (the Atomists) and those who did not. The Atomists were convinced of the indivisibility of atoms. Enter Arrhenius, who argued against both sides: He believed sodium chloride in solution broke down into sodium ions and chloride ions but that these ions were not the same as sodium atoms and chlorine atoms (Salzberg 1991). That is, the sodium was no longer reactive and metallic nor was the chlorine green and toxic. No wonder his ideas were rejected until the era of J. J. Thomson and the discovery of the electron.

**SCiLINKS.**
THE WORLD'S A CLICK AWAY
**Topic: conduction**
**Go to:** *www.scilinks.org*
**Code: JCSTC152**

## Ionic and Covalent Bonding

In the context of modern chemistry courses, a modification of the classic conductivity experiment is the one that is most useful. The lighting of the bulb after the addition of sodium chloride to the water is first used to demonstrate the existence of ions, thereby indicating the existence of ionic bonding in compounds. When the experiment is then repeated using sugar rather than salt, the bulb does not light. (To confirm the identity of the substances and to relate them to the everyday life of students, it is advisable to use grocery store sugar and salt rather than reagent bottles of the substances.)

The difference in behavior between the salt and the sugar solutions indicates the existence of a different type of bonding: covalent. The concept of ionic and covalent bonding is one of the roots of modern chemistry.

It is illustrative to do the experiment with a third substance, powdered chalk. The bulb remains unlit—but what is the conclusion? The naive thinkers will assume that chalk must contain covalent bonds. In fact, the test is inconclusive. It is this extra demonstration that shows compounds to be tested have to be soluble in water.

## Net Ionic Equations

The next opportunity to use the conductivity experiment comes with the teaching of net ionic equations. To illustrate, we often use double-replacement reactions. The driving force for these reactions is the production of a gas, a precipitate, or water. In the example to be used here, water and a precipitate are formed. This elegant reaction, between barium hydroxide solution and sulfuric acid, gives two products, water and solid barium sulfate.

$$Ba(OH)_{2(aq)} + H_2SO_{4(aq)} \rightarrow BaSO_{4(s)} + H_2O_{(l)}$$

The equation can be expressed in net ionic form:

$$Ba^{2+}_{(aq)} + 2OH^-_{(aq)} + 2H^+_{(aq)} + SO_4^{2-}_{(aq)} \rightarrow BaSO_{4(s)} + 2H_2O_{(l)}$$

The instructor may wish to note that barium sulfate is used in stomach X-rays. The barium ion is the absorber of X-rays but the ion is also highly toxic. Hence the extremely insoluble barium sulfate must be used to obtain the X-ray without killing the patient.

In the experiment, dilute sulfuric acid is added from a buret to a solution of barium hydroxide (Shakhashiri 1983). The base solution is stirred continuously and the lightbulb conductivity detector is inserted. Thus, as the equivalent quantity of sulfuric acid is added, the light becomes weaker as the concentration of ions is diminished. Finally, the light is extinguished; there are no significant quantities of ions remaining in the solution. Addition of excess sulfuric acid causes the bulb to relight, an indication of the presence of ions in the sulfuric acid itself.

## Weak Acids

The topic of weak acids and bases enables the lightbulb to be brought out again. In a qualitative comparison, immersion of the probes into ethanoic acid gives a weak glow to the bulb, whereas immersion in hydrochloric acid of the same acid concentration gives a bright glow. There is a fundamental weakness with this, as with many demonstrations: students have to accept the instructor's statements on faith.

It is only your word that one colorless liquid is a hydrochloric acid solution and that the other is ethanoic acid of an identical concentration. We often forget that, to the students, we are simply working with containers of colorless liquids. They have no real evidence as to the identity of the solutions. In this case, the vinegary odor of the ethanoic acid does give a qualitative indication to students that the two solutions are different.

## The Ion-Product

One problem in teaching chemistry is that it is like peeling an infinitely large onion. As we uncover the next layer, we reveal that what was previously stated as fact is not quite true.

Up to this point, we have considered that pure water is nonconducting. After all, the bulb did not light. However, we were cheating. We were using a testing device that required a high current to function; it only responded when the solution contained very high concentrations of ions. With a more sensitive multi-range conductivity tester, we can show that even distilled water conducts a small current. It is worth pointing out that the minuscule current is of the order of that of the heart muscle. Hence, the current might be too small to light a bulb but it is large enough to electrocute anyone foolish enough to touch an electrical circuit with wet hands.

Therefore, the pure water must contain some ions. This can be explained as being due to the presence of the hydronium and hydroxide ions satisfying the ion-product constant relationship:

$$H_3O^+_{(aq)} + OH^-_{(aq)} \leftrightarrow 2H_2O_{(l)}$$

However, this is not a compelling explanation. Many students would argue that the water conducts electricity simply because it is not pure enough and, in part, they are correct. The distilled water will contain dissolved carbon dioxide (in equilibrium with hydronium and hydrogen carbonate ions) together with low levels of salts leached from the container walls.

$$CO_{2(g)} + 2H_2O_{(l)} \leftrightarrow H_3O^+_{(aq)} + HCO_3^-_{(aq)}$$

They will have to take on faith that ultrapure water sealed under nitrogen still conducts electricity.

## Bonding Revisited

At the elementary level, we used the conductivity experiment to illustrate the idea of ionic versus covalent bonding. It is common to draw the conclusion that ionic compounds are formed by combinations of metals and nonmetals while covalent compounds are formed by combinations of nonmetals. In an introductory inorganic chemistry course, the same experiment (with different solutes) can be used to destroy this edifice on which much of general chemistry is based. Actually, there is no hard dividing line between ionic and covalent behavior but a bonding continuum.

To illustrate this point, solutions of magnesium chloride and mercury(II) chloride are prepared. (As mercury(II) chloride is only slightly soluble in water, 0.01 mol/L solutions of each reagent are used.) The solution of magnesium chloride causes the bulb to light, that of mercury(II) chloride does not. Mercury(II) chloride, like many metal-containing compounds, contains covalent bonds (Greenwood and Earnshaw 1984).

## Learning Can Be Elegant Yet Simple

Chemists are prone to devise more and more complex demonstrations in which the point of the experiment is often lost through the complexity of the equipment (O'Brien 1991). Here we have a series of experiments with one simple piece of apparatus. The results explore a crucial concept in chemistry—the chemical bond—and the observations can be placed within a historical context.

## Acknowledgment
*The author acknowledges with thanks the assistance of Dr. Julian Dust for his incisive comments on this manuscript.*

## References
Alyea, H. N., and F. B. Dutton. 1965. *Tested Demonstrations in Chemistry*. Easton, PA: Journal of Chemical Education.

Crawford, E. 1984. Arrhenius, the Atomic Hypothesis, and the 1908 Nobel Prizes in Physics and Chemistry. *ISIS* 75:503–522.

Greenwood, N. N., and A. Earnshaw. 1984. *Chemistry of the Elements*. New York: Pergamon Press.

Jaffe, B. 1976. *Crucibles: The Story of Chemistry*. 4th ed. New York: Dover.

O'Brien, T. 1991. The science and art of demonstrations. *Journal of Chemical Education* 68:933–936.

Salzberg, H. W. 1991. *From Caveman to Chemist*. Washington, DC: American Chemical Society.

Shakhashiri, B. Z. 1983. *Chemical Demonstrations*, vol. 3. Madison, WI: University of Wisconsin Press.

# La Fiesta Radioactiva

## Distinguishing Alpha, Beta, and Gamma Emissions from Orange-Glazed Dinnerware

Ruth N. Russo

It's 9 a.m. Spotlights are trained toward the front of the lecture hall on two pieces of pottery, pools of color gleaming against the matte black benchtop.

The instructor carries in a survey meter, a beige box roughly the size of a portable radio. She slides a red plastic cover from the detector, a thick paddle tethered to the box, and turns the detector toward the students, holding it in her right hand like a tennis player about to serve. With the left hand, she flicks a switch on the survey meter, and a quiet click...tick...click...tick records the sporadic passage of background radiation. The bustle of students settling into their desks tapers off.

The instructor holds the detector to the lemon-yellow curves of a gravy boat. Click...tick...click...tick. Background. She then steps toward a bulbous orange pitcher and the click-ticks come faster and faster until the detector screams a shower of radiation. The students shift in their seats, whispering.

One young man slides a piece of construction paper between the detector and the orange pitcher. The noise of the meter still frantically rips through the room. A young woman walks up to the bench and carefully molds a small aluminum bread pan around the pitcher. The survey meter's insistent whine decelerates into a percussive, rapid-fire staccato.

Another student picks up a heavy lead sheet the size of legal paper. He gently bends the lead, fashioning a tent over the orange pitcher. Suddenly, silence. Click...tick...click...tick. Background! The class erupts into cheering.

* * *

"Fiesta," a line of ceramic pottery manufactured by the Homer Laughlin Company, and "Ringware," Bauer Company's answer to Fiesta, are hot collectibles. This art-deco dinnerware, distinguished by rounded shapes and detailed with rings of concentric circles, sells in a handful of mix-and-match solid colors. One of today's

Topic: types of
radiation
Go to: www.scilinks.org
Code: JCSTC156

most desirable colors of pottery dates to the 1930s and early 1940s: a cheery orange-red. This hue, ranging in shade from pumpkin to rusty marigold, is produced by radioactive uranium oxide suspended in the glaze. Measuring the radioactivity emitted by Fiesta acquaints students with the rudiments of radiation detection and shielding and requires little preparation or in-class time. The few materials needed and the simple procedure are described below. Because this demonstration always prompts a lot of questions, I have organized the discussion in a question and answer format.

## Materials

- *Pottery.* Two pieces of Fiesta or Ringware are needed, one with the characteristic orange hue and one of *any shade but orange.* An authentic manufacturer's mark may appear on the bottom of the item (Huxford and Huxford 1996; Tuchman 1995). Orange pieces of "Early California," by Vernon Kilns, also work.

  This pottery is ubiquitous in antique stores and flea markets. Six-inch plates are inexpensive, currently valued at $5 to $7. A small pitcher sells at $24 to $28 in mint condition, while a gravy boat is valued at $40 to $45. Frequently one can find slightly damaged pieces for much less (Jill Emigh, Shady Lawn Antiques, personal communication).

  Glazed ceramic tableware is considered safe to store and handle, and is specifically exempted from the need for radioactive materials licensing and regulation in Washington state (Department of Health 1997). Instructors may check state regulations where they live.

- *Alternative materials.* Other materials can also serve as radioactive sources for the demonstration of shielding. Some turn-of-the-century clocks have dials with radium-laced paint, and iridescent Depression-era glass contains uranium. Samples of uranyl acetate or nitrate are available in most chemistry departments, the plastic lids and glass bottles of which shield radiation to different extents. Samples of uranium ores (e.g., pitchblende, uraninite, carnotite) may be found in geology departments and lapidary shops.

- *Survey meter.* I use a Ludlum Model 3 Survey Meter connected to a Model 44-9 Geiger-Mueller (G-M) Detector (Ludlum Measurements, Inc., Sweetwater, TX). This survey meter has an audio on/off button and a sensitivity range switch. The analog meter can be read in counts per minute or in milliroentgen (mR).

- *Shields.* Construction paper suffices to absorb alpha particles. To absorb beta particles, I fold several thicknesses of aluminum cooking foil inside a disposable aluminum bread pan. To absorb gamma radiation, I use a 1-mm-thick sheet of lead. VWR Scientific Products (800-9325000) sells 0.25 mm lead foil, or one could also use a 1-3/8" Plexiglas shield.

## The Procedure

- Appoint a student to read the analog meter and record the results on the chalkboard. Assign handling of the three shields to other students.

- The instructor should handle the survey meter since the sensitivity setting must be periodically changed. The mica window of the G-M detector is also fragile.

- Turn on the survey meter and take a background reading. Record the results.

- Place the G-M detector directly on the surface of the pottery. Compare the radiation emitted by the orange-glazed pottery and the control. Record the results. (Direct contact is necessary to detect alpha particles, which only penetrate several centimeters through air.)

- Slide construction paper between the detector and the orange-glazed pottery. Although there will be no apparent diminution of the audio signal, one can usually detect a slight decrease in the analog signal corresponding to shielding of alpha particles.

- Remove the paper and wrap the orange-glazed pottery with several thicknesses of aluminum to shield beta particles. Gently place the detector directly on top of the aluminum shield.

- Remove the aluminum foil and cover the orange-glazed pottery with lead foil or place it behind a Plexiglas shield. Gently place the detector directly on the shield. Record the results.

Table 1 summarizes the results of an experiment using an orange pitcher and a yellow gravy boat.

## Discussion
### What is radioactivity?

Some elements—like uranium—have inherently unstable nuclei and spontaneously emit small particles or energy as they decay to a more stable state. Alpha particles are helium nuclei (two protons and two neutrons), while beta particles are electrons. Only 1/1,800 the mass of a single proton, a beta particle is much less massive than an alpha particle. Gamma rays—simply high-frequency electromagnetic radiation—have no mass. All three types of radiation are ejected from decaying nuclei with kinetic energies that depend upon the identity of the element (Lillie 1986).

### Why do materials shield only some types of radioactivity?

The ability of any material to absorb radiation depends upon its electron density and upon the penetrating power of the radiation, which increases with decreasing mass, decreasing charge, and increasing kinetic energy.

Even though they have relatively large kinetic energies, alpha particles cannot penetrate

paper since they are massive and doubly charged. Beta particles and gamma radiation easily penetrate paper since they are less massive than alpha particles and have either one charge (beta) or no charge (gamma). Aluminum has sufficient electron density to absorb alpha and all but very high energy beta particles. Lead absorbs even very high energy beta particles and gamma radiation (Hill and Kolb 1998).

### What produces the orange-red color?

Uranium oxide, also known as sodium uranate, is a mixed oxide salt with the ideal composition $Na_2O \cdot 2UO_3 \cdot 6H_2O$ (Kautz 1934). However, since uranium exists in many stable oxidation states, the $UO_3$ in this formula is likely a mixture of $UO_2$, $U_3O_8$, $UO_3$, and other noninteger stoichiometries of oxygen to uranium (Cotton and Wilkinson 1980). When added to vitreous glaze in increasing concentration, uranium oxide produces colors from orange to light red to tomato red (Dodd 1967). The Fiesta color of the 1930s and 1940s was produced by 14 percent (w/w) uranium oxide suspended in the glaze (Huxford and Huxford 1996).

### Why is orange Fiesta radioactive?

Uranium exists as a mixture of isotopes—atoms with differing numbers of neutrons making up their nuclei. Ninety-nine percent of naturally occurring uranium is the unstable isotope U-238, which decays to Th-234 with the release of alpha particles. Th-234 decays to Pa-234, releasing weak beta particles and gamma radiation. Pa-234 emits highly energetic beta particles and gamma radiation as it decays to form U-234. The orange glaze contains all four of these isotopes (Crawley 1959).

### Is the orange color made any more?

Bauer reports having imported 450 lbs. of uranium oxide per week to use for orange glaze during the height of its popularity (Tuchman 1995), but this brisk business was halted by the

**table 1** Fiesta survey with detector in direct contact

| Sample | Shield | Average Reading (mR/hr) | Percent Radiation Shielded |
|---|---|---|---|
| Background | none | 0.02 | |
| Yellow gravy boat | none | 0.03 | |
| Orange pitcher | none | 10.0 | none |
| Orange pitcher | paper | 8.5 | 15 |
| Orange pitcher | aluminum foil | 6.5 | 35 |
| Orange pitcher | lead sheet | 0.03 | 100 |

Manhattan Project. Uranium ores were interdicted between 1943 and 1958, when the U.S. government allowed commercial use of uranium depleted of the fissionable U-235. Yet no U.S. company continues to use uranium ceramic glazes (National Council on Radiation Protection and Measurements 1987).

## How does the detector work?

The G-M detector used in this experiment has a thin mica window through which alpha, beta, and gamma radiation passes into a special chamber. Incoming radiation ionizes a gas filling the chamber, and every ionizing event causes a pulse of current that is detected and converted to analog and audio readings (Lillie 1986).

## What do the units mean?

One roentgen (R) is the amount of radiation that generates one electrostatic unit of charge in 1 $cm^3$ dry air (Lillie 1986). Technically, the roentgen is reserved for massless radiation (e.g., gamma rays). The gas-ionization chamber of a G-M detector is not efficient at measuring alpha and beta particles since they have different energies and lose this energy to the surrounding medium at different rates. Yet because the handheld counter is so portable, it is often the most convenient means of detecting all types of radiation. One must simply obtain an efficiency rating for a par-

ticular isotope: Ludlum Instruments, for example, gives the efficiency of the detector for U-238 as ~57 percent (personal communication).

## Is orange-glazed dinnerware harmful?

We need a means of expressing the dose of radiation in terms of its effect in biological tissue instead of its effect in producing electrostatic charge. One rem—from "roentgen equivalent man" (Hutchison and Hutchison 1997)—is the dose of any ionizing radiation that produces the same biological effect as one R of X-rays. Beta particles and gamma radiation have the same relative biological effectiveness as X-rays, meaning that they all do the same amount of damage.

One R of alpha particles, on the other hand, is about 20 times more damaging to biological tissue than one R of X-rays. Fortunately, alpha particles only penetrate up to 4 cm through air (Lillie 1986). A diner seated in front of a piece of orange Fiesta is probably more than 15 cm away from the pottery, and so receives no alpha radiation.

So what radiation dose is emitted by Fiesta pottery—a six-inch plate, for example? At 15 cm distance, a six-inch plate emits roughly 0.7 mR in an hour after correcting for the meter's efficiency (Table 2). Since this consists solely of beta and gamma radiation, 0.7 mR is equivalent to 0.7 mrem of radiation-induced biological damage. This is a relatively tiny dose, roughly equivalent

**table 2** Fiesta survey with detector at 15 cm

| Sample | Shield | Average Reading (mR/hr) | After Adjustment for Detector Efficiency (mR/hr) |
|--------|--------|--------|--------|
| 6" plate | 15 cm air | 0.4 | 0.7 |

to five hours of television watching, 1/14 of a chest X-ray, flying 1,750 miles by jet airplane, or living at sea level for five days (Joesten and Wood 1996).

It is such a small dose that, at least in Washington state, one doesn't need to post Radiation Hazard signs concerning the pottery since warning signs are required only if the source emits more than five mR/hr at 30 cm distance (Washington State Department of Health 1997).

In fact, one would have to remain by the plate for more than 1,400 hours in order to exceed one mR/year, which is the upper limit of acceptable external radiation exposure to the body according to the International Commission on Radiation Protection (Lillie 1986). In other words, Fiesta makes a dramatic but entirely safe table setting.

## Acknowledgments

*The author expresses her gratitude to Ann Coombs for inspiring this demonstration nearly 20 years ago. She also thanks Sam Fazzari and Carmen Lorenz for their gifts of Depression-era Fiesta, and Jill and Dave Emigh for allowing her to haunt their antique shop with a G-M counter.*

## References

Cotton, F. A., and G. Wilkinson. 1980. *Advanced Inorganic Chemistry.* 4th ed. New York: John Wiley and Sons, Inc.

Crawley, H. W. 1959. Radioactivity experiments for high schools using orange glazed ceramics. *Journal of Chemical Education* 36(4):202–204.

Dodd, A. E. 1967. *Dictionary of Ceramics.* Totowa, NJ: Littlefield, Adams and Co.

Hill, J., and D. Kolb. 1998. *Chemistry for Changing Times.* 8th ed. Upper Saddle River, NJ: Prentice Hall.

Hutchison, S. G., and F. I. Hutchison. 1997. Radioactivity in everyday life. *Journal of Chemical Education* 74(5):501–505.

Huxford, S., and B. Huxford. 1996. *The Collector's Encyclopedia of Fiesta.* 7th ed. Paducah, KY: Collector Books.

Joesten, M., and J. Wood. 1996. *World of Chemistry.* 2nd ed. Fort Worth, TX: Saunders College Publishing.

Kautz, K. 1934. The effect of glaze composition upon the colors produced by sodium uranate. *Journal of the American Ceramic Society* 17(8):8–10.

Lillie, D. W. 1986. *Our Radiant World.* Ames, IA: Iowa State University Press.

National Council on Radiation Protection and Measurements. 1987. *NCRP Report No. 95: Radiation Exposure of the U.S. Population from Consumer Products and Miscellaneous Sources.* Washington, DC: U.S. Government Printing Office.

Tuchman, M. 1995. *Bauer, Classic American Pottery.* San Francisco: Chronicle Books.

Washington State Department of Health. 1997. *Rules and Regulations for Radiation Protection, Radioactive Materials Edition.* WAC 246-232-0-1-0-c-ii-A and WAC 246-221-130-1.

# Demonstrating the Principles of Column Chromatography

## An Easy Introduction to a Useful Analytic Technique

Brian R. Shmaefsky, David Barnes, and Chris Martin

The isolation and analysis of chemicals by chromatography are fundamental principles taught in chemistry and biochemistry. Even introductory biology classes demonstrate the use of chromatography (thin layer) as a method for discriminating different plant pigments and amino acids. Lecture alone does not provide students with a basic understanding of the roles of the mobile and stationary phases. Students need to see a chromatographic separation to fully understand its analytic potential.

Thin layer chromatography is usually simple and quick to demonstrate in class. This is not true for column chromatography. Unfortunately, column chromatography media can be too expensive to use in the amounts needed to perform a sizable demonstration readily visible to a large

class. Additionally, one class period may not be enough time to either demonstrate a separation in class or perform it as a laboratory activity.

The authors have designed a simple, inexpensive, and rapid large-scale column chromatography setup for classroom demonstration. It is easy to build and reuse, and it accurately demonstrates the principles of liquid column chromatography. The setup can be adapted to demonstrations showing the effects of various mobile and stationary phases on analyte separation.

## Background

Column chromatography is a technique for separating different components of an inorganic or organic chemical mixture. The components can be separated based on differences in their molecular weight, size, solubility in various solvents, relative electric charge, and functional groups. In column chromatography, the mixture to be separated is placed on the surface of a column filled with a porous material (called the *stationary phase*). The stationary phase provides an environment that selectively permits or impedes the movement of the mixture components. A continuous flow of solvent (the *mobile phase*) is then passed through the column from top to bottom, forcing the chemical mixture into the stationary phase. The various components of the mixture travel through the column of porous material at different rates. The various components are then collected as they pass out of an opening at the column's bottom. The components travel through the column based on their interactions with the stationary and mobile phases. For example, components that dissolve readily in the mobile phase and travel unimpeded through the stationary phase pass out of the column quickly.

## Materials

The following materials are needed for one column chromatography setup:

### Column and Stationary Phase

- Fluorescent light protector shield (available in hardware and home repair stores; any length between 1 and 1½ m is acceptable for the demonstration)
- Small bag of playground sand (available at discount and gardening stores; 5 lbs. of sand are adequate for two large columns)
- Plastic funnel large enough to fit under the fluorescent light protector shield
- Large ring stand with two large clamp attachments
- Large bucket
- 32 cm × 32 cm piece of cheesecloth or muslin
- Two strong rubber bands
- Roll of duct tape
- Small rubber balloon or latex glove

### Mobile Phase and Analyte

- 20 L of tap water, or a large beaker and immediate access to tap water
- Large bottle of green liquid food coloring
- 10 mL pipette
- Several 100 mL beakers or clear plastic cups

## Column Setup

Construct the column by first folding the cheesecloth over twice into an 8 mm square. Secure the cheesecloth to one end of the column with the rubber band. The rubber band can be secured with one wrap of duct tape. This will form the bottom of the column.

Next, mount the column bottom side down on the ring stand. Tighten the clamps to secure the column to the ring stand. The bottom of the column should be at least 30 cm from the ring stand base. Now use duct tape to secure the funnel to the bottom of the column. Place the large bucket under the funnel to collect runoff.

Slowly add wet sand to the column until the sand is approximately 10–15 cm from the top of the column. Tap the column regularly to ensure even settling of the sand. Readjust the clamps to support the added weight to the column. Keep the large bucket under the funnel to collect the mobile phase. The setup should resemble the column shown in Figure 1. Pretreat the sand by gently flushing the water through the top until it elutes clear (this will take about 15 minutes to an hour). Once pretreated the column can be kept wet and used indefinitely.

## Running the Column

Saturate the sand by adding enough water to fill the column. Seal the column bottom by using a rubber band to secure a balloon or latex glove to the funnel tip. Next, add enough water to form a 3 cm layer above the sand.

Topic: chromatography
Go to: *www.scilinks.org*
Code: JCSTC162

**figure 1** The column chromatography demonstration setup is easy and inexpensive to construct and use.

Use the pipette to load the analyte solution by gently layering at least 20 mL of the concentrated food coloring onto the sand surface (underlying the water). Migration of the analyte is initiated by removing the seal from the funnel. Keep adding water to the top of the column as the water column moves within 1 cm of the top of the sand. Collect the clear fractions continuously in the bucket. Then use small beakers to collect fractions of the analyte.

## Results

The green food coloring will separate into discrete blue and yellow bands representing the dye components. These dyes are different enough in molecular weight (Blue #1 is approximately 800 and Yellow #5 is approximately 600) that band separation begins within a 10 cm migration through the sand. Complete separation is clearly evident after 20 minutes. The two dye components can be easily collected as they pass out of the column. The yellow dye travels fastest and comes out of the column first. The blue dye should pass out of the column after 40 minutes. This demonstration clearly shows the peak fractions containing the pure dye constituents and the tail fractions having combined dye constituents.

## Variations

Two columns can be simultaneously operated using different mobile phases. Water can be compared to a salt or alcohol solution. In addition, dye separation can be conducted comparing water adjusted to an acidic versus a basic pH. Stationary phase differences can be demonstrated by comparing dye migration in coarse sand versus fine silica sand such as that used in ashtrays or flower drying. Red food coloring dye (Red #2 and Red #40, both approximately 500 in molecular weight) will separate from a mixture of green and red.

## Acknowledgment

*The column was designed for use in a biotechnology teacher-training workshop funded by the National Biological Impact Assessment Program of the U.S. Department of Agriculture and sponsored by the National Association of Biology Teachers. The workshop was conducted at the Kingwood College biotechnology facilities.*

## Background Reading

Boyer, R. F. 1993. *Modern Experimental Biochemistry*. 2nd ed. Redwood City, CA: Benjamin-Cummings.

Lindsay, S. 1992. *High Performance Liquid Chromatography*. 2nd ed. New York: John Wiley & Sons.

# The Roles of Different Mobile Phases in Liquid Chromatography

## A Moving Demonstration of Chemical Interactions

Brian R. Shmaefsky, Timothy D. Shmaefsky, and Kathleen M. Shmaefsky

Teaching the basics of liquid chromatography to undergraduates in freshman biology and chemistry can be a nightmare. Explaining the relative roles of the mobile and stationary phases can be done quite lucidly, yet few students gain enough information about the theory to adequately design and troubleshoot a simple chromatography application. The inherent complexity of the mobile phase/stationary phase interaction makes it a difficult concept to learn without a visual presentation that demonstrates the interaction variables.

Liquid chromatography is a fundamental analytical tool in biochemistry and organic chemistry, and students continuing in upper-level undergraduate and graduate biology and chemistry classes need a thorough understanding of the subject. Ultimately, students who pursue careers

in chemistry will have to work with chromatography units or will interpret the results of chromatograms.

The following activity will demonstrate the role of mobile phase polarity on the separation of dyes having different solubilities in polar and nonpolar solutions. A paper chromatography system is used in this demonstration for simplicity and speed. It also models the same principles of low-pressure and high-performance liquid column chromatography.

### Background

Liquid chromatography is a method of separating chemicals in a dissolved mixture. It is highly specific for the particular component of a sample, or analyte, and is powerful enough to separate one analyte from a solution containing hundreds of molecules. The technique entails using a moving solvent, the mobile phase, to draw the analyte across a solid medium, the stationary phase.

The mobile phase is a solvent that continuously moves across the stationary phase. It acts to carry the analyte based on an interaction between the analyte's solubility in the mobile phase and its affinity to the stationary phase. The stationary phase is usually a solid matrix that alters the rate of travel of the analyte based on lipophilic properties, molecular size, polarity, or the possession of particular functional groups. The travel of the analyte through the system is dependent on its equilibrium between the two phases.

Adjusting the nature of the mobile phase can drastically affect the relative migration of different analytes in a chromatography system. This demonstration will show the effects of varying the mobile phase in separating the components of different writing materials. The stationary phase is kept constant for simplicity of the demonstration.

## Materials

### Analytes

- One black crayon
- One black dry-erase marker
- One black erasable overhead projector marker
- One black waterproof or permanent marker
- One blue dry-erase marker
- One blue highlighter marker

### Mobile phase

- 100 mL of distilled water
- 100 mL of acetone
- 100 mL of 50:50 acetone/distilled water mixture
- 100 mL of 9:1 petroleum ether/acetone solution

### Stationary phase

- Four 15 cm × 10 cm pieces of medium porosity, slow flow rate filter paper (Fisher Scientific P5 filter paper was used in this demonstration)

### Developing tank

- Four 600 mL beakers or comparable size glass jars

### Other materials

- (Optional) One long-wave ultraviolet light (UVA range)

## Procedure

The demonstration is very simple to set up and takes only minutes to obtain unambiguous results. The following steps should be followed for conducting the demonstration. First, number the beakers from 1 through 4, then label the beakers as follows: Beaker 1—Distilled water; Beaker 2—Acetone; Beaker 3—Acetone/Water; Beaker 4—Petrol/Ether. Cover the beakers with plastic wrap or foil to reduce evaporation. Take care to keep the acetone and petroleum/ether solutions away from heat or open flame.

Not more than 30 minutes before the demonstration make the analyte spots on the four stationary phase papers. Do this by gently touching the writing material to the filter paper. Follow the pattern in Figure 1 as a guide for placing the analytes. The analyte samples should be at least 3 cm from the bottom of the stationary phase paper. Make the spots as dark as possible without causing the marker ink to spread more than 1/2 cm from the center of the spot. A 1 cm spot is ideal for this demonstration.

Place one stationary phase paper in each beaker. The analyte spots must be toward the bottom of the beakers and the paper should stand erect. Gently pour in the respective

figure
1

Analyte placement on stationary phase paper

Black
crayon

Black
dry-erase
marker

Black
erasable
overhead
marker

Black
permanent
marker

Blue dry-
erase marker

Blue highlighter
marker

mobile phases without dripping any on the stationary phase paper. Cover the beakers with the plastic wrap and let sit until the solvent travels at least half the distance of the stationary phase paper. Remove the paper, now called a chromatogram, and let dry.

Lastly, draw the spotting pattern on the board or project on the overhead and pass the chromatograms around the class or display on an opaque projection device. You may wish to scan the chromatograms with the UV light to look for fluorescent dyes that are not visible under room light.

## Results

Have the students explain the relative migrations of different writing materials in each mobile phase. Then have them compare the differences in migration for an individual writing material in the different mobile phases. The black crayon should not have moved in any of the systems because its affinity to the stationary phase is greater than its solubility in any of the mobile phases. In the distilled water system, the components of the black erasable and blue highlighter markers should have migrated and separated. The acetone and acetone/water mobile phase system cause differential migration of the components of all the markers. Some nonpolar components separate from the black permanent marker in the petrol/ether mobile phase.

## Extension Activities

This demonstration can be developed into a laboratory activity in which students formulate a mobile phase for an unknown analyte solution. The solution should be composed of two or more analytes with slightly different solubilities dissolved in a common solvent. For example, red food coloring and Sudan III can be mixed in ethanol to create an analyte red solution. The red food coloring is carried best in a polar mobile phase while the Sudan III is carried best in a nonpolar mobile phase. Students should concoct a mobile phase that best separates the two compounds using a paper chromatography system.

### Background Reading

Bidlingmeyer, B. A. 1992. *Practical HPLC Methodology and Applications.* New York: John Wiley & Sons.

Lindsey, S. 1992. *High Performance Liquid Chromatography.* New York: John Wiley & Sons.

Scott, R. P. W. 1992. *Liquid Chromatography Column Theory.* New York: John Wiley & Sons.

Scott, R. P. W. 1995. *Techniques and Practices of Chromatography.* New York: Marcel Dekker.

Shmaefsky, B., D. Barnes, and C. Martin. 1995. Demonstrating the principles of column chromatography: An easy introduction to a useful analytical technique. *Journal of College Science Teaching* 25(2):150–151.

# A Limiting Reactant Demonstration

## Making a Stoichiometric Concept Visible for Beginning Students

Janet Z. Tarino

L imiting reactant problems in the stoichiometry chapter of general chemistry textbooks are often challenging for beginning
students. They can easily get lost in the
calculations and lose sight of the meaning of the concept. This demonstration helps
students grasp the idea that a reaction can only
proceed to the extent that there are sufficient
quantities of *all* reactants to generate it.

The demonstration employs this chemical
reaction:

$$Mg(s) + 2\,HCl(aq) \rightarrow MgCl_2(aq) + H_2(g)$$

The hydrogen gas is collected in a balloon,
and the size of the balloon provides a visual clue
about the amount of product formed (Dillard and
Goldberg 1971). When the demonstration is presented with the help of students' responses in
developing the accompanying table, the logic of
limiting reactant problems is clarified.

## Materials
- Three small-mouth bottles, 125 mL
- Three balloons
- Three rubber bands
- 1.0 M hydrochloric acid, HCl*(aq)*, 300 mL
- Magnesium, Mg*(s)*, turnings, approximately 5 g

## Demonstration
Place 100 mL of 1.0 M HCl*(aq)* (0.10 mole) in
each bottle. Mass out three portions of Mg turnings: 1.2 g (0.050 mole), 0.6 g (0.025 mole), and
2.4 g (0.10 mole). Transfer each portion of Mg
turnings into one of the balloons. A funnel will
facilitate this. Now fit a balloon over the neck of
each bottle, fastening the balloon securely with a
rubber band.

When ready, transfer the Mg turnings into
each bottle by lifting the balloons. Immediately
H$_2$*(g)* is generated, and the gas inflates the balloon. Comparisons of the sizes of the balloons
clarify the concept of limiting reagent and the

| table 1 | Before the demonstration, allow students to calculate the amount of Mg(s) needed to react completely with the HCl(aq), listed in the first column of this chalkboard diagram. | | | |
|---|---|---|---|---|
| **Bottle** | **Mg(s)** | **2 HCl(aq)** | **H₂(g)** | **MgCl₂(aq)** |
| A | 1.2 g<br>0.050 mol<br>stoichiometric<br>amount | 100 mL of 1.0 M<br>stoichiometric<br>amount | 0.050 mol<br>0.10 mol | — |
| B | 0.6 g<br>0.025 mol<br>limiting reagent | 100 mL of 1.0 M<br>0.10 mol<br>in excess | 0.025 mol | — |
| C | 2.4 g<br>0.10 mol<br>in excess | 200 mL of 1.0 M<br>0.10 mol<br>limiting reagent | 0.050 mol | — |

influence of the limiting reagent on the amount of product formed.

## Suggested Presentation

The success of this demonstration as a pedagogical tool requires that students help with calculations and make predictions about the eventual sizes of the balloons. Table 1 depicts a chalkboard diagram that can be filled in as the demonstration progresses. The volume and molarity of the HCl(aq) and the mass of Mg are provided to the students.

Allow students to calculate the mass of Mg needed to react completely with 100 mL of 1.0 M HCl(aq) (0.10 mol). This mass (1.2 g, 0.050 mol) is the stoichiometric amount of Mg in bottle A. The size of the A balloon represents the maximum volume of hydrogen that can be produced. This volume represents 0.050 mole $H_2(g)$ in the table.

Ask students what happens when we use half the stoichiometric mass of Mg (0.6 g, 0.025 mol). Will we get the same volume of $H_2$? Will the balloon be the same size? Most students predict that less $H_2$ is formed and are not surprised that the balloon is smaller on bottle B. Magnesium is the limiting re-

SCI LINKS.
THE WORLD'S A CLICK AWAY
**Topic: reaction rates**
**Go to: www.scilinks.org**
**Code: JCSTC170**

agent, and it determines the 0.025 mol of $H_2$ produced.

Now ask students what happens when we use twice the stoichiometric mass of Mg (2.4 g, 0.10 mol). Will we get twice the volume of $H_2$? No, because the extra Mg is in excess. The limiting reagent is HCl(aq). The balloon on bottle C is the same size as the balloon on bottle A, because again 0.050 mole $H_2$ is produced.

## Hints

Prepare a second set of bottles beforehand. Run the demonstration 30 minutes before class and bring this set of bottles with you in a covered box. These serve as a backup in case one of the balloons has a leak or some other catastrophe occurs. In addition, the reaction will be complete in this backup set so you can more easily show the status of the product mixture. In bottles A and B, the solution is clear; in bottle C, excess Mg is visible. It is difficult to see the excess Mg in bottle C at first because the solution is cloudy with gas evolution.

Finally, if you wish to add some excitement at the close of the demonstration, tie off the balloons and ignite them behind an explosion shield.

## Precautions

Instructors preparing and conducting this demonstration must wear latex gloves and chemical-resistant goggles. A laboratory coat or apron is recommended. Students near the demonstration should wear chemical-resistant goggles. Instructors wishing to ignite the balloons should do it in a well-vented room with the demonstration performed behind an explosion-proof barrier. It is recommended to keep a fire extinguisher nearby.

## Reference

Dillard, C. R., and D. E. Goldberg. 1971. *Chemistry: Reactions, Structure, and Properties. Instructor's Manual.* New York: Macmillan.

# List of Contributors

D. Blane Baker is an associate professor in the Department of Physics, William Jewell College. e-mail: *bakerb@william.jewell.edu*

David Barnes is a graduate of the Kingwood College Biotechnology Program.

Jan Benjamin is the laboratory coordinator at Kingwood College. e-mail: *Jan.Benjamin@nhmccd.edu*

Kimberly Boman, at the time she co-authored her article, was a scientist in the cell culture research lab of Genentech, San Francisco.

Barbara A. Burke is a professor of chemistry at California State Polytechnic University, Pomona. She served as editor of the "Favorite Demonstration" column from 1990 to 2000. e-mail: *baburke@csupomona.edu*

Ashley J. R. Carter is a postdoctoral researcher in the Department of Biological Science at Florida State University. e-mail: *ashley.carter.aya.yale.edu*

Theodor C. H. Cole, at the time his article was published, was a professor of biology at the University of Maryland, University College, European Division, Unit 29216, APO AE 09102.

Mitchel J. Doktycz is a senior member of the research staff at the Oak Ridge National Laboratory, Oak Ridge, Tennessee. e-mail: *doktyczmj@ornl.gov*

Veljko Dragojlovic is an associate professor, Oceanographic Center, Nova Southeastern University. e-mail: *veljko@nova.edu*

Brendan Flynn is a research associate in the Department of Chemistry at Binghamton University. At the time he wrote his article, he was a professor of chemistry and chair of the Department of Chemical Engineering Technology at Broome Community College. e-mail: *bflynn@stny.rr.com*

Marty Fox is an associate professor of biology at Edinboro University. e-mail: *mfox@edinboro.edu*

Mark Francek is a professor of geography and Earth science, Department of Geography and Earth Science, Central Michigan University. e-mail: *mark.francek@cmich.edu*

John J. Gaynor is an associate professor in the Department of Biology and Molecular Biology, Montclair State University. e-mail: *gaynorj@mail.montclair.edu*

Glenn Good is a professor in the Department of Physics, Ouachita Baptist University. e-mail: *goodg@obu.edu*

Robert M. Graham is a professor of physics at the University of Nebraska at Omaha. e-mail: *rgraham@mail.unomaha.edu*

Myra Hauben is an assistant professor of chemistry at the College of Staten Island. e-mail: *hauben@mail.csi.cuny.edu*

Douglas Hayward, now deceased, was an emeritus professor in the Department of Chemistry, University of British Columbia, at the time he wrote his article.

Douglas C. Johnson is the senior physics technician at California State Polytechnic University, Pomona. e-mail: *dcjohnson@csupomona.edu*

Marjorie A. Jones is a professor in the Department of Chemistry, Illinois State University. e-mail: *mjones@xenon.che.ilstu.edu*

George B. Kauffman is a professor of chemistry at California State University. e-mail: *george_kauffman@csufresno.edu*

James H. Larson is professor emeritus of science education, Viterbo College. e-mail: *jklars@msn.com*

Arthur M. Last is an instructor in the Department of Chemistry, University College of the Fraser Valley, British Columbia. e-mail: *arthur.last@ucfv.ca*

Roger M. LeBlanc is a professor in the Department of Chemistry at the University of Miami, Coral Gables, and director of the University of Miami Center for Advanced Microscopy (UMCAM). e-mail: *rml@miami.edu*

Vincent J. Lumetta is an adjunct biology instructor at Macomb Community College, Warren, Michigan, and a biology teacher at De La Salle Collegiate High School, also in Warren. e-mail: *vlumetta@hotmail.com*

John Luoma, now deceased, was an associate professor of chemistry at Cleveland State University at the time his articles were written.

Chris Martin is a graduate of the Kingwood College Biotechnology Program.

David P. Martin was an instructor in the Department of Physical Sciences, Auburn University at Montgomery at the time his articles were published. Now, together with his wife, he runs a small school for American students in Odessa, Ukraine. e-mail: *martins@paco.net*

Jillian L. McCarty is a graduate student at the Oceanographic Center, Nova Southeastern University.

Miodrag Micic is a senior application scientist at Veeco Instruments, Inc., Santa Barbara. e-mail: *mmicic@veeco.com*

Terry O'Brien is an assistant professor in the Department of Biological Sciences, Rowan University. e-mail: *obrien@rowan.edu*

Scott D. Pennington, a premedical student at the time he coauthored his article, is now a doctor of osteopathic medicine and a lieutenant in the U.S. Navy at the U.S. Navy Medical Center in Portsmouth, Virginia. e-mail: *spdo00@yahoo.com*

Geoff Rayner-Canham is a professor of chemistry at Sir Wilfred Grenfell College, Corner Brook, Newfoundland. e-mail: *grcanham@swgc.mun.ca*

Randy D. Russell is an assistant professor of physical sciences at Auburn University at Montgomery. e-mail: *rrussell@mail.aum.edu*

Ruth N. Russo is an associate professor in the Departments of Chemistry and General Studies at Whitman College. e-mail: *russorn@whitman.edu*

Judith Shillcock is a professor in the Department of Biology and Molecular Biology at Montclair State University. e-mail: *shillcock@mail.montclair.edu*

Brian R. Shmaefsky, the editor of this book and of the "Favorite Demonstration" column, is a professor of biology, Kingwood College. e-mail: *brian.shmaefsky@nhmccd.edu*

Kathleen M. Shmaefsky is a student at Atascocita Middle School in Humble, Texas.

Timothy D. Shmaefsky is a student at Humble High School in Humble, Texas.

Peter W. Slade is a professor in the Department of Chemistry, University College of the Fraser Valley, British Columbia. e-mail: *Peter.Slade@ucfv.ca*

Mary Jo Smith is in the district office of the Humble Independent School District in Humble, Texas. e-mail: *Maryjo.Smith@humble.k112.tx.us*

Robert Sproles is a doctoral student in the Applied Science Department at the University of Arkansas, Little Rock. e-mail: *rwsproles@ualr.edu*

Janet Z. Tarino is professor emeritus in the Chemistry Department, The Ohio State University at Mansfield. e-mail: *tarino.1@osu.edu*

Sharon L. Weldon is an assistant professor in the Department of Chemistry, Illinois State University. e-mail: *weldon@xenon.che.istu.edu*

Susan Yochum is an associate professor of chemistry and division chair for the Division of Natural and Health Sciences, Seton Hill University. e-mail: *yochum@setonhill.edu*

Kathryn Hajek Zuehlke is a science teacher at Salem High School in Conyers, Georgia. e-mail: *kzuehlke@bellsouth.net*

# Index

(Page numbers in **boldface** type refer to figures or tables.)

## A

Alleles
    genetic complementation, 43–46, **44, 45**
    genetic drift, 27–30
Allotropic modifications of sulfur, 143–145, **145**
Ammonia lava lamp activity to teach diffusion, 91–94, **93, 94**
Anatomy and physiology, brine shrimp as model organism for biology, 24
Antibiotics: microbial antagonism, 31–33, **33**
Aprons, 4
Arthropods: brine shrimp as model organism for biology, 23–25
Atmosphere
    "greenhouse effect," **57,** 57–62, **59–61**
    stopping a siphon action by reduction of atmospheric pressure, 95–97, **96**

## B

Biology
    brine shrimp as model organism, 23–25
    DNA structure, 73–76, **74, 75**
    genetic complementation, 43–46, **44, 45**
    genetic drift, 27–30
    heterochrony and heterotopy, 63–66, **64, 65**
Brine shrimp, 23–25

## C

Catalysis
    combustion of sugar cube with cigarette ashes, 86
    decomposition of hydrogen peroxide, 87–89, **88**
Chemical weathering, 41–42
Chemistry
    allotropic modifications of sulfur, 143–145, **145**
    ammonia lava lamp activity to teach diffusion, 91–94, **93, 94**
    catalytic decomposition of hydrogen peroxide, 87–89, **88**
    chemical evolution, 47–49, **48**

combustion of sugar cube with cigarette ashes, 86
    conductivity of solutions, **151,** 151–154
    demonstrating chemical processes with the transfer-tube model, 131–136, **132, 134–136**
    electrolysis, **85,** 85–86
    ester synthesis from butyric acid and pentanol, 86
    Le Châtelier's principle, 115–119
    Material Safety Data Sheets, 4, 5
    Remsen demonstration of nitric acid action upon copper, 99–104, **100, 101, 103, 104**
    stoichiometry: limiting reactant demonstration, 169–170, **170**
    sulfuric acid, 109–113, **112**
    visualizing chemical reactions with pop-it bead model, 125–129, **126, 127**
Chromatography, liquid
    principles of column chromatography, 161–163, **163**
    roles of different mobile phases in, 165–167, **167**
Combustion of sugar cube with cigarette ashes, 86
Complementation, genetic, 43–46, **44, 45**
Conductivity of solutions, **151,** 151–154
Conservation of energy: electricity calculations, 83–84
Conservation of matter: differential weathering, 41–42
Coveralls, 4

## D

Dangerous demonstrations, 3
*Daphnia,* 24
Demonstrations
    allotropic modifications of sulfur, 143–145, **145**
    ammonia lava lamp activity to teach diffusion, 91–94, **93, 94**
    brine shrimp as model organism for biology, 23–25
    catalytic decomposition of hydrogen peroxide, 87–89, **88**

chemical evolution, 47–49, **48**
of chemical processes with the transfer-tube model, 131–136, **132, 134–136**
combustion of sugar cube with cigarette ashes, 86
conductivity of solutions, **151,** 151–154
differential weathering, 41–42
distinguishing alpha, beta, and gamma emissions from orange-glazed dinnerware, 155–159, **158, 159**
DNA structure, 73–76, **74, 75**
educational role of, 3
electricity calculations, 83–84
electrolysis, **85,** 85–86
electrophoresis, **51,** 51–55
ester synthesis from butyric acid and pentanol, 86
fall leaf color changes, 69–71
floating spinach disks to teach photosynthesis, 35–39, **37, 38**
fluorescent dyes to teach solution-mixing techniques, 13–14, **14**
generating electricity using single displacement reactions, 79–81, **80**
genetic complementation, 43–46, **44, 45**
"greenhouse effect," **57,** 57–62, **59–61**
heterochrony and heterotopy, 63–66, **64, 65**
interactive genetic drift exercise, 27–30
Johnson DC Electric Motor, 105–108, **106, 107**
Le Châtelier's principle, 115–119
Lenz's law, 121–123, **122**
microbial antagonism, 31–33, **33**
principles of column chromatography, 161–163, **163**
radiation of heat by black vs. white paint, 137–141, **139, 140**
Remsen demonstration of nitric acid action upon copper, 99–104, **100, 101, 103, 104**
roles of different mobile phases in liquid chromatography, 165–167, **167**
safety precautions for, 3–5, **5**
seasonal size variations of Martian polar caps, 17–21, **18**
solar time calculation, 84, **85**

# Index

stoichiometry: limiting reactant demonstration, 169–170, **170**

stopping a siphon action by reduction of atmospheric pressure, 95–97, **96**

sulfuric acid, 109–113, **112**

thermodynamics fountain, 147–149, **149**

touch lamp activity to teach logico-deductive reasoning, **9**, 10–11

visualizing chemical reactions with pop-it bead model, 125–129, **126, 127**

Differential weathering, 41–42

Diffusion, ammonia lava lamp activity for teaching of, 91–94, **93, 94**

Disposal of hazardous waste, 4

DNA structure, 73–76, **74, 75**

### E

Ear protection, 4

Earth and planetary science

allotropic modifications of sulfur, 143–145, **145**

chemical evolution, 47–49, **48**

differential weathering, 41–42

"greenhouse effect," **57**, 57–62, **59–61**

seasonal size variations of Martian polar caps, 17–21, **18**

solar time calculation, 84, **85**

Ecology: microbial antagonism, 31–33, **33**

Electric motor, 105–108, **106, 107**

Electricity calculations, 83–84

Electricity generation using single displacement reactions, 79–81, **80**

Electrolysis, **85**, 85–86

Electrophoresis, **51**, 51–55

Emergency response measures, 4

Energy transfer

radiation of heat by black vs. white paint, 137–141, **139, 140**

thermodynamics fountain, 147–149, **149**

Equilibrium

demonstrating chemical processes with the transfer-tube model, 131–136, **132, 134–136**

Le Châtelier's principle: effects of stress on solution containing iron(III) thiocyanate ions, 115–119

visualizing chemical reactions with pop-it bead model, 125–129, **126, 127**

Ester synthesis from butyric acid and pentanol, 86

Evolution

chemical, 47–49, **48**

genetic complementation, 43–46, **44, 45**

genetic drift, 27–30

heterochrony and heterotopy, 63–66, **64, 65**

terms used in evolutionary biology, **64**

Explosions, 3

Eye protection, 4

### F

Face shield, 4

Fall leaf color changes, 69–71

Fiesta pottery, distinguishing alpha, beta, and gamma emissions from orange-glazed dinnerware, 155–159, **158, 159**

Fire extinguishers, 4

First-aid equipment, 4

Fluorescent dyes to teach solution-mixing techniques, 13–14, **14**

Foot protection, 4

Fuming reactions, 3

### G

Genetics

genetic complementation, 43–46, **44, 45**

genetic drift, 27–30

heterochrony and heterotopy, 63–66, **64, 65**

Geological timescale: chemical evolution, 47–49, **48**

Gloves, 4

Goggles, 4

Gowns, 4

"Greenhouse effect," **57**, 57–62, **59–61**

### H

Hand protection, 4

Hazardous situations, 3

Hazardous waste disposal, 4

Heat

"greenhouse effect," **57**, 57–62, **59–61**

radiation by black vs. white paint, 137–141, **139, 140**

thermodynamics fountain, 147–149, **149**

Hemophilia: genetic complementation, 45, **45**

Heterochrony and heterotopy, 63–66, **64, 65**

Hydrogen peroxide, catalytic decomposition of, 87–89, **88**

Hypothesis testing, touch lamp activity for, **9**, 10–11

### I

Incendiaries, 3

Infrared radiation

emission by black vs. white paint, 137–141, **139, 140**

"greenhouse effect," **57**, 57–62, **59–61**

Internet resources. *See also SciLinks*

safety precautions, 3–4

Io's volcanic surface: allotropic modifications of sulfur, 143–145, **145**

### J

Johnson DC Electric Motor, 105–108, **106, 107**

### L

Laboratory coordinator, 4

Laboratory Safety Institute, 3

Le Châtelier's principle

demonstrating chemical processes with transfer-tube model, 131–136, **132, 134–136**

effect of stress on a solution containing iron(III) and thiocyanate ions, 115–119

visualizing chemical reactions with the pop-it bead model, 125–129, **126, 127**

Leaf color changes, 69–71

Lenz's law, 121–123, **122**

Limiting reactant demonstration, 169–170, **170**

Liquid chromatography

principles of column chromatography, 161–163, **163**

roles of different mobile phases in, 165–167, **167**

Logico-deductive reasoning, touch lamp activity for teaching of, **9**, 10–11

### M

Magnetic fields, Lenz's law, 121–123, **122**

Mars, seasonal size variations of polar caps on, 17–21, **18**

Masks, 4

Material Safety Data Sheets (MSDS), 4, 5

Microbial antagonism, 31–33, **33**

Microscale demonstrations, 3

MSDS (Material Safety Data Sheets), 4, 5

### N

National Science Teachers Association, 4

Nucleic acids
    DNA structure, 73–76, **74, 75**
    electrophoresis, **51**, 51–55

**P**

Personal protective equipment (PPE), 4
Photosynthesis, floating spinach disks for
    teaching of, 35–39, **37, 38**
Physical weathering, 41–42
Plants
    environmental factors and fall leaf color
      changes, 69–71
    floating spinach disks to teach
      photosynthesis, 35–39, **37, 38**
Polymerization, DNA structure, 73–76, **74, 75**
Polymorphisms, interactive genetic drift
    exercise, 27–30
PPE (personal protective equipment), 4
Projectiles, 3

**R**

Radiation
    distinguishing alpha, beta, and gamma
      emissions from orange-glazed
      dinnerware, 155–159, **158, 159**
    emission of infrared radiation by black
      vs. white paint, 137–141, **139, 140**
    "greenhouse effect," **57**, 57–62, **59–61**
Redox chemical reactions, 79–81, **80**
Remsen demonstration of nitric acid action
    upon copper, 99–104, **100, 101,
    103, 104**
Research procedures
    electrophoresis, **51**, 51–55
    fluorescent dyes to teach solution-
      mixing techniques, 13–14, **14**
    principles of column chromatography,
      161–163, **163**
    roles of different mobile phases in liquid
      chromatography, 165–167, **167**
    safety precautions for, 3–5, **5**
Respirators, 4
Respiratory protection, 4
Ringware pottery, distinguishing alpha, beta,
    and gamma emissions from orange-
    glazed dinnerware, 155–159, **158, 159**

**S**

Safety checklist, 4–5, **5**
Safety officer, 4
Safety precautions, 3–5, **5**
Sample preparation, fluorescent dyes to
    teach solution-mixing techniques,
    13–14, **14**
Science Inquiry, 3–4
Scientific method, touch lamp activity for
    teaching of, **9**, 10–11
*SciLinks*
    acids, 109
    arthropods, 23
    atmospheric pressure, 96
    catalysts, 87
    chemical reactions, 102
    chromatography, 162, 166
    conduction, 152
    diffusion, 91
    DNA, 73
    electric motors, 105
    electrolysis, 83
    electrophoresis, 52
    factors affecting equilibrium, 116, 126,
      132
    genetic drift, 28
    genetic mutations, 43
    geological timescale, 48
    greenhouse effect, 58
    heterochrony, 63
    leaf structure and function, 70
    magnetic fields, 121
    Mars, 17
    microorganisms, 32
    photosynthesis, 35
    reaction rates, 170
    redox reactions, 80
    safety in the science classroom, 4
    scientific method, 10
    solutions, 13
    transfer of energy, 138
    types of radiation, 156
    weathering/erosion, 42
Seasonal size variations of Martian polar
    caps, 17–21, **18**
Single displacement reactions for
    generation of electricity, 79–81, **80**

Siphon action, stopping by reduction of
    atmospheric pressure, 95–97, **96**
Solar time calculation, 84, **85**
Solutions
    conductivity of, **151,** 151–154
    fluorescent dyes to teach mixing
      techniques for, 13–14, **14**
Stoichiometry: limiting reactant
    demonstration, 169–170, **170**
Stress effects on solution containing iron(III)
    and thiocyanate ions: Le Châtelier's
    principle, 115–119
Sulfur, allotropic modifications of, 143–145,
    **145**
Sulfuric acid, 109–113, **112**

**T**

Temperature
    emission of infrared radiation by black
      vs. white paint, 137–141, **139, 140**
    "greenhouse effect," **57**, 57–62, **59–61**
    thermodynamics fountain, 147–149, **149**
Thermodynamics fountain, 147–149, **149**
Touch lamp activity to teach logico-
    deductive reasoning, **9**, 10–11
Toxicology, brine shrimp as model organism
    for biology, 25

**U**

Uranium oxide, distinguishing alpha, beta,
    and gamma emissions from orange-
    glazed dinnerware, 155–159, **158, 159**

**V**

Virtual laboratory software, 3

**W**

Weathering, 41–42